The Cubalogues

UNIVERSITY PRESS OF FLORIDA

Florida A&M University, Tallahassee
Florida Atlantic University, Boca Raton
Florida Gulf Coast University, Ft. Myers
Florida International University, Miami
Florida State University, Tallahassee
New College of Florida, Sarasota
University of Central Florida, Orlando
University of Florida, Gainesville
University of North Florida, Jacksonville
University of South Florida, Tampa
University of West Florida, Pensacola

# THE CUBALOGUES

## Beat Writers in Revolutionary Havana

Todd F. Tietchen

University Press of Florida

Gainesville Tallahassee Tampa Boca Raton Pensacola Orlando Miami Jacksonville Ft. Myers Sarasota

Copyright 2010 by Todd F. Tietchen
Printed in the United States of America. This book is printed on Glatfelter
Natures Book, a paper certified under the standards of the Forestry Stewardship
Council (FSC). It is a recycled stock that contains 30 percent post-consumer
waste and is acid-free.
All rights reserved

15  14  13  12  11  10   6  5  4  3  2  1

A record of cataloging-in-publication data is available from the Library of Congress.
ISBN 978-0-8130-3520-8

The University Press of Florida is the scholarly publishing agency for the State
University System of Florida, comprising Florida A&M University, Florida Atlantic
University, Florida Gulf Coast University, Florida International University, Florida
State University, New College of Florida, University of Central Florida, University
of Florida, University of North Florida, University of South Florida, and University
of West Florida.

University Press of Florida
15 Northwest 15th Street
Gainesville, FL 32611-2079
http://www.upf.com

For my parents,
Barbara and Frank

True, indeed, behind this fantastic farce, enacted on the visible stage of society, solid things and stupendous labors are to be discover'd, existing crudely and going on in the background, to advance and tell themselves in time. Yet the truths are none the less terrible. I say that our New World democracy, however great a success in uplifting the masses out of their sloughs, in materialistic development, products, and in a certain highly deceptive popular intellectuality, is, so far, an almost complete failure in its social aspects, and in really grand religious, moral, literary, and aesthetic results. In vain do we march with unprecedented strides to empire so colossal, outvying the antique, beyond Alexander's, beyond the proudest sway of Rome. In vain have we annex'd Texas, California, Alaska, and reach north for Canada, and south for Cuba. It is as if we were somehow being endow'd with a vast and more and more thoroughly appointed body, and then left with little or no soul.

—Walt Whitman, *Democratic Vistas*

# Contents

# Acknowledgments

Long-term writing projects often send us vacillating between feelings of elation, disappointment, revelation, and even, at times, downright despair. Thanking all of those responsible for keeping us sane and focused along the way comes with its own elation and despair. While I cannot help feeling a great degree of joy and thankfulness toward those who have added so much to my life and work over the years, I am also profoundly aware of the fact that whatever I say will never capture the full meaning of what those individuals have meant to me. The brilliance of Nikhil Pal Singh, Bob Shulman, and Chandan Reddy never ceases to amaze me. Nikhil has been the most tremendous and supportive of mentors and teachers, and when called upon (in many situations) he has acted as the older brother I never had. Bob taught me the most elemental things regarding intellectual work, including the importance of keeping your own assumptions and conclusions under constant scrutiny. Chandan was (and continues to be) possessed by a trait exceedingly rare in academic circles: the ability to be as genuinely excited about the ideas of others as he is about his own. Thank you to each of you for being so generous with your time, ideas, and encouragement. This book could have never existed without you.

My conversations with Kathleen Woodward and Jodi Melamed added much to my intellectual range at a critical moment. I also had the privilege of crossing paths with Alys Eve Weinbaum, an incredibly insightful teacher and mentor whose lessons are weaved throughout the pages which follow.

Though I have long since left Seattle, I remain forever in debt to Brandy Parris, Rahul Krishna Gairola, and Brian Zindel, amazing friends whose ideas, excitement, commitment, and laughter always made the grayest of days bearable (and oftentimes blissful).

Many others have contributed to the realization of this book along the way. Bob Comeau, Tim McCracken, Naomi Liebler, Lee Bartlett, and Gary Harrison all played instrumental roles in my intellectual life, imparting lessons that I continue to value and that made this work possible. John Wargacki ("Peace, Brother"), Alyssa and Jim "Red" Yanchitis, Michael Nagy, Ann Marie and Wally Jarema, Robert and Adam Tietchen, Roberta Jasper, Christopher Jarema, Tom Caporaso, Tom and Marge McTighe, and Victoria and Bill Seesman also provided me with support, encouragement, advice, and respite at critical times during the completion of this project. My sister and her husband, Tracey and Jeff Merton, have always provided me with a safe and loving place to land (and oftentimes crash) over the years, and their sons, Zachary and Benjamin, consistently remind me of the most basic and grounding joys of life. I'm so very happy, Zac and Ben, that you joined us all on this journey when you did.

My acquisitions editor at the University Press of Florida, Amy Gorelick, has been incredible from the outset and I appreciate the belief she showed in the importance of the ideas that follow. At a critical point during the writing process, Daniel Belgrad and Sarah MacLachlan provided me with a series questions and comments that helped me bring the stakes of what I was involved in into clearer view. Zoe Trodd and Martha Carpentier also offered sage advice at crucial moments.

Sections from the introduction and chapters 1, 3, 4, and 5 previously appeared in an article titled "The Cubalogues (and After): On the Beat Literary Movement and the Early Cuban Revolution." Those sections have been reprinted from *Arizona Quarterly* 63.4 (2007) by permission of the Regents of the University of Arizona, and I thank them for granting that permission. *Mosaic, a journal for the interdisciplinary study of literature,* published a section of the introduction in "On the Waldport Fine Arts Project and the Aesthetics of Estranged Being" in volume 42.3 (September 2009), and I appreciate their willingness to introduce that material to their readers in advance of this book.

On a more personal note, my father, Frank, passed away in 2003, while this project was still in its embryonic stages, but not without leaving me with a lifelong love of reading, a respect for clarity in writing, and an ability to recognize the value and beauty in ordinary life. I continue to miss his presence intensely and hope that he'd be pleased with this accomplishment, which I wish we could've shared. My mother, Barbara, has incredible capacities for love and support, which I've miraculously failed to exhaust. I continue to admire her personal strength, her integrity and fairness, and her ability to keep laughing in the most trying of circumstances. It's been a bumpy but beautiful ride, Mom. We owned some great cars, didn't we?

# INTRODUCTiON

# The "Stranger Relations" of Beat

On June 30, 1961, Fidel Castro delivered his now infamous address, "A True Social Revolution Produces a Cultural Revolution" (or "Words to the Intellectuals"). Offered in the wake of the failed Bay of Pigs invasion, Castro's address represented a pivotal moment in Cuban intellectual and cultural history as his revolutionary government attempted, for the first time, to provide its national artistic policy with a more refined ideological blueprint. This newly pronounced ideological turn brought a decisive end to what Guillermo Cabrera Infante identified as a post-Batista "Cuban cultural renaissance," in which Havana had momentarily served as a vibrant and international cultural center for some of the most notable artists, writers, and thinkers of the mid-twentieth century.[1] Castro himself admitted as much in his June 30th address, in which he claimed that if Cuba's revolutionary leaders "were to review our efforts" toward culture "with a critical eye" they would soon admit that they had allowed Havana to become dangerously tolerant of outside political and cultural influences.[2] Castro attributed the presence of these influences—who ranged from Jean-Paul Sartre, Simone de Beauvoir, and C. Wright Mills to Maya Deren and the Maysles brothers—to the "improvised" fashion in which the early revolution had unfolded, leaving Cuba momentarily open to a host of politically progressive intellectuals from throughout the Americas and from across the Atlantic, thinkers whose commitments to actually existing socialism were ultimately suspect.[3] He further admitted that while he had just recently engaged in spirited exchanges with both Sartre and Mills on the importance of illimitable cultural freedom to his still-burgeoning revolutionary movement, the time for such conversations had come decisively to an end.

Officialdom typically moves a pace or so behind the trajectories of culture. But by June of 1961, Castro had finally found his legs in the stretch, using his ideological second wind to engage in some breakneck cultural maneuvering. One of the most significant outcomes of the June 30 address was the disbanding of *Lunes de Revolución,* the Cabrera Infante–edited journal which had anchored Cuba's new literary and artistic scene since the earliest days of Castro's revolution. As Cabrera Infante explains, once Castro openly declared his allegiance to the Soviet sphere (in April 1961) he simultaneously began to assert the revolution's newly pronounced socialist ideals as the only proper subject matter for Cuban artists, initiating a period of pronounced meddling in the island's cultural sphere. In turn, the content of *Lunes* was eventually denigrated as "decadent, bourgeois, avant-gardist and, the worst epithet in the Communist name-calling catalogue, cosmopolist." [4] According to Cabrera Infante's perspective, the initial years of the revolution were equivalent to the early years of the Weimar Republic, an incredibly brief yet incredibly prolific cultural upheaval that, in an earlier time and place, had left Germany's political reactionaries bemoaning the dangers of cosmopolitanism and the avant-garde within the midst of a momentarily bohemian Berlin. In Castro's Cuba, "avant-gardist" and "cosmopolist" tendencies would soon meet a similar fate as *Lunes,* which had published works by Sartre and a number of other writers from throughout the Americas since 1959, and was soon after replaced by the more politically orthodox *Union* and *La Gaceta de Cuba* at the center of the revolution's artistic culture. But while the "cosmopolist" interactions fostered by the literary, artistic, and intellectual culture of the early revolution may have proven transient and fleeting, they nevertheless had tangible effects on the direction of Castro's cultural policy and especially on the evolution of literary, intellectual, and political culture within the Cold War United States.

At the center of this cultural and intellectual history were the Cubalogues, an explicitly political subgenre of Beat travel narrative which included works such as Lawrence Ferlinghetti's "Poet's Notes on Cuba," Amiri Baraka's "Cuba Libre," and Marc Schleifer's "Cuban Notebook." Driven by a profound skepticism concerning the negative portrayal of Castro's revolution within the mainstream U.S. media, each of the Cubalogue writers decided to witness the revolution firsthand, recording their experiences of Cabrera Infante's "cultural renaissance" in works of autobiographical journalism which opened a revealing window into the earliest moments of revolutionary culture. The Cubalogues, in other words, are best understood as a politically engaged form of literary reportage in which stock features of Beat writing—ranging from the celebration of spontaneity, to the veneration of musical culture, to the glorification of the street hustler and unconventional sexualities—were explicitly recast against the backdrop of early revolutionary events as a politically vital set of values opposed to what their writers experienced as the rhetorical preconditions of the U.S. public sphere and its role in the production of Cold War public opinion. The Cubalogue writers were ultimately concerned with the extent to which Cold War pieties concerning nationhood and national belonging, bolstered by proliferating and durable appeals to national security and the superiority of American political institutions and "ways of life," placed telling limits on public expression, political subjectivity, and alternative renderings of collectivity (including those emerging from within the precincts of global anticolonialism). In response to what they viewed as a severely compromised public arena and cultural sphere at home, these writers configured the early Cuban Revolution as an inter-American repository— or a political dreamspace of sorts—for anti-imperialism, racial justice, sexual freedom, and a more expansive understanding of democratic philosophy and political belonging during what proved to be a climactic moment in Cold War geopolitics.

As rhetorical travelogues, the Cubalogues exemplified a mode of descriptive argumentation that Walter Fisher has identified as the "narrative paradigm." Fisher has been principally concerned with discovering an approach to human communication and public discourse not wholly dependent upon "practical reason"—or upon those argumentative outlooks which he identifies with the "rational world paradigm." He suggests that equally valid forms of reasoning— or of social and political thought—might "be discovered in all sorts of symbolic action."[5] That is to say, reasoned conversation or discourse is neither historically neutral (that is, based on pure and objective rationality) nor confined to the "argumentative prose" style of journalists, commentators, and politicians operating within the dominative public sphere, based as it is on "clear-cut inferential or implicative structures" indebted to Western conceptions of logical argumentation.[6] Film, literature, and other cultural forms might be equally understood, in other words, as making some claim or argument about our world, in the same way that slang, street style, graffiti writing, and urban fashion might represent nontraditional modes of social and political thinking, often denigrated for a lack of true sophistication or principled intent.

Narrative modes of rhetoric are invested in telling argumentative stories about the world and its meanings; in many instances, narrative arguments provide alternative outlooks on events or phenomena that seemingly cannot be explained by the official rationales of public discourse and mainstream debate.

To accept the narrative paradigm is to work from "a dialectical synthesis of two traditional strands in the history of rhetoric: the argumentative, persuasive theme and the literary, aesthetic theme."[7] This synthesis requires its practitioner to accept that storytelling might also be a form of argumentation (and vice-versa). The Cubalogues certainly fit within Fisher's narrative paradigm, as they attempted to narrate the early years of Cuba's revolution in a way that ran counter to popular, journalistic renderings of Cuban events within the mainstream U.S. press. Through autobiographical reportage, the writers of the Cubalogues challenged the public rhetoric of Cold War nationalism and its monolithic appeals to anti-Communism with a narration of the "real" meaning of the revolution as they experienced it. In the process, these writers also rewrote the Beat road narrative in explicitly political terms; the Cubalogues, that is to say, were marked at times by a profound skepticism regarding the ultimate usefulness of Beat disaffection. As works of literary journalism, they foreshadowed the New Journalism to come, pushing against the discursive and argumentative assumptions of the Cold War public sphere even as they attempted to rewrite the prototypical Beat narrative in a more overtly politicized way. Just as the journalism of Tom Wolfe, Norman Mailer, Joan Didion, Truman Capote, and Hunter S. Thompson would rely on personally invested narrative and the inclusion of actual dialogue (rather than paraphrasing) in ways that challenged the professed objectivity of mainstream reporting, the Cubalogue writers embraced first-person narration and eyewitness testimony while laying claim to a factuality or truthfulness they considered absent from mainstream accounts of the same historical events.

Nevertheless, the perspectives embodied in the Cubalogues owed some debt to the Fair Play for Cuba Committee (FPCC), which sponsored the Cuban trips of Ferlinghetti, Baraka, and Schleifer between 1959 and 1961. Founded by the liberal activists Robert Taber and Alan Sagner, the FPCC also counted Sartre, Mills, James Baldwin, W.E.B. Du Bois, and Shirley Graham among its members. Van Gosse has argued that the FPCC—a signal organization of New Left liberation movements in the United States—was animated by a high degree of "Fidelismo," which initially celebrated Castro and his revolutionary circle as American insurgents in the tradition of Ethan Allen's Green Mountain Boys.[8] This sentiment was clearly registered in Taber's film documentary "Rebels of the Sierra Maestra: The Story of Cuba's Jungle Fighters," which aired on CBS in 1957, portraying Castro and his guerilla army as romantic, young freedom fighters confronting their own version of the Red Coats.[9] Along with their lionization of Castro, the FPCC was convinced early on that military intervention was imminent in Cuba in order to secure U.S. interests in corporate entities such as the United Fruit Company and International Telephone and Telegraph. The FPCC contended, in turn, that the United States should begin divesting itself of its hemispheric ambitions by taking a noninterventionist stance toward the revolution. The federal government, so the FPCC argument went, should *strengthen* diplomatic ties with Castro in order to retain post-Batista Cuba as a trading partner, thereby defusing any possibility of Soviet influence within the American hemisphere. We all know that U.S. foreign policy and hemispheric history took a far different course, a course whose ramifications we still live with today. We know far less about the role U.S. artists and intellectuals—such as those affiliated with the Beat Movement—played in challenging the inevitability of this course and of imagining new approaches to democratic life, expressive culture, and social belonging during the initial years of the Cuban Revolution.

## Beat Politics

As Cuba came to embody U.S. fears regarding Communist penetration of the Americas—a position it has yet to fully relinquish—Havana also momentarily emerged as an inter-American haven, or oppositional public sphere, for a transnational intellectual culture that created an alternative public history of U.S. social inequality, media complicity, and world-ordering ambition during one of the defining moments of the Cold War era. As we shall see, the works explored in the following chapters represent a compelling inquiry into the limits of official forms of democratic life and attendant avenues of public expression, rendered, as they were, against the backdrop of Cold War national security concerns— an inquiry still of momentous value to a turbulent and war-inflicted present in which U.S. political culture continues to promote itself as the paradigmatic representation of the political good. By extension, then, the Cubalogues ask us to reconsider stereotypical renderings of the Beat Movement and its fellow travelers as politically immature, intellectually unsophisticated, or worse yet, completely naive.

To a large extent, dismissals of the Beats as "apolitical" can be traced to early characterizations of their writing in the *Partisan Review,* one of the central harbingers of artistic, literary, and political taste during the early Cold War years. In his Spring 1958 *Partisan Review* article "The Know-Nothing Bohemians," Norman Podhoretz famously derided the Beats as childish, irrational, criminal, overly sexualized, and lacking in social responsibility, while at the same time marked by "destructive impulses," which included open hostility to Western civilization.[10] Baraka immediately attempted to defend the movement's honor (so to speak) in the Summer 1958 issue of the *Review,* identifying Podhoretz's piece as "a kind of ill-concealed rant," a politically motivated polemic whose own excessive vitriol against the New Bohemia violated the very conditions of "rational, coherent discourse" that Podhoretz claimed to be defending and that the Beats, in their purported irrationality and silliness, were accused of continually and shamelessly violating.[11] Despite Baraka's rebuttal, the enmity of Podhoretz and the *Partisan Review* toward Jack Kerouac and his fellow Beats was subsequently condensed in Daniel Bell's excoriation of the Beat Movement in *End of Ideology* (1960), one of the defining works of Cold War liberalism. Citing Podhoretz, Bell declared that "Jack Kerouac, the 'spokesman' of the Beat Generation, is, it should be pointed out, thirty-seven years old—a curious reversal of role, since the effort of the Beats is, like Peter Pan, the denial of growing up. It is, of course, an apolitical movement."[12] As was the case with other Cold War liberals, however, Bell was operating under a diminished definition of political activity that confined politics proper within highly conventional notions of constitutional proceduralism, the two-party system, and a supposedly self-evident conception of pragmatic rationality in the era of the gray flannel suit. More preoccupied with "modish and flat" interests such as Zen Buddhism, Abstract Expressionism, and "progressive" jazz, Kerouac and his peers clearly lacked, in Bell's estimation, the sober maturity distinguishing the politics of Cold War common sense, rendering them childishly "apolitical" icons of a postwar youth culture lacking in worthy values.[13]

While Bell and Podhoretz may not have been completely amiss regarding Kerouac's lack of political sophistication—indeed, as we shall see, Ferlinghetti and Baraka would express similar misgivings against the backdrop of early events in Cuba—their dismissal of the Beat Movement en masse reveals more about liberal conceptions of Cold War political activity than it does about the variety of social and political outlooks circulating within the Beat orbit during that very same era.[14] Moreover, as shall become clear over the chapters that follow, the Beat Movement that Bell and Podhoretz admonished as a form of cultural philistinism—whose proper home was the dustbin of Cold War thought—actually generated a searing rebuttal of Bell and his liberal anti-Communist peers over the course of the 1950s and early 1960s (beginning with documents such as Baraka's letter to the *Review*). U.S. militarism and world-ordering ambition have never been lacking in liberal theorists and apologists, and the Cold War period was no exception. Indeed, Ann Charters has attributed the *Partisan Review*'s hostility toward the Beats to the recalibrated politics of "New York intellectuals who journeyed from radicalism to conservatism in their careers after the Second World War," and who served as the brain trust for the *Review*.[15] Moreover, Podhoretz went on to serve as *Commentary*'s editor-in-chief from 1960 until 1995, overseeing that journal's transformation from a beacon of Jewish secularism and liberal anti-Communism into one of the central organs of neoconservative political thought—a transformation which, on its own, seems to speak volumes about the underlying motivations of the Cold War liberal ethos. In other words, simply calling these figures "conservative" (or "neocons") masks over the nuances of Cold War political divisions during a period in which many of the New York intellectuals, despite their sudden hawkishness, remained professed progressives and liberals, though the various schools of Marxist thought they had embraced during the radical 1930s had been transformed, as Andrew Ross explains, "by the new exigencies of [Cold War] national culture, defensively constructed against foreign threats and influences, and internally [consolidated] by the declaration of [the Cold War] consensus, posed in the form of a common and spontaneous agreement" concerning the fundamental goodness of U.S. political and commercial institutions, along with the nation's standing as the benevolent defender and purveyor of social justice around the world.[16] No event clarified this liberal shift away from the Marxian-inflected, labor-based leftism of the 1930s and toward the patriotic centrism of Cold War National Security culture more than the *Partisan Review*'s 1952 symposium, "Our Country and Our Culture," "in which twenty-four leading intellectuals [including Bell, Podhoretz, and Arthur Schlesinger, Jr.] responded rather favorably to the editorial suggestion that they were exhibiting a more 'affirmative' attitude toward American institutions and American culture, an attitude that was interpreted as signaling an end of a long phase of alienation on the part of intellectuals. . . . Most of the respondents, with the exception of Norman Mailer and C. Wright Mills, saw fit to agree with the editorial assumption that, compared to the thirties and forties, intellectuals were now more centrally aligned, if not wholly identified, with American political, economic, and cultural institutions."[17] During the period in question, liberalism made its way home to the hawkish center, as the *Review* became highly invested in disowning its connections to the Marxist and Trotskyite Left of the previous decades through a newfound political seriousness based on moderation and pragmatism. Or put slightly differently, the era of liberal anti-Communism represented a flattening of social and political thought in the United States as previous polarizations between Right and Left in the years leading up to World War II converged toward a shared center of global ambition.

Cold War liberals such as Bell and Arthur Schlesinger, Jr.—among the upper echelon of public intellectuals of their day—advocated legislative gradualism, constitutional proceduralism, and corporatist consensus as the preferred modes of progressive political struggle, leaving the 1930s call for a revolutionary rupturing of U.S. industrial society (and all of its attendant inequities) decisively behind. Richard Rorty has since argued that Schlesinger and other Cold War liberals represented a shining example of the U.S. "reformist left," which operates according to the pragmatic spirit of the "American civic religion."[18]

According to Rorty's narrative, Marxian influences over the social movements of the tumultuous 1930s were misguided and disastrous departures from the true American leftism, which he identifies with the reformist tendencies of Cold War liberals who decisively refocused (or attempted to instrumentalize) political activism and social justice claims "within the frameworks of constitutional democracy" rather than calling for immediate and revolutionary upheavals of American social, economic, and cultural life.[19] That is to say, figures such as Bell and Schlesinger situated liberalism within a decidedly nationalistic ethos, asserting its institutional functionalism *solely* within constitutionally authorized legislative and juridical practices where social injustice and inequity would be rectified through congressional initiative and principled court decisions, which would in turn serve as democratic beacons to the rest of the world. Collectively, then, Cold War intellectuals aggrandized forms of institutional patriotism that channeled political thought and argumentation through a highly rigidified public arena, where the preservation of national unity against a myriad of "communist" or "totalitarian" or "anti-American" threats bracketed out any social or political demands that endangered the entrenched institutions and interest structure of the Cold War nation-state and its militaristic and corporate underpinnings, constituting a largely homogenous and buttoned-up "left" more easily at home within the hawkish political center of Soviet-inspired paranoia. Eric Lott has recently referred to this intellectual phenomenon as "liberal patriotism," or a politics confidently grounded in the official policies, procedures, and institutions of the territorial nation-state, thereby protecting exceptionally American expressions of progressive thought, that is, mainstream and centrist liberalism, "against a terrible left specter," or what we might refer to as "too much," or "too radical," or "too direct" an expression of democracy.[20] Moreover, this attempted channeling of political demands through official institutions and protocols required an attenuation of political subjectivity within a tightly bounded version of the public sphere, where the pragmatic or rational—or we might say that which was "doable" without rocking the ship of the U.S. state or its corporate payload too vigorously—set the horizons for political deliberation and action.

Confronted with the patriotic earnestness and pronounced hawkishness of mainstream liberalism—or what Baraka himself has recently described as the "right-leaning liberalism" of the 1950s and 1960s—the Beats suffered collateral damage in publications such as the *Partisan Review* for their overt playfulness and perceived lack of real commitment in an era of high political seriousness.[21] As shall become evident in the following chapters, however, the Beats also articulated a number of political stances actively opposed to the pronouncements, rigidities, and confident global triumphalism of their dismissive liberal contemporaries. The Cuban encounter remains an especially important catalyst in this regard, as it allowed for the crystallization of Beat attitudes toward Cold War domestic and foreign policy, a group pronouncement of dissenting outlooks that had been deemed irrational, non-pragmatic, and even un-American by prominent public intellectuals such as Bell and Schlesinger. That is to say, the Cubalogue writers were momentarily driven by the belief that the early revolution might realize forms of cultural, racial, and sexual freedom that had been stultified in U.S. political culture by a reformist or gradualist liberal agenda that consistently attributed its unwillingness to enact drastic programs of social change—or to acknowledge the validity of anticolonial movements proliferating throughout the world—to the threatening specter of the Soviet Union, which anchored the nationalistic paranoia of the Cold War National Security State. Cold War liberalism, according to Ferlinghetti, Baraka, and others, talked a good game regarding free speech and social justice but tended to play it politically safe, identifying anything that failed to correspond with its pronounced patriotism and carefully honed pragmatism as "too radical" or, as Lott argues, too directly democratic. Worse yet, Cold War liberals played too loosely with the term "communist"—the orienting epithet of the Cold War public sphere—applying it in a cavalier fashion to political outlooks and social movements whose desires and goals they failed in many cases to understand, and whose insights might have actually enhanced the realization of a more democratic life within the mid-century United States.

## Beat Worldliness

Operating under too limited a definition of political expression, Bell's stereotypical admonition of the Beats as hopelessly immature and apolitical also failed to acknowledge that literary and artistic movements are prismatic, possessed by ambitions and objectives that can never be generalized through the work of one representative figure, such as Kerouac. While writers, artists, and intellectuals might discover a collective purpose in a shared set of historical, cultural, or aesthetic concerns, those concerns tend to refract through their work in unique and differing ways. This is particularly true of the Cubalogues, which, in a sense, might be read as a corrective to the predatory treatment of Latin America—especially Mexico—in works such as Kerouac's *On the Road* or William Burroughs's *Junky,* where characters routinely participate in forms of ethnic/racial tourism replete with exorbitant drug use, poorly formed Spanish dialogue, and sexual encounters with exoticized and underage girls and boys.[22] The Cubalogues imagined a quite different manifestation of inter-American contact and, as such, remind us that literary and other cultural movements are rarely marked by a completely uniform purpose; they tend, instead, to represent sites of intense rhetorical or argumentative activity oriented by a collective interest in particular socio-cultural predicaments or dilemmas.

Guided by this realization, recent scholarship in the field of Beat Studies has been asking us to reorient our own notions of "Beat" identity and aesthetic practices within wide-ranging textual, historical, and cultural contexts. This pronounced reclamation has led to an ongoing and expansive reformation of the Beat canon, which has simultaneously resituated Beat cultural and political concerns within broader intellectual geographies and more extensive networks of influence. With its focus on the Beat interaction with revolutionary Cuba, this project adds to a robust reconstruction of the Beat canon that is already under way, epitomized in works such as Jennie Skerl's edited volume *Reconstructing the Beats* (2004), Ronna Johnson and Nancy Grace's *Girls Who Wore Black: Women Writing the Beat Generation* (2002), and Timothy Gray's *Gary Snyder and the Pacific Rim* (2006). In her revealing discussion of the conventional Beat canon, Skerl explains that up until fairly recently "Books by scholars consist mostly of biographies and single-author studies. Most publications focus on Kerouac, Ginsberg, and Burroughs and, to a lesser extent, on Gary Snyder, Lawrence Ferlinghetti, and Gregory Corso. The dozens of other writers and artists associated with the Beat Generation have received little attention. This publication history serves to reify a restricted (white male) canon that glamorizes a few legendary figures and perpetuates an academic dismissal of popular culture icons."[23] As Skerl suggests, the Beats, for nearly their entire critical shelf life, have served primarily as fodder for literary biography, a critical practice whose intense focus on life events and endless waves of personal anecdote venerates writers and artists such as Kerouac as neo-Romantic individualists in the era of mass conformity. Undeniable as that characterization may be at times, the limited focus of single-author studies has obscured a more encompassing network of artists and concerns, which evolving developments in Beat scholarship have located within broader cultural, social, and political history. By extension, these efforts pose a serious intellectual challenge to the work of figures such as Bell, who framed his dismissal not only around conventional understandings of political thought and action, but upon a highly reductive conception of Beat writing anchored in the figure of Kerouac as an icon of youthful and unabashed irresponsibility, or, to borrow the title of one of the era's most popular teen films, as a *Rebel without a Cause* (though Bell evidently found the inspiration for his dismissal in 1953's *Peter Pan*). Oddly enough, as Skerl so helpfully points out, much Beat scholarship has actually replicated Bell's reductionism at the cost of that work which most challenges his stereotypical rendering and the accompanying Cold War politics he advocated.

Widening the focus of Beat Studies has fostered an accompanying reevaluation of the cultural geographies within which Beat aesthetics and philosophies circulated, unmooring the movement, in some intriguing ways, from its conventional anchoring points in the Bay Area and New York. Daniel Belgrad's "The Transnational Counterculture: Beat-Mexican Intersections" (included in Skerl's *Reconstructing the Beats*) reasserts, for instance, the intercultural currents running through the writings of the Beats and Magical Realists such as Octavio Paz.[24] Most recently, Timothy Gray's *Gary Snyder and the Pacific Rim* has effectively situated Snyder and, by extension, Bay Area cultural production, within a trans-Pacific sphere of creative activity during a Cold War era that often wedded anti-Asian racial sentiment to anti-Communism. Gray goes on to argue, quite persuasively, that being too strident in our regionalism might mask over more extensive networks of contact and influence, putting his work in conversation with a wealth of contemporary scholarship that asks us to view national culture as something other than self-enclosed or as the end product of a geographically delineated exceptionalism. This pronounced transnational or globalizing turn within historiography, literary, and cultural studies has been guided by the supposition that the parameters and concerns of American intellectual and expressive culture are at times generated in places other than the United States—or that the contours, attitudes, and conditions of our local contexts are often challenged, enriched, and enhanced via interactions that outstrip our immediate proximity.[25] This study, focused as it is upon inter-American cultural contact, cannot avoid the implications of these current methodological and theoretical developments. In the process, I will also be testing, in a way which Skerl and others would appreciate, the limits of conventional Beat canonicity as the contemporaneous Cuba narratives of figures such as C. Wright Mills, Harold Cruse, Carl Marzani, and Robert Williams shall be read alongside the Beat Cubalogues in the chapters that follow; as we shall see, the ideas and insights of these figures intersected with those of the Beat orbit in pronounced, influential, and documentable ways that have yet to be fully understood. The early years of the Cuban Revolution helped foster this conversation, which also included Cuban intellectuals and artists, such as Cabrera Infante and Pablo Armando Fernández, and other Latin American figures, such as Nicanor Parra and Pablo Neruda, within its purview. Considered side by side, the work of these figures reveals a more nuanced cultural history of the early Cuban Revolution, in which U.S. literary, artistic, and political culture played a prominent role and was itself changed in notable ways.

## Robert Duncan's "Stranger Relations"

To a large extent, the evolution of this study has been guided by the ethos of what Robert Duncan deemed "stranger relations"—an ethos that is key to understanding the political outlooks of several of the Cubalogue writers, along with their cohorts within the Beat Movement and San Francisco Renaissance. Responding to the Korean War in his poem, "Writing at home in history," Duncan declared that "Now if in Korea we hear there is continual killing, / now if we rightly have no longer faith in our nations, now if we tire of futile decisions, / we are at home among stranger relations."[26] Locating the Beat writers within a more encompassing set of "stranger relations" has indeed been the guiding principle of new scholarship in the field, though I shall simultaneously, and not without significant historical justification, offer Duncan's call for stranger relations as a socio-political trope that gestures toward a new set of relations with "the stranger"—an activist epistemology that resonates not only with Duncan's anarcho-pacifist writings from World War II, but with Étienne Balibar's highly influential thoughts on nationalism and national subject formation. Balibar has been principally concerned with the extent to which the national subject has existed primarily as an exclusionary concept, foregrounded for much of its history against a supporting cast of entangled "others" who serve as a collective negative supplement to the "proper" national subject and mainstream political discourse; racialized and colonized subjects, drug users, dangerous immigrants and foreigners supposedly possessed by subversive political ideas, sexually independent women, and those judged deviant in myriad other ways roam the margins of national belonging as an inter-articulated roster of abjection—or what we might refer to as its estranged or "strange" remainders.[27] As we shall see, the trajectory of Duncan's own thinking in this regard prefigures Balibar and can be traced from the print culture of World War II pacifism through postwar Bay Area cultural institutions such as City Lights Books, where it helped set the cultural stage for early Beat perceptions of the Cuban Revolution.

Duncan's initial thoughts on alternative forms of political loyalty and expressive culture emerged from within the milieu of World War II conscientious objection in the form of his 1944 *politics* essay "The Homosexual and Society." Many conscientious objectors spent World War II interned in labor camps throughout the western United States, including the camp at Waldport, Oregon, which served as home to the Civilian Public Service System's Fine Arts Project and Untide Press. Along with Dwight Macdonald's anarchist journal, *politics,* the Waldport Fine Arts Project anchored a fairly prolific alternative print culture whose depths have yet to be fully mined. This wartime print culture was animated by three intersecting political beliefs, a set of orienting ideas that resonated across the anarcho-pacifist intellectual community: first, anarcho-pacifists identified the widespread destruction of the Second World War as the inevitable result of modern, acquisitive nationalism. While asserting that the militarized nation-states at the world's industrial center posed a significant threat to the future of the planet, they in turn argued that all of the world's peoples should openly refuse to participate in the war. Second, anarcho-pacifists viewed the further consolidation of mass culture and militarized nationalism as simultaneous events that had collapsed wider vistas of human potential through the willful elimination of competitive definitions of *being* in the world. This outlook was animated by a variety of political and philosophical stances: Christian humanism, antiracism, Gandhian anticolonialism, anarchist traditions of antistatism and antinationalism, and the insurgent cosmopolitanism of figures such as Duncan, William Everson, and Kenneth Patchen. Third, these stances coalesced, more or less, into a neo-Romantic call for new subjectivities and modes of collective life disconnected from the wartime public arena and its production of dutiful national subjects, as epitomized in the realist portrayals of patriotic war preparation proffered by the Office of War Information. As such, anarcho-pacifists viewed themselves (much like the Zurich Dadaists of World War I) as an avant-garde movement advocating for more radically open and decidedly cosmopolitan forms of public dialogue and expression. A more inclusive understanding of human kinship and loyalty would require a proliferation of new cultural venues and alternative press formations, especially as existent channels of culture had become so sutured to the needs of nationalistic warfare.[28]

Anarcho-pacifists such as Duncan, Everson, and Macdonald understood these developments as ushering in an unprecedented era of mass nationalism buttressed in ever more powerful cultural apparatuses which, despite their increased reach and breadth, left no room for a public dialogue regarding more expansive—or stranger—notions of political belonging and social policy. They believed, as Charles Taylor does, that the public sphere ideally functions as an "extrapolitical" space of interaction; while it serves explicitly political purposes in terms of fostering debate and revelation (of government abuse and untruth) its democratic strength, if it can be said to possess one, must ultimately rest in its stringent independence from the will of the state and its accompanying interests—an independence that helps secure dialogue, in as open and uninhibited a fashion as possible, as a central tenet of a democratic and liberated life.[29] During the period in question, the exigencies of economic crisis and war preparation had helped refashion public culture into a fairly extensive site of administrative contact and opinion-building, to which anarcho-pacifists responded with an alternative print culture bent on theorizing new expressions of anti-militarism and political amity. This commitment to new forms of political being and belonging found its most trenchant, and certainly its most audacious, rendering in Duncan's "The Homosexual in Society," which broadened anarcho-pacifist interests in anti-nationalistic thought to touch more specifically upon sexuality and racial politics. Duncan—who had been discharged from the Army as a Classification 8 in 1941—declares at the beginning of his *politics* essay that homosexuals, like African Americans, were "yet another group whose only salvation is in the struggle of all humanity for freedom and individual integrity."[30]Homosexuals, Duncan insisted, must locate their own causes within these larger struggles, or they must actively work to forge their concerns within a more complex and inclusive alternative collective, guided by the hope of generating a shared and more expansive vision of social justice and democratic life. In turn, he criticized U.S. homosexuals for participating in a "cult of homosexuality" whose logics of exclusion, in Duncan's estimation, mirrored at times the exclusionary and xenophobic practices of nationalism itself. In response, Duncan argued for the formation of an ineluctably diverse political coalition based not on the proletarian internationalism of an earlier generation, but on stranger relations—a convergence of marginalized and differentiated human subjects across horizontal points of contact.

Duncan's article proposed a mode of coalition building in which particular forms of social oppression might become universalized in a world struggle for emancipation excessive to the narrowed conditions of nationalistic belonging. Duncan, and other anarcho-pacifists, attempted to articulate a new pathway for democratic thought based in the humanistic and cosmopolitan claim that what "can be asserted as a starting point is that only one devotion can be held by a human being . . . and that is a devotion to human freedom, toward the liberation of human love, human conflicts, human aspirations. To do this one must disown *all* the special groups (nations, religions, sexes, races) that would claim [primary] allegiance."[31] The discourses of nationalism, sexism, and racism, Duncan argued, include by excluding, leading to various forms of human encampment and estrangement. Because these logics of exclusion place limits on a more extensive sense of humanness and human potential—including within the registers of racial thinking and sexual behavior—Duncan identified them as "inhumane."[32] An effective opposition to militarized public culture and global inhumanity, Duncan asserted, could only be mounted through a coordination of dissenting counterpublics, poised to embrace alternative cultural geographies and to theorize new ways of living together in the world.

While this organic and open-ended striving for democratic existence ultimately defied realization, the commitment of Duncan and his anarcho-pacifist peers outlived World War II to play a formative role in the Bay Area Renaissance of the late 1940s and 1950s. Upon being released from the West Coast CPS camps following the war, many anarcho-pacifists headed for San Francisco and Berkeley, bringing their legacy of political and cultural activism along. Most of them gravitated toward Kenneth Rexroth's Libertarian Circle, a collective of anarchist intellectuals that came to include former internees such as Everson, along with younger Bay Area figures such as Duncan, Ferlinghetti, Michael McClure, and Allen Ginsberg.[33] The poetry of Ginsberg's father, Louis, had in fact been included in a public exhibition of pacifist art and literature, held at the Waldport Camp in 1945. Lewis Hill, a former internee at California's Coleville Camp whose poetry had appeared in Untide's literary journal, *The Illiterati*, initially proposed his idea for a pacifist radio network at a meeting of Rexroth's Circle. That network became, and still exists as, Pacifica Radio.[34] Ferlinghetti's founding of City Lights Books and publishing was also energized by these meetings. Established in 1953 by Ferlinghetti and Peter Martin, son of assassinated New York anarchist Carlo Tresca, City Lights inherited the anarcho-pacifist commitment to alternative culture, solidifying a new cultural venue for the expression of pacifist, anarchist, and other dissenting outlooks during the earliest stages of McCarthyite cultural repression.

## The Itinerary

As shall become clearer in the pages that follow, the concerns of the Cubalogues (while not always pacifistic) can be contextualized within a long intellectual and cultural history guided by the spirit of what Duncan so aptly termed "stranger relations," an ethos of political activism and belonging redirected at the normative modes of subjectivity required by Cold War nationalism; or, put somewhat differently, anarcho-pacifists like Duncan had located the preconditions of political subjectivity and social belonging within the limited arenas of mainstream public expression, as secured against various internal and external threats to national cohesion and security. The work of the Cubalogue writers further explored the limiting nature of these preconditions, especially in relation to mid-century social justice claims, while formulating unconventional or "stranger" notions of political belonging and aesthetic intention at the height of Cold War geopolitical bifurcation. Ultimately, the Cuban encounter fed many streams as the Cubalogues encompassed—and in many ways anticipated—new and competing expressions of inter-American cultural collaboration, the growing importance of black nationalism to the larger African American freedom struggle, and the gathering concerns of queer political movements; while these streams diverge at times, or head into different territories of what I have called "the strange," they nevertheless discovered a shared impetus in early revolutionary events. Grounded in this insight, my first chapter, "Hemispheric Beats (in the Bay Area and Beyond)," cuts a new analytical path through the history of Ferlinghetti's City Lights books from its inception out of postwar anarcho-pacifist culture through the early years of the Cuban Revolution. This chapter argues that City Lights Books was a central alternative press formation of the early Cold War period, pushing against the rhetorical limits of an overly nationalistic public sphere as they materialized around the postwar Bay Area. Along with advocating for widened conceptions of sexuality and interracial contact, City Lights was immersed in a series of "stranger relations" with some of Latin America's most prominent political poets from the outset, as the second City Lights edition, Rexroth's *Thirty Spanish Poems of Love and Exile* (1956), included translated poetry by Nicolas Guillen and Pablo Neruda. The influence of figures such as Guillen and Neruda on the politics and poetics of Ferlinghetti and other Beat figures has been overlooked, as has Ferlinghetti and Ginsberg's relationship with the Chilean poet Nicanor Parra, whose work was also translated in the City Lights volume *Anti-Poems* (1960) and compels us to think more deeply than we have about the hemispheric aspects of Beat attitudes and aesthetics.

Ferlinghetti believed that the postwar Latin American political experience embodied an important corrective to U.S. claims of global benevolence and the inevitability of worldwide liberal democracy—or what might be referred to as *the* orienting ideas of mainstream political expression in Cold War America. City Lights attempted to supplement these overriding claims with dissenting voices from throughout the "other" Americas, and Ferlinghetti's intentions in this regard go a long way toward explaining his response to the early Cuban Revolution in "Poet's Notes on Cuba," an essay which appeared in A. J. Muste's pacifist political journal *Liberation* (an important forerunner of New Left ideas in the United States). *Liberation* had hailed the early revolution as a democratic alternative to a world rent down the middle by Cold War geopolitical divisions, and Ferlinghetti's Cubalogue celebrates the revolution's literary/print culture as the wide-open antithesis to the compromised public sphere he had been battling at home—most publicly in the *Howl* obscenity trials of 1956. "Poet's Notes on Cuba" recalls the time Ferlinghetti spent in Havana with Neruda and the members of the *Lunes de Revolución* collective, whom Ferlinghetti views as the kindred Cuban spirit of City Lights. Overall, he asserts that despite U.S. charges of cultural repression, the public culture of the revolution was far worldlier and far less ideologically constricted than the U.S. media had suggested. Ferlinghetti locates his proof for this assertion in the number of American writers, including the Beat poets, being translated and included in *Lunes* on a regular basis. He goes on to argue, in a way which resonates with C. Wright Mills's *Listen Yankee: The Revolution in Cuba* (1960), that U.S. politicians and liberal members of the mainstream media were unable to see early Cuban events for what they truly were as the result of a rhetorical and rational block—a figurative enclosure that reduced every oppositional political movement emerging from the colonial world to "Communism" and that had drastic effects on U.S. foreign and domestic policy, not to mention national understandings of actually existing democratic culture that at times might require a certain level of unruliness and agonism.

Ferlinghetti's Cubalogue idealizes the early revolution as possessed by a radically open democratic culture, as does Harold Cruse's initial assessment of revolutionary events in 1960's "A Negro Looks at Cuba." Cruse would emerge, over the course of the 1960s, as one of the key theoreticians of black nationalism and the Black Arts Movement, and the specter of the Cuban Revolution casts a long shadow over Cruse's work from that politically tumultuous era. Chapter two, "On the Crisis of the Underground and a Politics of Intractable Plurality," explores this period of Cruse's work, which many consider to be his most innovative and invigorated. When the revolution broke out, Cruse was actually living in Greenwich Village as a struggling playwright, and another 1960 article, "Race and Bohemianism in Greenwich Village," presents the Village Beats in a positive light, as a young and sexually brash interracial cadre, which upset the Village's older, professed white liberals—many of whom were associated with the *Partisan Review* and the fledgling *Village Voice*. According to Cruse, the overwhelmingly negative white liberal response to the interracial Beat presence in the Village revealed the improbability of establishing a truly oppositional Cold War counterculture within the confines of bohemian New York, and in turn signaled his ongoing interest in the liberating promises of the Cuban Revolution for years to come. Left with some serious apprehensions regarding the dubious liberalism of the Village's "Old Bohemians" whose claims had been compromised by their unwillingness to coexist across the color line with the "New Bohemia" of the Beat Generation, Cruse composed his first Cubalogue, "A Negro Looks at Cuba," which identified Castro's revolution as the paragon of "true nationhood," mostly on account of its professed beliefs in inter-cultural diversity, which Cruse hoped would help the island traverse its long-standing racial hierarchies (unlike the ongoing racism he had witnessed in the Village).[35]

As the 1960s continued to unfold, however, Cruse increasingly lost his faith in interracial politics, arguing that African American causes had become "absorbed" into white liberal alliances in ultimately self-defeating ways—a tendency he had previously identified in relation to the supposed cultural "underground" of Greenwich Village—while advocating for an independent black public sphere capable of confronting the white interest structure as its unbending and agonistic antithesis.[36] In 1962's "Revolutionary Nationalism and the Afro-American" and 1967's *The Crisis of the Negro Intellectual* Cruse reassessed the legacies of Cuba's revolutionary upheaval while simultaneously questioning the overriding racial logics of U.S. national culture. Ultimately the Cuban Revolution challenged Cruse's earlier commitments to pursuing political change through the procedural structure of the Cold War nation-state while the persistence of a racialized poverty gap and police brutality within America's black metropolises continually marginalized African Americans, in Cruse's view, as an inner colony—or a disenfranchised nation within a nation. As such, Cruse's writings from the period explored the inconsistencies and shortsightedness of Cold War liberalism from a variety of angles, while ultimately aligning the hopes of black liberation causes with other anticolonial uprisings—such as the one Cruse had witnessed in Cuba—rather than the integrationist ethic of the mainstream Civil Rights Movement.

Amiri Baraka followed a similar trajectory out of the interracial promises of 1950s New York bohemia and toward black nationalism and global anticolonialism. My third chapter, "Unsettling the Democratic Score: Music and Urban Insurgency," traces this evolution in Baraka's work, paying particular attention to the publication history of "Cuba Libre," which first appeared in *Evergreen Review* in 1960—when Baraka was still writing as LeRoi Jones—only to be considerably revised for 1965's *Home: Social Essays*. The substantial revision of "Cuba Libre" reveals much about the myriad ways in which the Cuban Revolution influenced Baraka's artistic and political development during the early 1960s, along with a whole generation of his peers within the Black Power and Black Arts Movements to come. Baraka's pronounced interest in the musical aspects of the Cuban Revolution in turn politicized long-standing Beat interests in jazz aesthetics and came to influence several of his subsequent historical, poetic, and fictional works, which valorized African American musical traditions as an alternative public culture, the repository of a marginalized history of oppression that might play an important role in U.S. freedom struggles. Upon returning from Cuba, Baraka's interest in the political stakes of black musical expression was fueled by his concern that the mainstream Civil Rights Movement had forwarded a watered-down version of black political demands in keeping with the pragmatic, deliberative, and integrationist goals of their white liberal peers within the Democratic Party; to a large extent, his Cuba-inspired reflections place him within a protracted debate within political and intellectual history which posits direct democracy—or what I will be discussing as the democratic propensities of the *demos*—in contradistinction to representative democracy and its attendant horizons of rationality that peremptorily bind political conversation in the dominative public sphere. In works such as "The Screamers," then, Baraka refigured the Cuban peasantry into the denizens of a Newark, New Jersey, jazz club who conga their way into a direct and violent street clash with the city's repressive white police force. The revolutionary spontaneity and immediacy which Baraka admired in the early revolution and other political movements throughout the decolonizing world inspired the "stranger" political scaffolding he began erecting in works such as "The Screamers" as he attempted to imagine a black politics more affiliated with the rationales of global anticolonialism than with the legislative and deliberative strategies of mainstream U.S. liberalism. Baraka's political conversion becomes even more pronounced in the 1965 revision of "Cuba Libre," as his initial focus on music and revolutionary carnival (as generative as it was) gives way to a more prevalent discourse of armed insurrection anchored in the figure of Robert Williams. Williams, who authored the proto-Black Power text *Negroes with Guns* while exiled in Havana, suddenly emerges as the U.S. equivalent of gun-toting Cuban revolutionaries in Baraka's revised Cubalogue—though Williams had only been mentioned briefly in the original version. Chapter three ends by exploring the reasons Baraka embraced Williams's political program of armed insurrection during a period that witnessed, on one hand, widespread urban rioting and the historical reemergence of black nationalism, and on the other, the passage of the most historically significant Civil Rights legislation in the history of the United States.

Robert Williams dictated the text that would become *Negroes with Guns* to Marc Schleifer, a freelance Beat journalist who also served as the founding editor of the New York literary journal, *Kulchur. Kulchur* included Baraka and Diane Di Prima on its editorial board and, in 1961, published an abridged version of Baraka's original "Cuba Libre." Chapter four, "Beat Publics and the 'Middle-Aged' Left," centers on Schleifer's epilogue to *Negroes with Guns* and his own "Cuban Notebook," both of which he composed while interviewing Williams in Havana. Schleifer's work from the period documented the Beats' importance to the emerging rationales of the New Left while situating them within a longer— and we might say "stranger"—intellectual and institutional history. Toward this end, chapter four contains an extended explication of the historical and institutional roots of Cold War liberalism, forged as they were by Arthur Schlesinger, Jr. within the cauldron of the Office of Strategic Services during World War II. During his tenure within the Office of Strategic Services (OSS), Schlesinger, Jr., who later played a pivotal role in formulating the Kennedy administration's policies toward Cuba, helped conceptualize the rationales of Cold War liberalism in response to his lingering anxieties over the 1930s Popular Front and Latin American political movements such as the Bolivian Revolution of 1943. Schlesinger, Jr. discovered his nemeses during this period in OSS cohorts Carl Marzani and Paul Sweezy, who eventually published Schleifer's Cuba writings (in Marzani & Munsell Press and *Monthly Review,* respectively) as hostilities between the United States and Cuba were reaching their head. To a large extent, then, this chapter demonstrates the ways in which the early revolution served as a flash point for arguments concerning public political expression that had been internal to U.S. progressivism since the 1930s, as the political outlooks of the Beats became situated within a print-based counterpublic which bridged the divide between Old and New Left political activism in some revealing (if largely overlooked) ways. Both generations, Schleifer argues, discovered their antithesis in the "Middle-Aged Left" of Cold War liberalism against the backdrop of world reactions to U.S. policies in Cuba and thus helped reinvigorate U.S. protest traditions on the other side of the McCarthy era.

While the events of the early revolution catalyzed a new and generationally diverse intellectual challenge to the Cold War consensus, Schleifer also expresses a great deal of skepticism regarding the Castro regime—and does so in typical Beat fashion. His "Cuban Notebook," that is to say, resists some of the initial excitement found in Ferlinghetti's and Baraka's versions of events. On one hand, he revisits the media misconceptions regarding the revolution, which he attributes to the "New Frontier" outlook of the Kennedy administration, as epitomized by Schlesinger, Jr., who had proven adept at using the *New York Times* as his personal mouthpiece. On the other hand, Schleifer wonders whether Castro's revolution has been revolutionary enough, as it has failed in his eyes to adequately address the situation of Cuban sex trade workers who had been placed in a historically precarious position after years of serving in various manifestations of sexual labor for U.S. tourists and soldiers during the Batista era. Schleifer, in other words, transforms the Beat interest in "outsiders" such as prostitutes and homosexuals into a political bloc or invisible class formation that the revolution had not yet included within its programs, prefiguring New Left attempts to elaborate a politics more far-reaching than Old Left concerns with the proletariat or industrial working classes.

Allen Ginsberg, in his "Prose Contribution to Cuban Revolution," which serves as the focus of chapter five, attributes the revolution's blind spot in regards to sexuality to Castro's continued adherence to puritanical outlooks— outlooks which Ginsberg, sounding much like Duncan at the end of World War II, ascribes to patriarchal and homophobic forms of nationalism, which replicated the repressive socio-political structures that U.S. artists and intellectuals hoped the revolution would ultimately shun. A socio-political revolution, Ginsberg exclaims, cannot be truly revolutionary unless possessed by a willingness to rethink conventional understandings of sexuality and gender, and Castro's policies toward homosexuality had invalidated what originally seemed promising about his political movement; while the Cubalogues of Ferlinghetti and Baraka criticize the political murkiness of Beat bohemianism, Ginsberg's "Prose Contribution" comes full circle and defends the Beat romance with "personal strangeness" and the social outsider as a viable political outlook lost on those, such as Castro, whose economic determinism had come to coincide with a heteronormative vision of nationalism already prevalent within the Cold War United States and Soviet Union. The core of this chapter explores Ginsberg's claims within the context of *Pa'Lante*, a one-issue journal that was dedicated to the art and literature of the early revolution and that also included works by Baraka and Michael McClure, alongside works by *Lunes* editors Guillermo Cabrera Infante and Pablo Armando Fernández. Published in New York by the League of Militant Poets, *Pa'Lante*'s single issue replicated the intercultural or "cosmopolist" idealism of the early revolution one final time, forwarding a vision of revolutionary culture ultimately at odds with Ernesto "Che" Guevara's notion of the "New Man," which not only formalized the cultural conditions of Castro's "A True Social Revolution Produces a Cultural Revolution" but helped establish machismo and a pronounced socialist aesthetic as intertwining revolutionary values. In turn, my closing chapter examines the journal's conflicted stance on the revolution alongside the events surrounding the banning of Sabá Cabrera Infante's short film *P.M.* and the subsequent disbanding of *Lunes de Revolución* events dually overshadowed with homophobic sentiments and a desire to rid revolutionary culture of its decadent Beat elements.

Many of the insights embodied within the Cubalogues, so my coda argues, remain on the table today, as was especially evident in the rhetorical posturing surrounding Cuba and the War on Terror during the latest U.S. presidential election, not to mention the use of the Guantanamo Bay detention center to house enemy combatants in the ongoing terror war. Ultimately, then, the Cubalogues offer us a revealing set of analytical lenses that might aid us in thinking about the long relationship between U.S. foreign and military policy and the rhetorical preconditions of the public sphere, not to mention the still protracted struggle for racial democracy and more encompassing forms of same-sex recognition against the backdrop of the highly reductive U.S. nationalism so aptly diagnosed by all of these figures years ago.

# 1

# Hemispheric Beats
# (in the Bay Area and Beyond)

At a 1961 meeting of the Fair Play for Cuba Committee, Lawrence Ferlinghetti unveiled one of his most well-known poems: "One Thousand Fearful Words for Fidel Castro." Composed upon Ferlinghetti's return from Havana the previous year, the poem warned Castro that he would soon be overthrown and assassinated, much like his boyhood hero Abraham Lincoln. In a telling allusion to the Spanish-American War, Ferlinghetti declared that "Hearst is Dead but his great / Cuban wire still stands: 'You / get the pictures, I'll make the / War.'"[1] As was the case with Theodore Roosevelt's foray up San Juan Hill, Ferlinghetti believed that U.S. military intervention was a foregone conclusion augured by the yellow journalism of his time. Or as Ferlinghetti so bluntly put it: "They're going to fix [Castro's] wagon / in the course of human events."[2]

The political thrust of "One Thousand Fearful Words for Fidel Castro" was animated by the concerns of Ferlinghetti's audience: the Fair Play for Cuba Committee (FPCC), a politically active group of intellectuals, led by Robert Taber and Alan Sagner, who had taken a noninterventionist stance toward the revolution and hoped that the federal government would work to establish friendly economic and political ties with Castro's new government. Ferlinghetti's concerns for Castro and revolutionary Cuba were also influenced by his experiences on the island in December of 1960, experiences captured in his "Poet's Notes on Cuba" and published in the pacifist journal *Liberation* in March 1961. Founded by A. J. Muste in 1956, *Liberation,* a vigorous supporter of the FPCC, featured the longtime peace activists Bayard Rustin and Roy Finch (one of the cofounders of Pacifica Radio) on its editorial board, and was one of the most innovative political monthlies of the Cold War period. As the editors explained in their inaugural editorial, "Tract for the Times," they were primarily interested in theorizing a "Third Way" for democratic thought and practice in the Cold War world. The *Liberation* brain trust considered both U.S. capitalism and Soviet Communism politically bankrupt, dually characterized by an overdependence upon militarism, over-bureaucratized state structures, and severely compromised (because hyper-nationalized) public spheres. Arguing that "a central part of any radical movement today is withdrawal of support from the military preparation and activities of both the dominant power blocs," the editors asserted that rather than support Soviet-styled Communism or U.S. visions of liberal democracy, North American intellectuals should attempt to foster cooperative relationships with activists in "Western Europe, Asia, Africa, and Latin America, peoples who live 'in between' the two atomically armed power blocs."[3] Further citing the activities of "Asian Socialist parties, the Gandhian Constructive Workers . . . , non-violent responses to Colonialism in Africa . . . and the June, 1953, workers' revolts in East Germany" as political templates, the editors implored U.S. intellectuals to align themselves with a Third Camp or Third Democratic Way "striving not only to avoid war but to build a socio-economic order and culture different from both Communism and capitalism."[4]During the initial years of the revolution, Cuban reforms in the areas of literacy, the criminalization of racism, universal healthcare, and land redistribution were heralded by the *Liberation* contributors as raising the possibility of a nonideological and democratic Third Way in the Americas—or what Robert Duncan might have referred to as a political topography "stranger" than that represented on either side of the U.S.-Soviet ideological divide.

While Ferlinghetti was impressed with Castro's early reform programs, his "Poet's Notes" begin with a critique of the federal government, the CIA, and the U.S. public sphere, with liberal members of the mainstream press absorbing the most stinging blows. Poking fun at the masthead logo of the *New York Times,* Ferlinghetti begins his article by asking:

> Are we not to believe our own free press that publishes all the news that's fit to print? Unless our Leaders and our newspapers have been deceiving us and spreading great monstrous evil lies about Cuba—unless the United Press International and the Associated Press and Time, Inc. and the CIA and all the radio commentators and all the big newspapers from the *New*

*York Times* to the *San Francisco Examiner,* are wrong—unless even most "liberal" writers in the United States are wrong in condemning Castro or in failing to back him—unless they along with most everyone else in the United States have been "brainwashed by news blackout" and, worse still, don't even know it or won't admit it—then I'm a naive fool.[5]

Ferlinghetti's article attempted to dispel the myth of dictatorship, and the accompanying loss of civil and cultural liberties, which mainstream press accounts had identified as taking place in Castro's Cuba. While Ferlinghetti supported the social programs initiated under the early revolution, his Cuba notes focus much of their attention on the diversity of public revolutionary culture, especially its inter-American or cosmopolitan aspects. Against the backdrop of the U.S. public sphere and its insistence on military intervention in Cuba—an insistence documented in the article's opening lines—Ferlinghetti portrayed Cuba as a site of robust and transnational intellectual exchange. In turn, his article presents Cuba's revolutionary press as transcending the Communist-capitalist divide, based instead on maverick or "stranger" forms of cultural interaction, which the *Liberation* editors were so interested in fostering, and which, as we shall see, Ferlinghetti had himself been fostering in City Lights Books since its earliest years.

In typical Beat argot, Ferlinghetti's Cubalogue describes the general Cuban population as "'turned on,' a kind of euphoria in the air."[6] Despite mainstream press accounts of Castro as an enemy of free speech, Ferlinghetti asserts the public openness of the events taking place outside his hotel window: "At one A.M. they're still at it, at two they're still at it. Still later, I look out from hotel room and see the crowd still there, the Revolution being argued out in the night, in what looks like Free Speech."[7] He then asks, with a pronounced sense of sarcasm, "Where's the Iron Heel of the Dictator crushing the People today?"[8] While Ferlinghetti's earlier characterization of the U.S. press had questioned its complicity in "news blackout," he was quick to point out the opposite about Cuba, where "United States papers for sale in the center of Havana include the anti-Castro *Miami News* and *Miami Herald* and the *New York Times.*"[9] Free speech issues—or questions regarding what could and could not be expressed in public venues—were obviously of intense interest to Ferlinghetti, who throughout his Cubalogue attempts to correct misinterpretations of Castro's initial cultural policies while pointing out U.S. shortcomings in the same area. As a result of his own cultural activism over the course of the 1950s, Ferlinghetti was intimately aware of his own nation's deficiencies in this regard, which goes a long way toward explaining the intensity of his interest in early revolutionary affairs.

## Ferlinghetti's Cultural Activism

Ferlinghetti had spent much of the 1950s challenging what he saw as the rhetorical limits and hypocrisies of postwar U.S. culture through his participation in a variety of reportorial venues and publishing ventures—a set of commitments that eventually placed him at the center of one of the most publicized censorship trials of the Cold War era as he defended his right to publish Allen Ginsberg's *Howl and Other Poems* (1956). His first public foray into Cold War cultural politics had actually come four years prior to the *Howl* controversies, with the publication of his article "Muralist Refregier and the Haunted Post Office" in *Art Digest*. Ferlinghetti's article decried the congressional attempt at removing Anton Refregier's federally sponsored murals—documenting a populist-inflected history of California—from the Rincon Annex Post Office in San Francisco. Refregier's panels were originally commissioned under the Works Progress Administration (WPA) and were reminiscent of the populist murals of Thomas Hart Benton, with a great deal of attention focused on California's laboring classes. On account of wartime funding shortages, however, Refregier was unable to complete his project until 1948, and by that time, as Ferlinghetti explains, the United States had undergone a marked political makeover, and "Refregier's subjects came into increasingly acute focus as disputable symbols of American life."[10] Backed by organizations such as the American Legion and the Veterans of Foreign Wars, Representative Hubert Scudder (R-California) introduced a congressional resolution asking that the panels be excised from the post office walls. According to Refregier's account of the incident, Scudder was greatly offended by a panel titled *War and Peace*, which included the flag of the Soviet Union alongside the flags of the other allied powers, including of course, the flag of the United States. Citing a 1951 House Committee on Un-American Activities (HUAC) report, which listed Refregier as affiliated with twenty-three Communist-based organizations, Scudder proclaimed that the Rincon Post Office murals were "definitely subversive and designed to spread Communistic propaganda" and demanded that they be immediately removed from public display.[11] The post office was "haunted," in other words, by an earlier political moment in which the Federal government counted the USSR as its ally and actively financed art depicting working-class subject matter (through programs such as the Federal Arts Project). Ferlinghetti saw the attempt at exorcising this cultural ghost—a symbol of U.S. political and artistic history barely a decade old—as an orchestrated effort at erasing state-sanctioned populism and amity toward the Soviet Union from public memory.

Scudder's appeal to the House of Representatives was indicative of the swelling McCarthyite tide of the period, in which an intensifying wave of anti-Communist sentiment, fostered by the United States' increasingly turbulent relationship with the Soviet Union, authorized, in Ferlinghetti's eyes, the whitewashing of recent political and cultural history. The leftist political leanings of artists such as Refregier, whose work had been put to extensive use by both the WPA and the Office of War Information (OWI), had suddenly become "un-American" within the context of the rampant anti-leftism inspired by geopolitical competition with the Soviet Union, and Ferlinghetti was concerned with the extent to which the new anti-Communist consensus might place new restrictions on what could be expressed under the moniker of U.S. culture into the foreseeable future. Nevertheless, Scudder's resolution failed to pass, due primarily to a tremendous outcry from Bay Area intellectuals skeptical of the anti-Communism pervasive in the Federal government, for they feared, and rightly so, that it represented a new and pronounced attempt at the sanctioned repression of dissenting viewpoints and culture.

The Refregier Affair remains integral to understanding the political evolution of Ferlinghetti in the years leading up to the Cuban Revolution, especially as it has been largely underappreciated by scholars of the American Left such as Van Gosse. Gosse has identified Ferlinghetti's 1961 unveiling of "One Thousand Fearful Words for Fidel Castro" as a pivotal moment in the development of the Beat Generation's political outlooks. According to Gosse's narrative of Cuban events, the early revolution provided a venue in which key figures within the Beat Movement "went South" and "went Public," as "the act of physically or metaphorically going to Cuba" allowed Ferlinghetti and others to emerge from their Bohemian chrysalis as newly engaged critics of U.S. Cold War policy.[12] While the Cuban encounter undoubtedly refashioned or clarified Beat political commitments, the metamorphoses of figures such as Ferlinghetti and Allen Ginsberg were not as drastic as Gosse would have us believe. Gosse's version of the Beat encounter with revolutionary Cuba relies far too heavily on a stereotypical rendering of these writers as "thoroughly antipolitical . . . interested exclusively in unmediated experience and perhaps liberation via sex, drink, drugs, bop, and hitting the road," an overgeneralization that echoes the dismissal of the Beats by figures such as Daniel Bell and from which these figures, fresh from their Cuban experience, could only emerge as sober-minded public intellectuals guided, for supposedly the first time, by truly pressing political concerns and newly pronounced internationalist sympathies.[13] Indeed, Gosse's characterization does a great discredit to Ferlinghetti's legacy as a publisher and activist in the years prior to the Cuban Revolution, a period in which he had already taken a principled stance against the paranoia of the Cold War National Security State and the cultural shortsightedness it helped foster. That is to say, revolutionary

Havana did not represent the first time in which Ferlinghetti went either "public" or "south"; rather, the early revolution allowed him to further elaborate on a number of commitments that had been at the forefront of his cultural activism and intellectual life since the early 1950s.

Considering his political lineage, Ferlinghetti's position on the murals was nevertheless unusual. Ferlinghetti had come of political age within a postwar cultural milieu highly indebted to the tenets of wartime anarcho-pacifism as theorized by a number of artists and intellectuals who, at the height of the Second World War, had quite vociferously rejected the New Deal cultural legacy preserved in works such as Refregier's panels. Figures such as William Everson, Kenneth Rexroth, and Robert Duncan equated New Deal culture with state-sanctioned expressions of nationalism, which had foreshadowed the nationalistic mass cultures of the Second World War—a cultural turn of events that compromised more worldly or cosmopolitan expressions of human community in favor of a culturally anchored and monolithic imaginary of naturally coherent nation-states possessed by competitive geopolitical interests, and willing to bomb each other into near oblivion in order to secure those interests. Their wartime pacifism was based, in other words, on rejecting the most recognizable forms of political affiliation secured under national symbols such as the "common people" and the flag—symbols which they blamed, in part, for the widespread death and destruction of the Second World War, and from which Duncan felt especially estranged.

Rexroth, who was affiliated with Everson's Waldport Fine Arts Project, became one of Ferlinghetti's principal mentors in the years following the war, spearheading a Bay Area intellectual collective known as the Libertarian (or Anarchist) Circle. Reflecting upon his own time within the Circle, Ferlinghetti's poetic peer Michael McClure points out that Rexroth "was like Godwin was to early nineteenth-century England—an anarchist, teacher, political figure, litterateur. He was a very brilliant man and put many of us on our feet with a stance we could grow with."[14] The guiding hope of the Circle, much like Muste's *Liberation,* was the establishment and maintenance of a forum for political discussion unencumbered by the nascent political rhetoric of the Cold War. The Circle's philosophy in this regard was deeply indebted to the wartime outlooks of anarcho-pacifism, especially in its efforts at creating cultural arenas opposed to the habitual anti-Communism of the postwar U.S. media even as it was still taking shape. Rexroth himself admitted as much when he identified the wartime culture forged by William Everson and other Waldport artists as the wellspring for the anarchistic and civil libertarian elements of San Francisco culture during and after the war.[15] Rexroth's Circle provided an informal—though intellectually charged—setting in which an earlier generation of antiwar activists mingled with younger Bay Area artists and intellectuals. Regular participants included prominent members of the anarcho-pacifist movement such as Everson, Robert Duncan, Morris Graves, Roy Finch, and Lewis Hill (the cofounders of Pacifica Radio, who had both published antiwar poetry in *Illiterati* during World War II), along with up-and-coming poets such as Ferlinghetti, Michael McClure, and eventually Allen Ginsberg.

Ferlinghetti's City Lights Books emerged as one of the more tangible fruits of this inter-generational convergence. Ferlinghetti founded City Lights in 1953 (the same year as his Refregier article) with Peter Martin, the son of assassinated New York anarchist and labor agitator Carlo Tresca. It was the first all-paperback bookstore in the United States, committed to providing affordable editions of imaginative and political literature to a non-academic readership. Ferlinghetti points out that "our bookstore had an anarchist background from the beginning. We sold the Italian anarchist newspapers, and I remember that one of the people who bought these papers was the garbageman."[16] From the outset, Ferlinghetti stocked the shelves with paperback editions of the works being discussed by the Circle, as Rexroth's extensive library of volumes by figures such as Emma Goldman and Peter Kropotkin became the prototype for the early City Lights inventory.[17] As such, the bookstore provided a site of public contact for the ideas being discussed in the Circle, as did Hill's KPFA/Pacifica Radio (which featured a weekly program hosted by Rexroth). Forwarding Waldport's commitment to free speech—especially in those times during which the government declares a national crisis or identifies a pronounced threat to U.S. national security—City Lights was dedicated to maintaining a cultural space for oppositional dialogue in the politically repressive climate of the early 1950s.

Ferlinghetti's participation in the Circle, along with the subsequent founding of City Lights, facilitated a sea change in his political outlooks that had begun during the closing years of World War II. Unlike Everson and his anarcho-pacifist peers, Ferlinghetti had been an active combatant in the Second World War, enlisting in the U.S. Navy, where he was initially assigned to a sub-chaser, then eventually took command of a small navy vessel which participated in the Normandy invasion. As the war was winding to a close, Ferlinghetti served in the Pacific as a navigator on an attack transport and took part in the occupation of Japan. Arriving on the Japanese coast six weeks after the nuclear attack on Nagasaki, he traveled to the bombed-out city hoping to witness the devastation firsthand, only to be emotionally overwhelmed by the lingering death and destruction. It was at this point, he later claimed, that he first gave serious thought to pacifistic philosophy.[18] Then, in 1950, attracted by the burgeoning artistic and literary scene in northern California, Ferlinghetti migrated from Paris (where he had attended the Sorbonne on the G.I. Bill) to San Francisco.

He became acquainted with Rexroth in 1951 and immediately began attending Circle meetings. All things considered, Ferlinghetti's wartime experiences might explain, in part, his defense of Refregier. To a large extent, he was more historically invested in the visual culture of World War II than his eventual mentors, who had rejected the symbols of militarized national life and followed, to one extent or another, the call of conscientious objection. Whatever his reasons may have been, they initially inspired him to paddle against the gathering McCarthyite maelstrom, thereby inheriting a tradition of free speech activism that catalyzed the founding of City Lights Books and sent him on a political trajectory that eventually forfeited the symbolic trappings of Cold War nationalism for a politics more strictly in line with his anarcho-pacifist peers and mentors within the Libertarian Circle.

### "Howling" Across the Bay Area

City Lights Books anchored one hub of a political and aesthetic culture that soon flourished in North Beach coffee houses, taverns, small art galleries, and public poetry performances. Suspicious of the mainstream political rhetoric of the McCarthyite period—as documented by Ferlinghetti in his 1953 *Art Digest* article—North Beach culture propelled the anarcho-pacifist quest for antinationalistic conceptions of human community and "stranger" expressions of political subjectivity far into the Cold War period. Toward this end, City Lights also became a small press publisher of poetry in 1955, and one of the chief outlets of the region's poetic renaissance. Ferlinghetti's own *Pictures of the Gone World* represented the first volume in what would become the press's worldrenowned Pocket Poet series, paperback volumes of poetry cut to fit into the back pocket of their owner's denim jeans—or sized, in other words, for going easily "on the road." Allen Ginsberg's *Howl and Other Poems* was published as volume 4 of the Pocket Poet series, and the ensuing censorship trials surrounding its publication further foregrounds the stakes of early Beat politics, while providing a valuable cultural backdrop to Ferlinghetti's eventual veneration of Cuba's early revolutionary culture.

Ginsberg himself had arrived in San Francisco in 1954 bearing a letter of introduction addressed to Rexroth from William Carlos Williams. On account of Williams's significant reputation, this letter granted Ginsberg immediate access to the Circle and its corresponding political and cultural scene. Everson explains that it was Rexroth who originally "attracted Ginsberg [to San Francisco]. He liberated Ginsberg, you might say. Ginsberg came from an environment where people like Lionel Trilling, people like that at Columbia—they weren't radical in any sense. They were politically liberal, but Kenneth was *radical*."[19] The political ramifications of these shifting loyalties should not be understated. Trilling and his wife Diana, as Everson notes, were central figures of Cold War liberal culture, key players in an influential cadre of artists and intellectuals whom Rexroth identified as his nemesis, and to whom he derisively referred, on account of their pronounced hawkishness, as the "Drop the Bomb Now Boys."[20] The Trillings had taken a leading role in Sidney Hook's American Committee for Cultural Freedom (ACCF), a CIA front organization that was virulently anti-Communist and involved in promoting "properly American" culture abroad through exhibitions, and at home in publications such as the suddenly patriotic *Partisan Review,* whose contributors, such as Norman Podhoretz, consistently excoriated Beat writing during the same period (and whose founding editor, Philip Rahv, also became associated with the ACCF during the 1950s).[21] Trilling's initial response to "Howl," a draft of which Ginsberg mailed him from San Francisco, was overwhelmingly negative. Calling the poems "dull" and lacking in "real voice," Trilling explicitly rejected the poem's "doctrinal element," complaining that "I heard it very long ago and you give it to me in all its orthodoxy, with nothing new added."[22] Ginsberg's corresponding embrace of Rexroth was in essence an embrace of a different literary and political community operating in the Bay Area, as San Francisco's elder statesman of anarchist poetics would prove a more supportive mentor of Ginsberg's radical leanings than had the Trillings.

*Howl and Other Poems,* composed in San Francisco during 1955 and 1956, was largely a product of Ginsberg's new cultural and political milieu aligned, as it was, against the hawkish consensus at the heart of U.S. political and intellectual culture. Michael McClure has described the political and cultural concerns of this emergent underground—or literary counterpublic—in the following way: "We were locked in the Cold War and the first Asian debacle—the Korean War. My self-image in those years was of finding myself—young, high, a little crazed, needing a haircut—in an elevator with burly, crew-cutted, square-jawed eminences, staring at me like I was misplaced cannon fodder. We hated the war and the inhumanity and the coldness. The country had the feeling of martial law. An undeclared military state jumped out of Daddy Warbucks' tanks and sprawled over the landscape."[23] In McClure's estimation, Bay Area artistic and literary culture represented an alternative, poetic public, a cultural oasis much like the one Everson and others had imagined at the outset of the Second World War. Along with City Lights Books, this literary counterpublic was embodied in Bay Area journals such as *Ark* and *Circle,* the former of which was published by ex-Waldport internee Jim Harmon, and which helped extend the political and cultural goals of Waldport into the postwar period. *Ark's* leading editorial, for example, declared that "Today, at this catastrophic point in time, the validity if not the future of the anarchist position is more than ever established. It has become a polished mirror in which the falsehood of political modes stand naked."[24]

Public poetry performance also provided shape to Ginsberg's new milieu. The assertion of poetry as public performance was based on a simultaneous rejection of isolated, university poetry culture—lorded over by liberal figures such as Trilling and the more conservative New Critics—and the public culture of the Cold War, which was viewed as the propagandistic extension of the anti-Communist, military state. Bay Area readings were in turn understood as an alternative cultural medium marked by an oppositional poetics, speaking to and forging a counterpublic that rejected Cold War rhetoric and the Korean War (ostensibly the first toppled piece in Eisenhower's "domino theory" of foreign policy). No poetry reading was more important—or has been more mythologized—in this regard than the October 1955 Six Gallery reading in which Ginsberg recited "Howl" publicly for the first time. McClure, Philip Lamantia, and Gary Snyder were also on the program, with Rexroth serving as master of ceremonies. But it was Ginsberg's poem that made the largest impression on the crowd of approximately three hundred that had crammed into the North Beach garage become art gallery. McClure later reflected that the Six Gallery reading represented "Allen's metamorphosis from quiet, brilliant, burning bohemian scholar trapped by his flames and repressions to epic vocal bard."[25] The event represented, in other words, Ginsberg's emergence as a public persona in the Bay Area, and eventually American culture in general.

Ferlinghetti was also present at the Six Gallery readings and immediately decided to publish a volume by Ginsberg, with "Howl" as its centerpiece. The first edition of *Howl and Other Poems* was printed by Villiers in England, then seized by U.S. customs agents, on March 25, 1957, as "obscene" under section 305 of the Tariff Act of 1930. On account of the book's open homoeroticism and frank portrayals of drug use, accompanied throughout by a quite tangible condemnation of the Cold War national security state, Ferlinghetti had expected trouble and had in fact contacted the American Civil Liberties Union (ACLU) beforehand.

His trepidation was understandable, especially given the conflation of homosexuality with Communism and political subversion during the period in question—a phenomenon I will address in some detail in chapter five. Of more immediate concern is Ferlinghetti's defense of his decision to publish Ginsberg's poetry, in the May 19, 1957, edition of the *San Francisco Chronicle*, at which point he also demanded that U.S. Customs immediately release the seized copies. William Hogan allowed Ferlinghetti to use his Sunday column space, "Between the Lines," for his explanation and appeal. Writing in Hogan's space, Ferlinghetti declared that what custom agents found truly obscene about the work was its explicit critique of "atom bombs and insane nationalisms, billboards and

TV antennae," a set of critiques that followed in the World War II tradition of anarcho-pacifism espoused by "Henry Miller, Kenneth Patchen, [and] Kenneth Rexroth."[26] *Howl's* seizure, Ferlinghetti further explained, was symptomatic of a larger problem concerning U.S. Customs and the circulation of unpopular cultural and political viewpoints, which they attempted to stop at the borders through a variety of tactics (including the well-worn "obscenity" charge). Moreover, Ferlinghetti made clear that Rexroth "on his KPFA program has regularly castigated the Customs for such seizures," of which *Howl* was only the most recent example. Customs, that is to say, had become a site for weeding out "foreign" ideas and culture according to the dictates of paranoid Cold War nationalism. It is worth pointing out, however, that Ferlinghetti noted the ultimately self-defeating nature of the Customs seizure as he thanked San Francisco's customs officials "for seizing Allen Ginsberg's *Howl and Other Poems* and thereby rendering it famous."[27] Ferlinghetti's prescience in this regard was soon verified by the public outpour of support for both him and Ginsberg. The ensuing public outcry in the Bay Area, accompanied by the legal pressures applied by the ACLU and Lewis Hill's broadcast of Ginsberg's poetry on KPFA/Pacifica, resulted in a decision by the U.S. Attorney at San Francisco to release the seized copies into Ferlinghetti's possession.

But Ferlinghetti's troubles did not end there. Soon after the Villiers editions were released, members of the San Francisco Police Department's juvenile division showed up at City Lights and purchased a copy of *Howl and Other Poems* from Shigeyoshi Murao, a former Japanese internment camp prisoner who ran the day-to-day operations of the North Beach bookstore. Shortly afterward, Murao and Ferlinghetti were both arrested and charged with selling lewd material that threatened the well-being of San Francisco's children. This time the trial was covered by the national press. Over the course of the trial it became rather obvious that the prosecutors were concerned about two poems in particular: "Howl" and "America." As part of Murao and Ferlinghetti's defense, their ACLU attorney requested that literature professors and notable poets write opinions concerning the poetry's social and cultural value. Those who answered this request included: Duncan, Rexroth, Patchen, San Francisco State professor Herbert Blau, editor of *Poetry* Henry Rago, and University of California Professors Mark Schorer and Leo Lowenthal.[28] One of the great ironies of the trial, then, was that it compelled professors to consider "Howl" and "America" as serious works of literature. That is to say, the testimonies and opinions given in Murao's and Ferlinghetti's defense represent the first scholarly work on Ginsberg's poetry. Moreover, the national publicity the trial received actually introduced Ginsberg's poetry and City Lights Books to a readership far beyond San Francisco, a development that flew in the face of the original goal of seizing the work. In the end, Murao and Ferlinghetti were ultimately found innocent by Judge Clayton Horn, who viewed the poem as an important humanistic "indictment of those elements in modern society destructive of the best qualities of human nature; such elements are predominantly identified as materialism, conformity, and mechanization leading toward war."[29]

## "Howling" Across the Americas

Contrary to Gosse's characterization of Ferlinghetti's political epiphany in Cuba, the young poet, journalist, and publisher had been working at the forefront of Cold War public intellectualism throughout the 1950s. Moreover, the Havana trip did not represent Ferlinghetti's first foray into the Latin American cultural scene—or it was not the first time, to use Gosse's phrase, that Ferlinghetti had "gone South." In 1959, Ferlinghetti and Ginsberg had attended the International Writers' Conference at the University of Concepción in Chile, a conference attended by representatives from twenty-five other American nations. Conference sessions focused predominantly on the artist's role in forwarding egalitarian political change within the American hemisphere and one of the chief points of discussion was the recent revolutionary upheaval in Cuba, which participants openly debated as a possible blueprint for Latin American autonomy.[30] Overwhelmed by Latin American poverty, and deeply impressed by the political zeal of his inter-American peers, the conference deepened Ferlinghetti's understanding of U.S. foreign and economic policy. Despite governmental claims of benevolence and inter-American economic development, Ferlinghetti admitted upon returning to the states that he now considered the United States "a great, fat, omnivorous crab . . . sitting on the top of the Pan American hemisphere, sucking the marrow from its soft underside."[31] Ferlinghetti further admitted his disgust over being duped by the mainstream press, which had helped consolidate the image of U.S. benevolence in the national perception of Latin American affairs. The widespread poverty and sickness witnessed by Ferlinghetti was in stark contrast to media portrayals of the United States as the munificent hemispheric purveyor of liberal democracy and prosperity. Ferlinghetti was so moved that he traveled back to San Francisco through Central America, hoping to gain a fuller understanding of the "crab-like" tendencies of U.S. policies throughout the region.

The Second World War had allowed for a pronounced expansion of U.S. interests and influence throughout Latin America, though in traveling across the region in 1959, Ferlinghetti failed to see the positive ramifications of this historical shift. During the war, the federal government agreed to bank the troubled Brazilian steel industry and in return Brazil had allotted territory to the United

States for the Army Air Corps base at Natal—the base that launched the most air sorties during World War II.[32] Aside from these new financial arrangements, in which U.S. dollars were brokered for large parcels of Latin American property, the war had tightened the inter-American trading system in two other prominent ways: first, Latin America became a major supplier of raw materials for the war effort, cementing the influence of U.S. industrial and financial firms throughout the American hemisphere. Second, these new relationships corresponded with the dismantling of Latin American–European trade, due mostly to submarine warfare in the Atlantic. Britain and Germany, who had been two of Latin America's central trading partners prior to the war, were ill-equipped to restore these ties in the wake of fighting, as their industrial infrastructures had been severely compromised.[33] As a result, U.S. firms became more firmly entwined in the business of Latin America than ever before. They forged new business relationships with Latin America's landowning elites and military castes, who maintained a significant disparity in income over the peasantry and poor they employed in export businesses (mostly agricultural) whose main beneficiary was the United States.[34] Through these new and expanded relations, the United States was able to maintain the economic superiority the war had helped solidify; by extension, the Cold War fear of Latin American political movements, traveling under the rhetorical motifs of anti-Communism, was anchored in the desire to maintain the economic and political geographies of the American hemisphere in a hierarchical configuration.

Ferlinghetti was so taken with the Latin American situation that upon returning to San Francisco, City Lights Books published a volume of pocket poetry by the Chilean poet Nicanor Parra, whom Ferlinghetti had befriended at the University of Concepción conference. Ferlinghetti hoped that the 1960 publication of Parra's *Anti-Poems* would introduce a broader U.S. audience to Parra and Latin American political poetry in an affordable, translated edition. In a highly important sense, though, the Parra translations simply built upon the inter-American connections City Lights had established as early as its second published volume, a short collection of translations by Kenneth Rexroth titled *Thirty Spanish Poems of Love and Exile* (1956), which had included poems by Pablo Neruda and Nicolas Guillen. That is to say, Ferlinghetti's efforts at situating Beat poetics within a more expansive inter-American context began prior to his ever stepping foot in Chile; released in 1955, Rexroth's translations speak to the "stranger," inter-American interests of Ferlinghetti's publishing house from its founding moments. The poems contained within *Thirty Spanish Poems of Love and Exile* are exactly as advertised—thirty poems by Spanish and Latin American poets who had all, for one political reason or another, been uprooted from the exigencies of clearly delineated national belonging, a collective trait that resonated with the willed anti-nationalism of wartime anarcho-pacifism and the thinkers surrounding *Liberation*. Rexroth's translations included poetry by Rafael Alberti and Arturo Serrano Plaja, both of whom had been exiled from Spain following the Spanish Civil War, alongside the selections by Neruda and Guillen. The inclusion of these poets in a single volume is interesting for the simple fact that it bridges the Spanish Civil War—an important symbol for the Old Left of the 1930s—with political poetry from postwar Latin America, which would emerge as an important site of contact for the American New Left in places such as Cuba.

Guillen was an especially important figure in this regard. Concerned with racial justice for Afro-Cubans his entire life, Guillen had been a close associate of Langston Hughes, and as a young poet had elevated Afro-Cuban vernacular into poetic form—much as Hughes had done for black vernacular speech at the height of the Harlem Renaissance. Also like Hughes, Guillen had a lifelong love affair with jazz and Afro-Cuban musical genres, helping to establish Cuba's contribution to Black Atlantic cultural forms as worthy of contemplation and emulation. He ran for the Cuban Senate as a member of the Communist Party in 1948 but spent most of the 1950s abroad, predominantly in the Communist bloc beyond the reach of Fulgencio Batista, who wanted Guillen jailed for his leftist politics. Rexroth points out in his introduction that Guillen—an expatriated "world citizen"—had spent the 1950s traveling through Russia, the Balkans, and China, though his translation of Guillen's poem "Satchelmouth" deserves the most attention in the current context. As a paean to jazz aesthetics, bearing some obvious traces of the homoerotic, the poem anticipates thematic concerns that would become closely associated with the U.S. Beat Movement beginning with *Howl and Other Poems* (which joined the City Lights catalog later that year). In his inter-American address to U.S. jazz artist Louis Armstrong, Guillen informs the trumpet player that "You know you got sweet lips," while simultaneously lamenting Armstrong's loyalty to his wife, who, we are told, keeps the musician well-satiated.[35] Or as the poet puts it: "Your old lady keeps you nice, / Cause you give her all of it."[36] Guillen's deceptively simple poem addresses outsider sexuality within a transnational aesthetic topography which was important to figures such as Duncan and, as we shall see, was to become equally important to Ginsberg, Baraka, and others. Moreover, Rexroth's short volume of translations embedded these concerns within a corresponding interest in Latin American poetics, with a special emphasis placed on leftist poets such as Alberti, Plaja, Neruda, and Guillen just as the engines of McCarthyism were kicking into high gear. In each of these ways, *Thirty Spanish Poems of Love and Exile*, published during the founding moments of City Lights Books, asks us to reconsider the Bay Area Renaissance as something more extensive than a regionally based bohemianism, while providing us with a valuable urtext for exploring the "strange" Cold War concerns of a group of figures whom many continue to identify as "apolitical."

Michael Davidson has described the Bay Area Renaissance as a utopian movement searching for a new sense of cultural community in the wake of the destruction of World War II and the cultural backwardness of Truman-McCarthyism.[37] The early publishing activities of Ferlinghetti undoubtedly attest to this search, though Davidson's characterization confines Bay Area cultural yearnings within the borders of an isolated and regional bohemianism. Rexroth's early City Lights translations, along with the subsequent publication of Parra as a fellow inter-American writer, asks us to rethink the cultural geography of the American Beat Movement beyond the national and regional boundaries which have often been conventionally assumed—cultural boundaries whose efficacy and worthiness had been challenged by Rexroth and his anarcho-pacifist peers since the height of World War II .[38] Much like Neruda and Guillen, Parra had a long history of radical aesthetic commitments in the Americas. As Fernando Alegria has explained, Parra served as the principal intellectual and artistic catalyst of Chile's "Generation of 1938," a modernist movement with deep proletarian sympathies, whose poetic creations were marked by "eccentric imagery [and] . . . humorous bitterness . . . with which they [broke] the facade of the bourgeois institutions' condemnation and [arrived] at the creation of a poetic atmosphere of lucidity and dynamic disorder."[39] Coming of artistic age during Chile's Popular Front period, Parra described himself as a "non-militant leftist," influenced by the Dadaists and Surrealists, who had dedicated himself to becoming a "spontaneous, natural poet, within reach of the ordinary public."[40] Parra branded his poetry "anti-poetry" on account of its interest in public contact and its corresponding opposition to academicism, a goal shared by his contemporaries in the U.S. Beat Movement who had resurrected the popular idiom and public performance as two of the hallmarks of their own poetics.

Parra's commitments, and their relationship to Beat aesthetics and politics, are clearly evident in "Vices of the Modern World," the opening poem of Parra's City Lights volume, Anti-Poems. Set in an unnamed Latin American city, the poem unfolds in an anarchic urban space gripped by "modern delinquents," resembling the collective anti-hero of Ginsberg's "Howl," who have sent the police "flee[ing] in terror" as they burned the city to the ground.[41] The opening lines of the poem capture a list of grievances which have set this rioting and burning in motion: "Vices of the modern world: / The automobile and the movies, / Racial segregation, / Extermination of the redskin, / The slick tricks of big bankers, / The catastrophe of the aged."[42] Parra's poetry resembles Ginsberg's Howl and other Poems in both its cataloging of political

36   The Cubalogues

complaints and incantatory nature, as well as its portrayal of U.S. aggression as a "phallic" exercise. I am thinking here of Ginsberg's famous admonition, in the poem "America," that the United States "Go fuck [itself] with [its] atom bomb."[43] U.S. capitalist extraction in Latin America, Parra tells us, is based upon the "Deification of the phallus, / International policy of open legs backed by the reactionary / press, / Lust for power and lust for profit, / The rush after gold, / The fatal dance of dollars."[44] As with the atom bomb in Ginsberg's "America," Parra cast the United States as a penetrating phallus, aroused by cooperative Latin American governments and journalists who willingly surrender to corporate lust.

Ferlinghetti's and Ginsberg's attendance of the 1959 writers conference—along with their ensuing relationship with Parra and subsequent interest in Cuban political events—stands in stark contrast to other (and some may say more conventional) Beat interactions with Latin America, especially in the road narratives of figures such as Jack Kerouac and William Burroughs. To a large extent, Kerouac's road novels and stories recast the economic outcasts of the 1930s (such as the Dust Bowl migrants) as young outsiders, helping to feed the expanding consumer needs of Cold War youth culture. As Morris Dickstein has explained in *Leopards in the Temple,* postwar economic growth had led to increased disposable income for American teenagers and the U.S. culture industries responded by creating new forms of entertainment and amusement for these deep-pocketed teens; Kerouac ultimately became a central producer and mythical figure of this brash, new youth culture, alongside other commercial and literary figures such as James Dean, Marlon Brando, and Holden Caulfield. A culture of commercially sanctioned disaffection, haunted by the spectral figures of Depression-era migration and the wandering, returning soldier, was passionately embraced by a generation of automobile- and motorcycle-obsessed youth "on the go," searching for carnal elation at tremendous speed, their collective affect vacillating between cool apathy and the ardent intensity of the recently converted.[45] Fittingly, when Kerouac's youthful characters travel south of the U.S. border, as in *On the Road* (1957), their chief interest lies in new drug experiences and vaguely defined, quasi-religious ecstasy—along with a sexual encounter or two with prostitutes (usually underage). Burroughs's *Junky* (1953) and *Yage Letters* (1963) are also illustrative in this regard. While these narratives obviously attested to physical and spiritual needs that had previously gone unmet by a burgeoning consumer society, they tended to offer fleeting modes of ecstasy—oftentimes based on objectifying an extensive cast of racial and economic others as drug providers and a sexual servant class—as the principal response to postwar feelings of social alienation.[46] But during the very same period, figures such as Ferlinghetti and Ginsberg also traveled into Latin America looking not for "cheap kicks" and guiltless gratification, but inter-American amity and new expressions of democratic culture.

## Spontaneity in Transnational Havana

Infused by these hopes, Ferlinghetti's *Liberation* article lionizes Cuba as home to a cosmopolitan and transnational literary culture, which included the work of the Beats and an extended international cast of writers and intellectuals within its purview. One of Ferlinghetti's initial stops on his tour of revolutionary Havana was at the office of *Revolución*—the official periodical of the revolution—where he spent time conversing with several unnamed Cuban writers and members of the editorial staff, gathering their impressions of the revolution's aims and goals. During this rather telling conversation, a few members of the staff informed Ferlinghetti that they had recently met with C. Wright Mills during his Cuban visit. While they admit that Mills seemed "pretty naïve" about the events of the revolution to that point, they applauded the American sociologist for his diligence and interest in talking to everyone he could regarding the revolution's direction.[47] The book that resulted from Mills's Cuban visit, *Listen, Yankee!* (1960), had yet to appear in a Spanish-language edition (it would later in the year), but Ediciones R (the Revolution's publishing house) had just finished translating Jean-Paul Sartre's *Visita A Cuba*, along with publishing a new volume of stories by Guillermo Cabrera Infante, the chief editor of *Lunes de Revolución*, whom Ferlinghetti would encounter later in his visit.

While the editorial staff of *Revolución* considered Mills naive, Ferlinghetti obviously held the Columbia professor in high regard, as witnessed in his elegy to Mills, "Parade Tirade," published in *Liberation* shortly after the sociologist's death in 1962. It is fairly safe to assume that the leather jacket–clad, motorcycle-riding professor participated in a politics of style that must have resonated deeply with the Beat writers—not to mention Che Guevara, who had once toured South America on a motorcycle.[48] *Listen, Yankee!*—which might be identified as a book-length Cubalogue—couched itself as an intervention into media misrepresentations of the revolution, while promising to insert "sound information" into the public record.[49] Mainstream journalists, according to Mills, lacked the intellectual and theoretical background necessary to understand the varieties of leftist politics emerging in the global scene and instead reverted to tired critiques of Communism—framed in nationalist habits of Cold War thought—in order to explain away happenings that were beyond their narrow comprehension. Mills explains that "to most [journalists], judging by our newspapers, it all appears as just so much 'communism.' Even those with the best will to understand, by their very training as well as the restraints upon their work, are not able to report fully enough and accurately enough the necessary contexts, and so the meanings, of revolutionary events."[50] What was emerging in Cuba, according to Mills, was not conventional, party-driven Communism, but the voice of the "hungry-nation bloc" or global anticolonialism, which included emergent nations throughout Latin America, Asia, and Africa. If we accept Mills's account, this miscomprehension on the part of the U.S. media was attributable to a false political analogy that collapsed the rationales and histories of anticolonialism into Soviet Communism in order to dismiss them as antithetical to the U.S. plan for the world—and to anchor the militaristic defense of U.S. hemispheric interests and national security if need be. The perception of Cuban events was obfuscated, in other words, by the *analogical Cuba;* rather than serving as a clarifying comparison, the joining together of the *analogue* (the Soviet Union) and the *target* (Cuba and the hungry-nation bloc) provided a convenient figurative shortcut across a gap in training or experience, a lacuna in which the production of public opinion emerged in support of an increasingly hostile U.S. stance toward Castro's young government.

Mills viewed the Cuban Revolution as a spontaneous anti-capitalist democracy in its becoming—a series of events unfolding prior to their strict political theorization. That is to say, Mills was engaging in an act of counterimagination whose own analogical framework was tuned to other anticolonial demands, out of which, as the editors of *Liberation* also imagined, might emerge a third way for thinking about global relations in the Cold War world. Resisting the U.S. model of liberal, free-market democracy *and* the Soviet model of highly centralized state socialism and its attendant "labor metaphysic," the early Cuban Revolution, according to Mills, exemplified the efforts of other decolonizing societies to autonomously re-create their political and cultural life-worlds as they went along.[51] As we shall see, Castro's own vision of the Revolution in its early moments corresponded with Mills's vision of political and cultural spontaneity, a vision that came officially to a halt only after the Bay of Pigs invasion. According to Mills, the U.S. press was unable to recognize the spontaneous and nonideological nature of the Cuban situation on account of a cognitive block, a rational (and thus rhetorical) restraint that could only identify the seizure of U.S. corporate interests as just another Communist threat to U.S. national security. The authors of the article-length Cubalogues come to largely the same conclusion: the Revolution could not be openly discussed in the U.S. public sphere as a result of Cold War habits of thought that foreclosed on the meaning of Castro's actions long before they had reached an explicit formulation or theorization.

What is particularly striking about Mills's diagnosis of the revolution as an improvised and nonideological event is that it resonates not only with Beat interests in the social and political value of spontaneity, but with an ethics of spontaneity which, as Daniel Belgrad has pointed out, provided the framework for so much of postwar intellectual and artistic production within the United States. Spontaneity and improvisation, according to Belgrad's take on Cold War intellectual and cultural history, were the central gestures or animating ethos of the postwar avant-garde, emerging in an oppositional or resistant fashion against the backdrop of an expansive mass culture that "fostered an image of American supremacy based on a combination of wartime and Cold War xenophobia (a fear of 'un-Americanism') and pride in America's material prosperity ('The American Way of Life')."[52] Those artists and thinkers who embraced spontaneous gestures were largely assuming a confrontational stance against what they considered to be increasingly pervasive cultural, social, and political rigidities grounded in the groupthink of the anti-Communist consensus, the ascendency of corporatism, and an ever more bureaucratized approach to national life. Spontaneity and improvisation were socially and politically significant, in other words, to not only the Beats but artists such as Miles Davis, Jackson Pollock, Robert Rauschenberg, and Larry Rivers, and as shall become abundantly clear, this pervasive ethics of spontaneity goes a long way toward explaining why figures such as Ferlinghetti, Mills, and Baraka configured the fledgling Revolution as largely unpremeditated—and thus powerfully open and free—in its attitudes toward culture and politics.

In any case, Mills's notion of an analogical block at the core of Cold War reportorial culture brings me back to my earlier discussion of Walter Fisher, especially his critique of the "rational world paradigm." The rational world paradigm assumes that human communities faced with pressing social and political issues are capable of rational argument; rational argumentation, pursued through precise and unambiguous "inferential structures," is understood as the most advanced model of collective decision making.[53] But Fisher also suggests that rational limits correspond with the reproduction and interests of the national community, and it is here that his work sheds much light on the Cubalogues as vital transnational narratives. Fisher suggests that the "actualization of the rational world paradigm . . . depends on a form of society that permits, if not requires, participation of qualified persons in public decision-making. It further demands a citizenry that shares a common language . . . [and] general adherence to the values of the state. . . . Because the rational world paradigm has these requirements and because *being rational* (being competent in argument) *must be learned,* an historic mission of education in the West has been to generate a consciousness of national community and to instruct citizens in at least the rudiments of logic and rhetoric."[54] Fisher's characterization of the rational world paradigm asks us to consider the extent to which the discursive boundaries of rationality are roughly congruent with the geopolitical boundaries of modern nationality in the West. He suggests, in other words, that the limits of rationality (that is, what can and cannot be accepted as a legitimate rational argument) are neither neutral nor ahistorical, but related to "the values of the state" and preservation of national community.[55] The speaker (or journalist or political candidate) can be judged as rational only in the case that the speaker reflects values and outlooks that are recognizable to the other rational members of the nation-state (comprising what Benedict Anderson has famously called the "imagined community"). This is precisely what is at stake in Mills's characterization of the reportorial restraints on the mainstream press in the United States. Thanks to the long-standing relevance of Cold War political logic, journalists were stunted in their ability to portray Cuban events. The anti-Communist consensus, or what Mills oftentimes referred to as the "main drift" of Cold War intellectual and political culture, had established preargumentative or prediscursive limits on the discussion of world politics, limits that the dominant interest structure—stinging from Castro's nationalization of U.S. enterprise in Cuba—was all too willing to accept.

Generally speaking, the Cubalogues rejected the argumentative prose of the rational world paradigm for a narrative approach to Cuban events in which eyewitness testimony—framed within a mutated form of Beat travel narrative—attempted to formulate a new political imaginary on the other side of the discursive (and national) horizon. Escaping Cold War habits of thought required escaping the discursive constraints of the peremptory public sphere, as the writers of the Cubalogues relied on the alternative press (represented by journals such as *Liberation, Evergreen Review,* and *Monthly Review*) to disseminate their unconventional renderings of Cuban events. In a sense, these alternative renderings were products of the transnational intellectual climate fostered by the Revolution in its early years. Ferlinghetti's "Poet's Notes on Cuba" is principally interested in documenting this open climate in contradistinction to reportorial portrayals of the revolution as the enemy of cultural freedom. This becomes particularly evident in his treatment of the revolution's literary journal, *Lunes de Revolución.*

On his fourth day in Cuba, Ferlinghetti met with Pablo Armando Fernández, the assistant editor of *Lunes.* As the cultural centerpiece of the early revolution, *Lunes* was distributed weekly in the Monday edition of *Revolución* from 1959 through much of 1961. At the height of its popularity *Lunes's* circulation reached 250,000 copies, making it, as William Luis has pointed out, "the most widely read literary supplement in the history of Cuban and Latin American literatures."[56] From the outset, *Lunes* attempted to be as inclusive as possible in its editorial policies, as the editors claimed in the opening essay of the inaugural issue that "We are not part of a group, neither literary nor artistic. . . . We do not have a defined political philosophy, although we do not reject certain systems which approach reality—and when we speak of systems we are referring, for example, to dialectical materialism or psychoanalysis, or existentialism."[57] If, as Luis has explained, *Lunes* could be said to have had a politics, it was informed by a commitment to broadly conceived notions of an anti-imperialistic American hemisphere, along with an embrace of modernity and its intellectual and cultural trends (such as Existentialism) purposely situated within an international context. What was meant in this case by "modernity," then, was an attempt "to incorporate the latest literary and artistic currents of the time," rather than confining content solely to Cuban writing or art—especially writing or art that dealt exclusively with the Cuban past or Cuban folkways.[58]

This embrace of "the modern," rather than some prelapsarian search for an authentically Cuban culture that existed prior to the long history of dictatorship and U.S. cultural imperialism, was understood by *Lunes*'s editorial board as key to imagining a new, forward-looking Cuban society whose future would not be decided through ideological rigidities—or which, to return to my previous point, had yet to be settled, or was still spontaneously unfolding. Thus, *Lunes's* loyal support of the Revolution in its earliest years was dictated by a political vision that contained a high degree of intellectual slack, matched by broad editorial policies with which someone like Mills or Ferlinghetti would have easily concurred.[59]

Fernández himself had come to admire Beat writing from the time he had spent in a self-imposed New York exile during the Batista era. By the time he met Ferlinghetti, however, Fernández was largely critical of the Beat Movement, explaining to his American guest that "he read a lot of Kerouac and others and dug their weird dissent but has lately gotten disillusioned with them since they won't come far enough out of their private lives and commit themselves (like Revolutionary writers for instance)."[60] Ferlinghetti immediately reflects on Fernández's charge in an aside, confessing that "Before I left the States, Kerouac told me on the phone from Long Island: 'I got my own revolution out here—the American Revolution.'"[61] In his personal notebooks, Ferlinghetti further admitted that Kerouac's view of an American revolution—being waged in isolation somewhere out on a suburban U.S. island—was not only naive, but "a typically selfish view."[62] Ferlinghetti leaves his interaction with Fernández questioning the limitations of Kerouacian dissent, as he comes to identify Kerouac's "American Revolution" with aimless self-indulgence and a conscious embrace of irresponsible (though politically inconsequential) behavior in the era of the gray flannel suit.

Ferlinghetti later accompanies Fernández to the *Lunes* offices where he meets the journal's chief editor, Guillermo Cabrera Infante. *Lunes*, Ferlinghetti discovers, has recently published an international poetry anthology critical of the nuclear arms race, an issue on the American Beats, an issue of African American writing, and an issue titled "USA vs. USA," which included critical appraisals of U.S. racism and global ambition by William Faulkner, Henry Miller, Langston Hughes, and Allen Ginsberg. Indeed, over its short history *Lunes* featured writing by an extensive international cast of figures, including Neruda, Jorge Luis Borges, Julio Cortázar, Federico García Lorca, Sartre, Albert Camus, Simone de Beauvoir, James Joyce, T. S. Eliot, Marcel Proust, and Franz Kafka.[63] These writers fit neatly within the broad editorial parameters of *Lunes,* which considered "poetic being" and the search for new expressions of human consciousness as the proper cultural accompaniment to what was momentarily an organically evolving revolutionary program (as understood by Mills). Cabrera Infante suggests in his memoirs that the purest Cuban expression of this aesthetic and political ethos was contained in José Baragaño's volume of poetry, *Poetry, Being's Revolution,* published by Ediciones R (the revolution's literary publishing house, of which Cabrera Infante was also the managing editor).[64] Again, the implication here is that the Revolution's vitality could be located in its open, diverse, and poetic nature, or the extent to which it still remained resistant to what might be called the prosaic nature of conventional (and reified) political realities or crystallized dogma—or an Existentialist, such as Sartre, de Beauvoir, or Camus, might say the extent to which it remained open to the multiple proclivities of human existence, incompatible as such proclivities are with rigid dogma or ideology, at least not without a high degree of bad faith (which consists in adhering to preapproved notions of being in violation of our freedom to refashion human existence and community anew). Baragaño himself, writing in a 1959 edition of *Lunes,* had declared that the purpose of evolving Revolutionary culture was to "compose a new consciousness" in a global moment marked by Cold War ideological bifurcation—a hope echoed by Ginsberg in "Prose Contribution to Cuban Revolution."[65] *Lunes* was attempting, in other words, to maintain a cultural space that had yet to be fully "rationalized" (to use Fisher's term) toward particular political and aesthetic ends; as a result of these editorial aims, the free, spontaneous verse of figures such as Ginsberg and the jazz poetics of figures like Hughes discovered a perfectly suitable home in *Lunes.* Moreover, despite Fernández's growing distaste for Beat literature, and contrary to U.S. charges of Cuban cultural repression, Ferlinghetti's conversation with the *Lunes* editors reveals the extent to which U.S. literary culture remained a vital part of the revolution's complex and international cultural scene.

While Mills has not been traditionally canonized as a Beat—motorcycle and leather jacket aside—*Listen, Yankee!* was guided by a similar set of motivations, and as was the case with the editors of *Liberation* and *Lunes,* Mills hoped that Havana would emerge as an open forum for political and cultural dialogue which might, in turn, allow the peoples of the world to think themselves beyond what seemed like impending nuclear disaster, along with the global social inequities that seemed destined to emerge under a reconstructed colonial system (under the auspices of the Soviet and U.S. spheres). Consider, for example, Mills's characterization of early revolutionary culture in *Listen, Yankee!*: "We want our new cultural establishments to be part of our revolution, and so, like the revolution itself, we want them to be free and useful and beautiful and fluent. So we are thinking about it now, debating quietly among ourselves this great social problem of culture."[66] As Castro eventually indicated in his "Words to the Intellectuals" address, Mills found himself on the losing end of this debate as the Bay of Pigs invasion compelled Castro to circle the ideological wagons around Cuban cultural production. To Mills's credit, he predicted this cultural turn of events beforehand, lamenting that the most significant threat to the flourishing of cultural freedom in Cuba came not from Castro's revolution but from the "menacing" behavior of the United States, which would compel Cuba to eventually seek protection from the USSR—and which would undoubtedly come at the cost of cultural, and indeed ideological, openness.[67]

Nevertheless, the earliest moments of the revolution represented a utopian space—a momentary blank spot, figuratively speaking, on the world political map—for figures like Mills and Ferlinghetti who were searching for a less ideologically constrained and more worldly public arena. Or as Mills puts it, many of the artists and intellectuals who had visited the island during this period hoped "to make revolutionary Cuba into a real intellectual and cultural center of the world," a capital of a new world culture that would not only overcome the "laziness of stereotypes" dividing the Cold War world, but "smash them" and the restrictions they imposed on human thought and action. What Mills was imagining was a "true world forum" that would be "absolutely free" from the type of analogical block he had located within the mainstream U.S. media, a political and cultural space "in which new minds can form themselves, and then solve problems we don't yet even know about." The realization of Mills's new world forum would require the founding of an international university in Havana, its curriculum developed by "a world-wide faculty" that would encourage "Chinese Communist Party members" to openly debate "the meanings of freedom" with "North American Republican Party members" in the university's imagined great hall. He also envisioned Polish economists collaborating with Cuban economists on the problems of collective ownership, and Latin American oil experts cooperating with representatives from Standard Oil of New Jersey on the issues of energy conservation and workable forms of nationalized industry. Though these conversations would be facilitated by Havana's new international university, Mills envisioned disseminating their findings worldwide by putting "it all on tape. Print it in the newspapers of Cuba. Make it available in translations for the press of the world. Make books out of it. Make Cuban intellectual life a truly international, a truly free forum, for the *entire* range of world opinion, study, art, judgment, feeling."[68]

In his long rumination on Cuba as home to a "world forum," Mills imagined an open, international university anchoring a globally oriented—or "stranger"—public sphere in which debate would not be preempted by the entrenched and dogmatic divisions structuring contemporary geopolitics. Labeling his transnational public sphere "a new zone of freedom in the Americas," Mills hoped it would become the most significant contribution of the young revolution to world culture.[69] Implied within both Mills's and Ferlinghetti's critical appraisals of the U.S. mass media, and their accompanying valorization of Cuban revolutionary culture as a type of political and rhetorical dreamspace, was an argument for a more complex and diverse media ecology in their domestic cultural scene—an argument anchored in the belief that agonism, ineluctable diversity of opinion, and protracted debate represent the fundamental characteristics of democratic life. While Mills imagined Cuba fulfilling this role by becoming home to a new "world forum," Ferlinghetti documented the complexity and range of actually existing Cuban cultural life, paying primary attention to the revolution's official literary journal, *Lunes de Revolución,* whose commitments in this regard were given additional weight by Ferlinghetti's encounter with Pablo Neruda. Upon being introduced to Ferlinghetti by Cabrera Infante at the *Lunes* offices, Neruda—whose poetry had been translated into English by Rexroth in *Thirty Spanish Poems of Love and Exile,* and who was presently in Havana overseeing the publication of a manuscript by Ediciones R—revealed that he closely followed the news of Ginsberg and Ferlinghetti's trip to Latin America the previous winter, then subsequently invited the younger poet to attend a public reading of his poetry. En route to the reading, Neruda, sounding much like Mills, requested that Ferlinghetti assemble a list of U.S. poets, writers, and editors of all political stripes, which would then be used to elicit submissions for Cuba's literary and political journals.[70] During Neruda's reading, which was prefaced by an outdoor speech by Juan Almeida (the Cuban Chief of the Army), Ferlinghetti found himself incredibly moved, and years later he fondly remembered Neruda speaking "his poetry to several thousands of multi-ethnic Fidelistas . . . in the great government hall where the late dictator had held forth. His rapport with the masses was evident in every poem he spoke. . . . Neruda had told me before the reading, 'I love your wide-open poetry'—by which he meant, I believe, the poetry . . . that we had published in San Francisco and some of which had been published in translation in *Lunes de Revolución*. And I answered, 'You opened the door.'"[71]

Ferlinghetti's recollection, published as the preface to a recent City Lights volume of Neruda's poetry, speaks to the inter-American aesthetic economy circulating through the Bay Area and Latin America. San Francisco's poetry scene, according to Ferlinghetti's recollections, owed an aesthetic debt to Neruda's experiments with free verse, a debt acknowledged early on in Rexroth's contribution to the City Lights catalog. It is this transnational and inter-American literary community—producing "wide-open poetry" for a political situation perceived as "wide-open"—which Ferlinghetti's "Poet's Notes on Cuba" celebrates as antithetical to the ideologically constricted public arena he had been confronting at home since the mid-1950s.

## *Lunes de Revolución* (Deferred)

Ferlinghetti's and Mills's experience of the early revolution as a "wide-open" and improvised cultural situation was not without historical legitimacy. Samuel Farber has recently observed that the revolution emerged from Cuban history as a "multiclass antidictatorial political movement" that did not begin its explicit transformation into a socialist or Communist revolution until 1961.[72] The energies of the early revolution often lacked well-defined contours, fed, as they were, by conflicting, if intertwining, political currents, attributable to what Farber further identifies as "the two wings of the Cuban Left."[73] At the outset of the revolution, Castro was primarily a populist "adventurer," guided by José Martí's tradition of Cuban populism, which "usually addressed itself to an amorphous 'people' and spoke of conflicts [as populism typically does] between the poor and the rich rather than workers and employers [as Marxian political philosophies tend to do]."[74] Martí's populism had been tempered during the 1895–1898 war of independence, during which poor Cuban blacks and whites fought together "in a far more socially inclusive manner than [was evident] in previous Cuban uprisings"—forging a "color blind" alliance that was neither socialist nor Communist, but based on anti-imperialist sacrifice and heroism from below.[75] Castro's populism found its counterbalance in the already sophisticated Marxism of Guevara and Raúl Castro, the latter having been a member of the Cuban Communist Party (established in 1925) since the mid-1950s, unlike his older brother, Fidel. The inclinations of Guevara and Raúl Castro—both of whom were open to Soviet influence from the outset—eventually won Cuba's political day, but these conflicting viewpoints within the revolution's early political dynamics did not come decisively to an end until Fidel's "founding of the united Cuban Communist Party in 1965."[76]

Yet this ideological restructuring (or consolidation) had already found its footing within the spheres of Cuban cultural life not long after Neruda's reading, as evinced in Castro's own admissions in 1961's "A True Social Revolution Produces a Cultural Revolution (Words to the Intellectuals)." In the months following the Bay of Pigs Invasion, Cabrera Infante and the *Lunes* editorial board found themselves at the center of Cuba's cultural storm as Castro openly embraced the Soviet sphere and began stripping Cuban revolutionary culture of its "cosmopolist" elements, especially those influences that could be traced to the United States and Beat culture. Toward this end, Farber has identified *Lunes* as "one of the most interesting and independent left-wing literary supplements [to have appeared] in Latin America," pointing out that while the independent politics of the *Lunes* collective may have resonated with Castro's professed aversion to sectarian Communism during the revolution's earliest moments, its editors found themselves suddenly suppressed in the ideological upheavals which took on a more urgent tone in the wake of the Bay of Pigs.[77] Fueling these suddenly pronounced controversies over suitable revolutionary content—a cultural showdown from which Castro emerged the victor—was the short film *P.M.*, co-directed by Sabá Cabrera Infante (Guillermo's brother) and Orlando Jiménez Leal. Guillermo Cabrera Infante has identified *P.M.* as a "free cinema" essay on the nightlife of Havana at the end of 1960.[78] Sabá Cabrera Infante and Jiménez Leal's cinematic vision was highly influenced by Albert Maysles, as both had been exposed to Maysles's camera work on Robert Drew's *Primary* (1960) and *Yanki No!* (1960) while Albert had visited Havana in 1959, hoping to make a film (which never materialized) on a day in the life of Castro. As such, *P.M.* was a document in the inter-American influence of cinema verité, possessing all of its stock features: handheld camera work, unrehearsed and spontaneous action/acting, long takes, loose plot lines, and on-location shooting. Jiménez Leal's camera documented a group of young men out on the town, hoping to capture the nightlife of everyday Cubans. The film, that is to say, was guided by a populist sensibility, and featured drinking, fistfights, and scenes of "seedy cabarets," a geography of male bonding that was also a conventional aspect of the Beat aesthetic.[79] In short, it portrayed a people's culture that Cuban authorities suddenly considered counterrevolutionary: a version of Cuban nightlife supposedly tied to the legacies of United States–inspired cultural decadence, shot in an improvised style that revealed Havana as an open environment of drinking, jazz dives, and dancing.

*P.M.* has been hailed by avant-garde filmmaker and critic Jonas Mekas as an important document of postwar underground cinema. But as Guillermo Cabrera Infante explains, his brother's short film also represented "the lever of a whole upheaval in the annals of culture under Castro."[80] The controversies surrounding the film helped bring an end to what the elder Cabrera Infante identified as a post-Batista "cultural renaissance" in which figures such as Ferlinghetti, Mills, and the Maysles briefly played a brief but luminous part. The formal alliance with the Soviets in the wake of the Bay of Pigs effectively shut down Havana as the site of an open and improvised inter-culture, which appears, by Castro's own acknowledgements in his June 1961 address "A True Social Revolution Produces a Cultural Revolution," to have been the revolution's de facto cultural policy in its earliest days. Castro delivered his address at the tail end of an "unofficial" trial in which the Cabrera Infantes, Jiménez Leal, and various other figures associated with *Lunes* were accused by newly empowered members of the Cuban government of producing counterrevolutionary, bourgeois culture. Shortly after the Bay of Pigs incident, the Communist Party of Cuba became officially absorbed into Castro's Revolutionary Party of the 26 of July Movement, and the CP's Council for Culture, which had been an ancillary organization up until that point, emerged as the official governing body of Cuban cultural life. One of its first actions was to immediately ban *P.M.*, which had been broadcast on *Lunes*'s television station (Cuban channel 4), while insisting that the *Lunes* editorial board cease its petition efforts on behalf of the film. The *Lunes* petition had arisen when the Comisión Revisora (Cuba's official film institute) refused permission for a public exhibition of the film (after which the *Lunes* board defiantly aired it on their television station). The Comisión Revisora, Cabrera Infante explains, had been in Castro's ear over the content of *Lunes* since its inception, as the Comisión's members considered the journal too cosmopolitan and avant-gardist in its leanings, and thus not fully committed to revolutionary principles. Cabrera Infante, in turn, admits that the *Lunes* board viewed the Comisión Revisora as "despicable bureaucrats, a bunch of ignoramuses with artistically reactionary ideas and no taste at all."[81] But backed by the CP's Council for Culture, the Comisión Revisora had its day in the ideological sun as *Lunes* was disbanded and *P.M.* was censored virtually out of existence.

Following upon the *P.M./Lunes* trial, Guillermo Cabrera Infante was assigned (or we might say "politely exiled") to Brussels as a Cuban cultural ambassador. After returning to Cuba in 1965 for his mother's funeral, he left the island for England (where he died in February of 2005). As the managing editor of *Lunes*, Cabrera Infante helped foster an inter-American and trans-Atlantic artistic culture during the early years of the Cuban Revolution, a culture which favored open dialogue, unrestricted creativity, and aesthetic experimentation over the cultural dogmatism that began to establish itself more fully in the wake of the Bay of Pigs. This cultural renaissance (to use Cabrera Infante's designation) attempted to momentarily exceed the stubbornly entrenched ideological encampments of Cold War geopolitics and their attendant public spheres on a search

48   The Cubalogues

for more complicated and expansive notions of being and belonging, though the era's political orthodoxies—in spite of the cultural dreaming of Ferlinghetti, the Cabrera Infantes, and Mills—eventually reemerged in Cuba with censorious force. We are still left, however, with Ferlinghetti's and Mills's Cubalogues which, despite the dashing of their visions for a forward-looking "world forum" in Havana, have much to tell us about the unrestrained idealism inspired by early revolutionary culture, while revealing the foundational paradigms of the peremptory public sphere in the Cold War United States in some useful and compelling ways.

# 2

# On the Crisis of the Underground and a Politics of Intractable Plurality

According to Ronald Sukenick's classic text on the Greenwich Village underground, *Down and In* (1987), postwar bohemianism and defiant intellectualism were mobilized in opposition to the white picket realities of the heteronormative nuclear family and the "waves of superpatriotism [that] were emanating from Washington." "Pinkos and faggots" and a large cast of their artistically inclined friends, Sukenick asserts, "were in trouble in the provinces" and thus retreated to bohemian and artistic strongholds like Greenwich Village and San Francisco's North Beach in droves, allured by histories of nonconformity and politically principled creativity that promised a life "stranger" and more unconventional than the Cold War ordinary.[1] For many Cold War Americans—and I number myself among the final generation capable of claiming that moniker— the underground represented an exceptionally powerful idea, as it spoke to a fervent hope for worthy forms of retreat and ennobled defiance, the possibility that dissatisfied outsiders might somehow flee the constricting aspects of Cold War normality for vibrant urban spaces more in tune with their desires, inclinations, and aspirations. To a large extent, this quest for other spaces represents the collective pursuit of the figures treated in this book, all of whom eventually extended their search from the American underground to revolutionary Havana, where they continued to seek out less inhibited (or "stranger") forms of cultural, social, and intellectual life during one of the defining moments of Cold War hostilities.

The life and work of Harold Cruse—who has not typically been affiliated with the Beats on either coast—nonetheless serves as a telling example of this geographically extended pursuit from the mid-1950s through the early 1960s. Cruse initially hoped, during this period, to integrate his own artistic and political dreams within the precincts of what remained the predominantly white bohemia of Greenwich Village. Born in Virginia at the outset of the First World War, Cruse had first arrived in New York during the Interwar (or Great) Migration of rural blacks to the industrial north, and by the 1950s he had already worn (and worn out) a number of political coats. A proud and mercurial autodidact conversant across a range of disciplines, Cruse passed through an enthusiasm for 1930s populism and the New Deal, had served in the armed forces in Italy during World War II, and in 1947 became a member of the Communist Party USA (CPUSA). Cruse's experiences within the CPUSA, however, left him permanently jaded concerning the white Left in America, as he believed they employed the black experience merely as an opportunistic chip in a class-based ideology that ultimately failed to address the role of white supremacy in a protracted history of race-based social terror. Racism, that is to say, possessed some economic roots and had undoubtedly structured U.S. class formations in ways that needed to be rectified in the name of social justice. Nevertheless, the freedom struggles of American blacks could not be neatly internalized (and thus flattened) within the general struggles of the industrial working classes, especially in the American South where injustice had historically been connected to the race-based distribution of property in rural, agricultural economies that had smuggled the hardships and dependencies of sharecropping through the backdoor of slavery's demise.[2]

Leaving the CPUSA in the mid-1950s, Cruse moved from Harlem to Greenwich Village in order to test his skills as a playwright, though the four plays he wrote during that period never saw the stage.[3] This period was nevertheless a generative one for Cruse, as he began to establish his reputation as a highly original and influential essayist and public intellectual. Anchored in Cruse's writings on Greenwich Village and the Cuban Revolution, this chapter reconstructs Cruse's evolution from a committed racial integrationist into one of the primary theorists of 1960s black nationalism—an evolution catalyzed by Cruse's perceptions of first the Beat Generation, then early events in Castro's Cuba. In the most famous of his works, *The Crisis of the Negro Intellectual* (1967), Cruse identifies these two strains—integrationist and nationalist—as the orienting poles of African American political thought and intellectual history. The prototype of integration was, according to Cruse's schema, Frederick Douglass, "the great Negro Abolitionist, and there is almost a direct line of development from him to the NAACP and the modern civil rights movement," whose rationales Cruse ultimately came to oppose.[4] The second strain—"the rejected, or nationality strain"—can be attributed to Martin Delaney (Douglass's peer) and courses through the post-NAACP work of W.E.B. Du Bois and on to the emergence of Malcolm X, focused as it was on forms of pan-African political striving. This nationalist strain, in which Cruse would comfortably settle over the course of the turbulent 1960s, identified African Americans as an internal colony or nation within a nation and thus favored (often in broadly rendered ways) uncompromising black political independence from white society, as opposed to integration into mainstream America helped along by white liberals and their commitments to "racial uplift" (a tendency which, in Cruse's mind, animated the integrationist approach back to Douglass's relationship with white abolitionists).[5]

## Harold Cruse's Village

Chief among Cruse's early essays—and representative of the early but deteriorating integrationist hopes that Cruse had carried through his New Deal and CPUSA years—was "Race and Bohemianism in Greenwich Village." Appearing in *The Crisis* in January of 1960, Cruse's frank assessment of Village life and its racist undercurrents provided a heroic yet disillusioned chronicle of New York Beat culture from the mid- to late 1950s. Oddly enough, Cruse's insightful treatment of the Beat milieu at the apex of its New York period has yet to be included in any of the numerous anthologies of Beat writing or in any of the collections of period essays concerning the Beats and their cultural scene. Cruse, nevertheless, inhabited this milieu at a critical time, following his own artistic inclinations during the cresting moments of the more extensive New York School. If scholarship on the Beats is to expand upon its recent commitments to contextualizing the Beat aesthetic and intellectual ethos within more extensive cultural geographies, the work of Cruse needs to be given its proper due—as I hope to do in what follows.

Upon leaving the CPUSA, Cruse gravitated toward the Village—as did many of the pivotal figures of the Beat Generation—owing to the neighborhood's long-standing reputation for political openness and cultural experimentation. The weight of that reputation is difficult to deny, especially during the neighborhood's long heroic period, which ran from the mid-nineteenth century through the 1970s (when it noticeably dissipated, after the Stonewall Riots and the punk movement constellated around CBGB). For over a hundred years, Greenwich Village held its place as an eastern Mecca of U.S. experimental culture and forward-looking intellectualism, a site of immense cultural, social, and political possibility. Within the confines of the Village, ideas and creative passions had converged over a number of generations, each of which, in its own historical epoch, sought to redefine the avant-garde, theorize new radicalisms of all sorts, and embrace expansive notions of sexual identity and freedom just beyond the watchful eyes of mainstream morality and political conventionality. Indeed, some of the most pivotal figures in U.S. cultural and literary history spent formative portions of their careers in the Village and its surrounding environs: Herman Melville, Walt Whitman, Eugene O'Neill, Emma Goldman, Djuna Barnes, John Reed, Randolph Bourne, Kenneth Burke, Hart Crane, Thelonious Monk, Charlie Parker, Mark Rothko, Charles Mingus, Jackson Pollock, Frank O'Hara, Philip Glass, Steve Reich, Robert Wilson, Lou Reed, and Patti Smith. From the late 1940s through the mid-1960s, the Village emerged as the artistic home of the East Coast Beats, as figures such as Baraka, Diane Di Prima, Gregory Corso, Allen Ginsberg, John Clellon Holmes, and Jack Kerouac contributed to the creative explosion that helped New York displace Paris as the capital of the Western avant-garde and a wellspring of alternative culture at the height of the Cold War; in a sense, then, the Village and its denizens generated an artistic and intellectual home of incredible consequence on the margins of Cold War normality, much as Ferlinghetti and Rexroth had done in the Bay Area. At the time, Cruse also called the Village home, though his writings regarding this period tend to question how imaginative or forward-looking Village culture actually was, sketching, at times, a critical portrait of the Village's professed white liberals who had failed, in Cruse's estimation, to fully live up to their maverick and nonconformist reputation.

In the opening sentences of "Race and Bohemianism in Greenwich Village," Cruse declares that "Villagers have a provincial, chauvinist attitude toward their community, which seems anomalous in cosmopolitan New York."[6] At first glance, Cruse's indictment of Village provincialism seems counterintuitive, for while the Village has undoubtedly been an enclave, or a city within a city, for much of its existence, it has typically been perceived as one of Manhattan's more worldly or cosmopolitan neighborhoods—or as Cruse later puts it, the Village has traditionally been lauded as "New York's version of Paris' Left Bank."[7] As becomes evident over the course of the essay, however, it is this very perception of cosmopolitan Village life that Cruse hopes to call into question, as he reflects upon the flourishing racial unrest—or "the problem of Village race relations"—which shook the bohemian enclave over the summer of 1959.[8]

At the heart of this racial unrest was the appearance, over roughly a four-year period, of what Cruse terms the "New Bohemia," a multiracial and multiethnic cadre of young people grouped together under the extended moniker of the Beat Generation (this moniker is assigned, in the case of Cruse, to not only the core artists of that generation, but to the more general youth culture swirling around them). Having lived in the Village since 1953, Cruse admits that

the racial situation did not become tense until circa 1955. What started it was the influx of members of the "New Bohemia." And much to the surprise of old-time Villagers was the influx of many Negroes from Harlem, who were only twenty minutes and a subway fare from the heart of the Village. There were also many young Jews from the Bronx, Brooklyn, and the lower East Side. These young people were fleeing their ghettos both geographically and psychologically. Culturally, the Negro's contribution was both "racial" and linguistic. Post-war bohemia became known as the "beat generation," whose lingo was made up of choice phrases and words originally coined by Harlem "hipsters" (people in the know). Although most Villagers did not know the origin of "beat" (which was Harlemese for "exhausted" or "broke"), and cared less, they quickly identified "beat" with those manifestations of Village life which met with their disapproval.[9]

Throughout his essay, Cruse portrays the young Beats as a racially integrated cultural and social scene. That is to say, the Beat Generation constituted an interracial counterpublic—including in its sexual mores and proclivities, which meets with the tremendous disapproval of older Villagers. In what can only be read as celebratory language, Cruse exclaims that "the 'New Bohemia,' therefore, soon approximated America's mythical 'melting pot.' But it was the Negro ingredient in the pot that soon put the Village's traditional racial liberalism to the test."[10] Cruse's statement references the Village's older generation of white liberals—or what we might identify as the Village's Brahmin class—the neighborhood's historical caretakers of socially liberal beliefs, holding their territory within a largely homogenous bohemian enclave. Or as Cruse explains (in a punning fashion), "the increase in interracial sex was pricking the hidden nerves of prejudice. . . . Such amorous activities across racial lines were regarded [by those crossing the lines] as rebellion against conventional middleclass habits" of which the elder, Brahmin class, in Cruse's estimation, was not completely ready to relinquish, cleaving a pronounced generational rift or "generation gap" into the bohemian continuum which ultimately subdued the promise of a fully integrated oppositional culture in the Cold War Village.[11]

Sukenick has employed Malcolm Cowley's designation of "Upper Bohemian" to elucidate the generational rift running through 1950s Village culture, a rift epitomized by Mary McCarthy's mid-1950s *New York Post* article on the "new village scene" in the San Remo Bar—a bohemian tavern famously fictionalized in Kerouac's aptly named *Subterraneans* (1958), a roman à clef whose narrative conflicts hinge on an interracial sexual relationship between the white Leo

Percepied and black Mardou Fox (based on Kerouac's short romance with Alene Lee, though Kerouac resituated the narrative in San Francisco while renaming the Remo "The Masque"). As was the case with other intellectuals within the *Partisan Review* orbit (such as Bell and Podhoretz), McCarthy dismisses the Beat milieu gathered regularly in "the Remo" on account of the fact that "its habitués Do Nothing." As Sukenick explains, McCarthy's article negatively juxtaposed the Beats to her "generation of Bohemians, the political intellectuals around the *Partisan Review*," the representatives of "Upper Bohemia," who were, in McCarthy's view, more explicitly "tuned-in . . . to 'the battle of ideas and standards.'"[12] Cowley had himself used the term "Upper Bohemia" in his 1934 novel *Exile's Return* to refer to those intellectuals who held radical ideas regarding aesthetics (that is, the High Modernist avant-garde), while maintaining conventional middle class attitudes toward party-based politics, competitive individualism, and the pieties of conventional domestic life.[13] These middle-class attitudes, which Cruse identifies as the primary culprit in the "Upper Bohemian" aversion toward interracial sex, leave him, in the short run, suspicious of his adopted neighborhood's persistent claims to cultural and social openness, and in the long run more generally suspicious of white liberals, as shall become increasingly evident over the course of the chapter. Throughout his early Village essay, Cruse counterpoises this aging bohemian class (attached, in Sukenick's mind, to the *Partisan Review*) to the racially crossed "migrant class" of young Beats, animated by new forms of cultural fusion or syncretism whose exuberance and relevance was lost on an older generation that could not find its way around a provincial sexual block. As is clear from his comment on the black linguistic contribution to the Beat Movement—including the word "Beat" itself—Cruse considered this youth culture heavily indebted to a Harlem-based hipster culture that stretched back to that neighborhood's Renaissance of the 1920s and 1930s. At the same time, however, Cruse viewed the bond between young artists such as Baraka, Ted Joans, Ginsberg, Di Prima, and Corso as a genuine interracial and intercultural bond cemented through the "Negro" bohemian rebellion "against convention" on account of "prejudice and racial discrimination" and an accompanying white bohemian rebellion "against the spiritual impoverishment of [an] American society" hitting its corporatist and militaristic stride.[14]

This ebullient and interracial bohemia, Cruse further laments, had been victimized by violent street attacks since first appearing in the mid 1950s, attacks aimed predominantly at mixed-race couples. Diane Di Prima, who resided in the Village while involved in an amorous relationship with Baraka, supports Cruse's assertion, attributing such violence to the conservative Italian American population also inhabiting portions of the Village at this time (and serving as the proprietors of many of the Village's legendary bars and restaurants). As she explains in her memoir, *Recollections of My Life as a Woman* (2002): "I had seen plenty of [racism] in the Village of 1953–54, when the Italians would swarm up MacDougal Street en masse from below Bleecker to threaten or wipe out a Black man for coming to the Village with a white woman. The outcome of such encounters, if any of us was foolhardy enough to call the police, was that the Black man was arrested (after he'd already been beaten up) and the local hoodlums went home."[15] Ronald Sukenick concurs with Di Prima's assessment of the era's racism, explaining that from the late 1940s through the 1950s "underground people" of different generations inhabited the Village alongside a profusion of Italian American families who were threatened by the bohemian presence and had reacted violently against it for quite some time. As Sukenick explains, "the Italians were very insular. Tribal. Hoods loafing around storefront social clubs directing deadly looks at Bohemian interlopers, especially if they seemed to be gay or, in their view, worse, were like Ted Joans [or Baraka], Black."[16] Cruse does not deny that the Village "hoods" discussed by Di Prima and Sukenick were primarily responsible for the violence, though he attempts to dissect the problem of these racially motivated attacks within the petri dish of Village intellectual culture, arguing that in the past, "hoodlum attacks" against racial and ethnic minorities were met with more vociferous protest from the neighborhood's white liberal bohemians. As the 1950s progressed, however, the growing silence of the neighborhood's long-entrenched white liberals—according to Cruse— helped foster a more supportive environment for the prevailing racial animus of "the hoods," which Cruse attributed to deep-seated anti-black and anti-Semitic hostilities. As evidence of liberal complicity in racial violence, Cruse offers a brief discussion of a New York radio segment dealing with the 1959 attacks in which an (unnamed) editor of "the Village newspaper" (presumably the *Village Voice*) expressed his own social anxieties toward interracial sex "despite his liberalism," an attitude "typical of many [Village] residents."[17]

Several years later, in his compendious *The Crisis of the Negro Intellectual*, Cruse names the *Voice* more explicitly in relation to these attitudes. In his treatment of Village culture in *Crisis*, Cruse again dismisses the supposedly interracial attitudes of the white liberal milieu through a more focused indictment of the *Voice* and the cultural compromises made by "integrationist" artists such as Loraine Hansberry, who, in the mid- to late-1950s, was a darling of the *Voice* literati, along with American culture at large. Cruse explains that while Hansberry, who reached the zenith of her popularity when *Raisin in the Sun* appeared on Broadway in 1959, chose to reside in the Village alongside its young black hipsters and Beat elements, she also chose, unlike these more unruly elements, to embrace a "middle class literary ethos" more fully aligned with *Raisin*'s Younger family and its efforts to relocate from the South Side of Chicago to the exclusive white suburb, Clybourne Park. Hansberry's work and lifestyle, in Cruse's estimation, epitomized the integrationist strain coursing through the mainstream Civil Rights Movement, whose political protocols (that is, legislative gradualism) and advocacy of middle-class tastes and values were more palatable to white liberals, a point that will become central to Cruse's work as the 1960s progressed.[18] In any case, on account of what Cruse viewed as Hansberry's support of integration into the white picket fence and nuclear family structure of a "featureless" postwar suburbia, he argues (in a tone that itself approaches Beat vernacular and phraseology at times, especially that of Ginsberg's "Howl") made her far more palatable to the white liberal Village establishment than "the social behavior of the déclassé Negro, the Beat, the uninhibited, free-wheeling escapee from the ghetto whose psychological mood found its counterpart across the color line among the alienated whites. There these Ghetto-wrought Negroes found soul communion in another subterranean world: the world of marijuana fumes and esoteric jazz-buffing to the formalistic tunes of 'new jazz sounds' for the connoisseurs of the hip and the beat: the world of interracial sex of all modes of expression; the world where the trend of the Beat Generation made the old style Village Bohemian [seem] 'square.'"[19]

While the *Voice*, Cruse continues, claimed to set the trends for "hip" New York liberalism—or educated progressivism "in the know"—it tended to champion the less threatening "middle class type" embodied in Hansberry, rather than the Beat writers (and their fellow travelers within the Village milieu) who had been simultaneously rebuffed by the "middle-class world of the cultural arts in America."[20] Or as Cruse, approaching his most accusatory, puts it: "From the point of view of *The Village Voice* (and most of the solid, but liberal, middle-class Village citizenry) much of what Negroes were doing in the subterranean Beat world was very unwholesome" and not worthy of serious consideration within its pages, despite the fact that the Beat's "new style" represented a convergence or hybridization of cultural styles, or a *stranger conception* of social and cultural relations far more interesting to Cruse than the precincts of middle-class comportment underwriting the integrationist ethic and what he viewed as Hansberry's suburban dreams.[21] Indeed, in its earliest years, the *Voice* often branded the young bohemia as an interloping force from the other boroughs and other Manhattan neighborhoods (such as the solidly working-class Lower East Side), pointing out that most of the Beats and their fellow travelers lived elsewhere and were not truly of the Village.[22]

Ultimately, Cruse's portrayal of Greenwich Village and its white liberal press was symptomatic of the growing and general distrust of white liberalism which helped catalyze and popularize black nationalism as a political and cultural strategy over the course of the 1960s, a development particularly pronounced in the work of not only Cruse but in the emergence of Malcolm X and organizations such as the Black Panthers. Cruse played a major role, as a cultural activist and intellectual historian, in codifying these emergent black nationalist trends, a role directly attributable to his contact with the Cuban Revolution at the very moment he was tiring of the Village's racial strictures and hypocrisies. In his parting shot to the Village, within the pages of *Crisis of the Negro Intellectual*, Cruse argued, in his inimitably dismissive way, that the aspirations of figures such as Hansberry should not be permitted to speak for the aspirations and desires of all African Americans, who remained the most poverty-stricken of U.S. ethnic or racial groups—a statement that, as we shall see, goes a long way toward explaining the impetus for various expressions of Black Power, including the Black Arts Movement.[23] To scratch Cruse's rhetorical surface a bit more deeply, it might be said that he was ultimately pondering the aesthetic preconditions of the era, through which black expressive practices, held up to the mirror of middle class "taste," became codified within the exclusive domains of white liberal expectations in limiting and limited ways—at least at the cultural center, whose rationales, in Cruse's estimation, still held sway over much of Village life. Or we might say, in today's multicultural parlance, that Cruse was searching for *a more diverse diversity* of cultural and political thought than he ultimately found within the Village mainstream, despite his being initially impressed with certain facets of Beat culture.

## Harold Cruse's Cuba

In turn, Cruse seems to initially locate this more diverse diversity—or a "stranger" conception of cultural relations—in Cuba shortly following upon the summer of 1959. Cruse's experience of Village racial violence and its attendant cultural mores colored his original conception of Cuban Revolutionary culture in some obvious ways. Having visited Cuba in July of 1960 as part of the same FPCC tour as Amiri Baraka and Robert Williams, Cruse's Cubalogue, "A Negro Looks at Cuba" (1960), celebrates the public culture of the early revolution as home to diverse outlooks and concerns, operating across a number of overlapping cultural geographies. Or put somewhat differently, Cruse configures the revolution, in what he asserts as its non-ideological and non-Communist infancy, as a heterogeneous contact zone for interracial, internationalist, and black transnational cultural forms coexisting in a *not yet fully defined* public arena that nevertheless signaled the "coming maturity of true nationhood" in Cuba, based, in Cruse's point of view, on an ability to integrate widely differentiated cultural voices and hues into an evolving conversation on the ultimate direction of social and political life.[24] As was the case with the other Cubalogue writers, Cruse idealizes the cultural aspects of the early revolution as a promise that has not yet "come-of-age," while nevertheless embracing the revolutionary situation with a level of descriptive exuberance missing from his portrayals of his white liberal neighbors in Greenwich Village.[25]

In the essay's initial treatment of Cuban culture, Cruse references the island's indebtedness to Black Atlantic culture—much as he had focused on the Beat Generation's indebtedness to Harlem hipster culture—hoping that Cuba might fully embrace this heritage in order to become a repository "for a new phase of inter-American cultural relations involving those of African descent."[26] Cruse anticipates—in a way that is consistent with his cultural aspirations regarding a proliferation of black expressive practices within the Unites States beyond the aesthetic preconditions of middle-class taste—that Cuba might eventually provide a welcoming and expansive contact zone for African American culture and Afro-Cuban culture, and he views his own contingent of African American artists and intellectuals as representative of an initial step in that direction.[27] As Cruse's time in Cuba was limited to a few days, his essay tends more toward general optimism than actual cultural examples, though he admits being particularly impressed with the National Theater's performance of "a ballet, 'El Milagro de Anaquille,' based on Negro dance-forms," immediately following Castro's commemorative address in the Sierra Maestra (which Cruse attended with the American contingent and others).[28] The program, Cruse tells us, also featured the performance of two cantatas, one of them being "Cantata a de Santiago," which "was written in New York in 1958 by Myriam Acevedo and revised by Pablo Armando Fernández, two Cuban poets and leading figures in the new cultural movement in Havana."[29]

While Cruse equated the early revolution with the promise of a new sense of Afro-diasporic cultural community in the Atlantic, a promise he sees underwritten in the inclusion of his African American contingent in the early commemoration of the July Movement, he simultaneously framed this promise within an interracial and international cast of thinkers and activists whose convergence was made possible by the loosely defined rubrics of the early revolution. In "A Negro Looks at Cuba," Cruse employs the train ride to the Oriente Province, where Castro and others will speak, to dramatize the carnivalesque and diverse aspects of revolutionary culture, admitting to have been "caught up in a veritable groundswell of revolutionary zeal," as the train pushed across the Cuban mainland. Of course, the train ride, or "hopping the rails," was also a stock feature of Beat aesthetics (inherited from Dos Passos and other Depression-era writers), and Cruse's Cubalogue employs that convention to carousing effect. Describing his fellow passengers, Cruse reveals that they not only included numerous members of the international press, but "Latin American youth delegates from other countries, visiting dignitaries, and special visitors from Europe and the United States. Francoise Sagan, the youthful authoress (*Bonjour Tristesse*) was with us. Simone de Beauvoir was reported on the way but, for some reason, didn't arrive. . . . The international composition of my train intrigued me. All the more so since I realized that my group was the de facto American delegation."[30] The American delegation, that is to say, to an international celebration of the revolution's anniversary, and Cruse in turn acknowledges what he sees as the significant value of openly discussing the meaning of revolution and the future of Cuban national life with intellectuals, journalists, and activists from throughout the world, leaving him with an impression of the early revolution as "an international adventure story."[31] It is on the train ride, where passengers also shared their concerns regarding the inequities of U.S. foreign and domestic policy against a backdrop of singing and dancing, that Cruse further admits: "I fell in love with Cuba."[32] At the tail end of this "international adventure," Cruse informs us that he and his international compatriots were invited to accompany Castro and the other revolutionary leaders on stage at the planned revolutionary celebration, providing an international and interracial backdrop for Castro's oratory broadcast on Cuban television.[33]

This final scene of Castro's public address to the Cuban peasantry, foregrounded as he was against a cadre of intellectuals, journalists, and artists from throughout the Americas and Europe, epitomizes Cruse's initial excitement for the revolution as a paragon of collaborative, ineluctably pluralist "nationhood"—the promise of which had previously eluded him within the deceptive racism of Greenwich Village, despite Beat efforts to realize functioning forms of interracial community against the deeply ingrained prejudices of the older or "Upper Bohemia." But this dream or promise proved, over the long run of the 1960s, untenable to Cruse, and not long after his initial assessment of the revolution, he notably altered his original rhetorical course. Cuban events instead came to anchor what would become his more intellectually sustained interest in black cultural nationalism, which involved, in a sense, prying free the Afro-diasporic promise he originally experienced in Havana from his interest in more extensive and racially integrated collaborative frameworks or coalition-building, just as, as Baraka would go on to explain, the Black Liberation Movement was prying itself completely free from the mainstream Civil Rights struggle as a result of a collective frustration over its pacifism.[34] Given some additional time to percolate within the increasingly heated political climate of the early 1960s, Cruse's interest in "stranger relations" became reconfigured along a more racially pronounced axis and began to resonate more fully with the global anticolonialism celebrated by figures such as Malcolm X and Frantz Fanon. As U.S.-Cuban relations soured completely following the Bay of Pigs, a notable shift in perspective appeared in Cruse's work as well, as he embraced black nationalism and unapologetically rejected integrationist political striving in 1962's "Revolutionary Nationalism and the Afro-American" and 1967's *The Crisis of the Negro Intellectual*—both of which also radically reframed Cruse's understanding of the Cuban situation as a critical hemispheric and world event.

## Harold Cruse's Cuba (Revisited)

"Revolutionary Nationalism and the Afro-American" originally appeared in the New Left journal *Studies on the Left,* only to reappear in Cruse's own *Rebellion or Revolution?* (1968). It was also published in *Black Fire* (1968), edited by Baraka and Larry Neal, which was one of the central achievements of Black Arts Movement print culture. In the opening paragraphs of "Revolutionary Nationalism and the Afro-American," Cruse admits to pondering the anticolonial and anti-imperialist imperatives of the Cuban Revolution for "a new idea or a fleeting spark of creative theoretical inspiration apropos of the [black] situation in the United States."[35] He finds that "fleeting spark" in his "domestic colonialism" thesis, grounded in the assertion that "the Negro has a relationship to the dominant culture of the United States similar to that of colonies and semi-dependents [which is where Cruse placed Cuba] to their particular foreign overseers: the Negro is the American problem of underdevelopment."[36] As Cruse further explains: "The American Negro shares with colonial peoples many of the socio-economic factors which form the material basis for present-day revolutionary nationalism. Like the people of the underdeveloped countries, the Negro suffers in varying degree from hunger, illiteracy, disease, ties to the land, urban and semi-urban slums, cultural starvation, and the psychological reactions to being ruled over by others not of his kind. He experiences the tyranny imposed upon the lives of those who inhabit underdeveloped countries."[37]

Cruse argues that U.S. blacks had always existed as "colonial beings," created during the protracted expansion of European empire that had installed an African colony within the confines of the southern United States. Thus, Cruse further asserts that a truly revolutionary approach to racial inequity in the United States would require a political and cultural movement capable of theorizing African Americans as a nation or colony forcibly contained within an oppressive state form. Cuban (and other) revolutionary events, that is to say, ultimately provided Cruse with a medium through which he began to work out a new set of ideas concerning black political possibilities against the backdrop of a protracted racially repressive history. Moreover, Cruse located corresponding traces of this emergent consciousness—as did Baraka—within an increasingly pronounced dissatisfaction with "NAACP-Martin Luther King-student legalistic and 'passive resistance' tactics," which identify political power with "integrated lunch counters, waiting rooms, schools, housing, baseball teams or love affairs."[38] Symptomatic of a growing disillusionment with the mainstream wing of the black freedom struggle, Cruse's 1962 essay asserts that "real power" can only be equated with increased black agency and autonomy—a quantifiable and ever-expansive ability for African Americans to actively determine the conditions of their political, economic, and cultural lives.

While in a "Negro Looks at Cuba" Cruse had celebrated the Black Atlantic possibilities of the budding revolution—even as he sublated Afro-diasporic concerns within the multifarious make-up of a public culture he viewed as more attuned to "true nationhood" than the cultural situation of the United States—he now, like so many other activists and intellectuals of his generation, surrendered hope in cross-racial cooperation. "Revolutionary Nationalism and the Afro-American" represents Cruse's abandonment of the "integrationist strain" for the "nationalist strain" as he increasingly advocated for independently functioning black cultural and political organizations adamant in their refusal to subordinate themselves to any "white groups" invested in political paternalism or talk of integration within the U.S. status quo. In turn, Cruse hoped that an autonomously rendered black politics might provide the sustained public pressure needed to "[alter] the structural form of American society" in the way in which anticolonial and anti-imperialist struggles throughout Latin America, Asia, and Africa had become openly invested in restructuring the global dynamics of underdevelopment and tilted, acquisitive economic arrangements.[39] Cruse argued, in other words, that it would be through the efforts of a black revolutionary vanguard, whose "new organizational forms" had yet to fully emerge from the oppositional margins of the public arena (where they were still overshadowed, from the integrationist center, by MLK and the NAACP), that U.S. society in general would eventually be compelled to articulate fully equitable social, political, and cultural arrangements, which might ultimately require significant changes to the political and economic proclivities of the existent constitutional nation-state and its attendant corporate structure.[40]

Cruse admittedly does not know what such a society might look like at the end of the long political day, affixing his work (here and elsewhere) with a vagueness and imprecision that present a serious challenge to scholarly attempts at mining his oeuvre for programmatic alternatives. But while his essay lacks an identifiable agenda, Cruse had begun to spread his wings as a cultural theorist who quite deftly linked the agonistic democratization of the public sphere to more extensive, and ultimately well-intended, democratic imperatives (an impulse that runs through all of the other Cubalogues in varying inflections). I believe this to be Cruse's signal and lasting achievement, visible, as Nikhil Pal Singh points out, when one foregrounds Cruse's assertion "that black movements needed to recognize the integral relationship between black autonomy and the democratization of U.S. public culture [in general]. Black separateness in both programmatic and institutional terms was the necessary corollary of America's democratic revolution."[41] That is to say, the realization of racial democracy, and thus of democracy in general, would require, Cruse argued, a more robust set of voices and arguments than could be heard coming from "integrationist" organizations such as the NAACP—or from "middle class artists" such as Hansberry—and he dedicated much of his intellectual energy to theorizing more space for what he viewed as the less conciliatory "nationalist strain" within a more complexly rendered black cultural sphere.

This is most pronounced in *Crisis of the Negro Intellectual*, where Cruse, largely inspired by C. Wright Mills's theorization of the "cultural apparatus," asserted that the "cultural front" was of utmost importance to ongoing black freedom struggles.[42] Over the course of *Crisis*, Cruse elaborated this argument regarding the black cultural front—or we might say a new black underground—in relation to his Cuban experience, as he recalls, in an earlier chapter, "the long journey from Havana to Sierra Maestra" with Baraka and the others in his contingent.[43] One of Cruse's primary concerns at the time was with how Baraka, as a "Greenwich Village Beat poet" long familiar with the neighborhood's white liberal hypocrisy, "would relate politically, artistically, ideologically to this foreign revolution," and he correctly intuited that the young Beat would eventually become enamored with Robert Williams's outlook on the necessity of revolutionary violence to black political struggle (an outlook I will be exploring in far greater detail in the following chapter).[44] Cruse's ideas diverged from Baraka's in this regard, as he claims in the *Crisis* version of his Cuban encounter to have realized (in the Sierra Maestra) that the actual force and violence required by revolutionary upheaval throughout the decolonizing world (or within "foreign territories") might be productively transmuted in the United States into a cultural (rather than explicitly violent) revolution equally invested in ridding the African American "inner colony" of the harmful paternalism of its white overseers across the political spectrum. Working from Mills's definition of the cultural apparatus as both the media forms enabling mass communication and "an organized network of functions that are creative, administrative, propagandistic, educational, recreational, political, artistic, economic and cultural," Cruse declared that "only the blind cannot see that whoever controls the cultural apparatus—whatever class, power group, faction or political combine—also controls the destiny of the United States and everything in it."[45] Contrary to the 1970 declaration of Gil Scott-Heron, Cruse's revolution would be televised—and printed in newspapers and journals, disseminated over the airwaves and through the nation's ever more extensive electronic circuitry, screened in neighborhood movie houses and acted out on agitprop street corners. Leaving behind his earlier beliefs (tenuous as they appear at times) in cultural and political collaboration across the color line, Cruse now argued that "there can be no real black revolution in the United States without [a] cultural revolution," which overturns the white "Anglo-Saxon" monopoly on mass cultural production and its narrowed conception of national values, national self-image, and national purpose.[46]

In a more general sense, then, Cruse's work from this period added a racialized component to Mills's critique of mass opinion-making, while dovetailing in compelling ways with the insights of postcolonial theory. Literary theorist Mary Klages has argued for this oft-overlooked resonance between African American critical theory and postcolonial theory quite succinctly in her assertion that

> both look at how a hegemonic white/Western culture came to dominate a non-white culture, and at how the subordinated culture reacted to and resisted that domination. The history of black-white relations in the United States is quite different from [the colonial British relations which still dominate postcolonial studies], because in the United States whites imported blacks from Africa as slaves, rather than urging whites to go and settle in Africa to "civilize" the indigenous peoples. But while the dynamics of racial and cultural politics are different, some of the effects are the same: in the United States, slavery and racism produced a hegemonic white culture which enforced its systems and values on the non-white population, and that non-white population both obeyed and resisted those systems and values [as they did within the British colonies].[47]

Klages goes on to connect the concerns of postcolonial theory primarily to Henry Louis Gates's notion of the "Signifying Monkey," though it should be clear from the writings of Cruse that the "strong connection" Klages elucidates runs through a deeper intellectual vein, one traceable to the very rise of anticolonialism as a pronounced and transnational political optic within Black Atlantic thought (nearly three decades prior to Gates's well-known theoretical contribution). Cruse's notion of the inner colony in need of pronounced and immediate cultural independence—announced as it was against the backdrop of Cuban, Asian, and African anticolonialism—was actually possessed by older antecedents in the seminal postcolonialism of figures such as Aimé Césaire and Frantz Fanon, especially in their own attempts at theorizing cultural independence from the legacies of European colonialism.[48]

As much as it was influenced by the imperatives of global anticolonialism, including its Caribbean and Atlantic manifestations, Cruse's arguments regarding oppositional and autonomous black culture were also influenced by Randolph Bourne's most well-known essay, "Trans-National America"(1916). In "Trans-National America," Bourne argued against U.S. notions of the "melting pot" (an animating feature of Cruse's integrationist strain) in favor of a "federated" vision of U.S. intercultures marked by divergent—rather than convergent—nationalistic loyalties, outlooks, and sympathies. According to Bourne, who, oddly enough, was one of the most prominent Greenwich Village intellectuals of the 1910s, the melting pot was shorthand for an ongoing attempt, by the "cultural makers of opinion," to meld the multiple societies (or nations within a nation) comprising U.S. national life into an overarching "Anglo-Saxon" value system and political and economic rationalities.[49] If something approaching true democracy were ever to be realized within the United States, Bourne insisted, it would require an acceptance of the United States as primarily a site of overlapping diasporas and migrations, which might anchor a proliferation of cultural outlooks openly competing to determine the direction of national life and culture, along with what its overarching "structural" (that is, governmental and organizational) principles might be or become.

One of the more interesting implications here, viewed through the protracted arc of Cruse's work on the Village, is that Bourne was more advanced in his cultural and political thinking than were many of his professed bohemian heirs of the 1950s. Secure in Bourne's assessment of U.S. society and his agonistic vision of cultural democracy, Cruse now declared that "American group reality demands a struggle for democracy among ethnic groups," a declaration that reconfigured Bourne through Cruse's experiences in Cuba and his comprehension of the more general anticolonial fervor of the period in question.[50] The time had come to admit, Cruse insists throughout Crisis, that "Negro intellectuals have been sold a bill of goods on interracialism by [both] white Communists and white liberals," and needed instead to find their cultural counterpart in the rising "Third World nationalism" of places such as Cuba, developments that might aid "the African foster-child in the American racial equation" to outgrow the psychological bonds of "intellectual paternalism."[51] Inspired by the ways in which anticolonial intellectuals were attempting to throw off the long-standing influences of their imperial/colonial overseers, along with the heavy baggage of alien cultural and political values, Cruse argued that American society could not realize its own democratic claims without the "complete democratization of the national cultural ethos," which he ultimately equated with an unapologetic and intractable pluralism.[52] Cruse's cultural vision, that is to say, celebrated the assertion of ethnic and racial cultural differences—or unassimilated "group identities" or racial blocs—over and against integration within mass produced social and political values which most Americans (of various ethnic and racial backgrounds) had no role in authoring. Hoping to conjure a more agonistic (that is, less integrationist) and financially autonomous black public sphere involved in a cultural Darwinist battle over social and political ideas, Cruse once again questioned the politics of Cold War liberals like Daniel Bell, whom Cruse discusses at length alongside Bourne and Mills. Bell, as Cruse points out, had oddly (and quite famously) declared an "end of ideological battles" within the U.S. domestic scene, claiming that the American people had finally become unified in their beliefs regarding the inherent rightness of U.S. institutional and governmental forms. This claim, Cruse adroitly observed, came at the very moment in which black political movements of increasing diversity—inspired by anticolonial movements operating beyond the bounds of the domestic political culture and Cold War consensus that Bell had sanctified in *End of Ideology* (1960)—were actually gaining momentum and visibility, leaving Cruse with some serious doubts regarding Bell's objectivity and motivations.

The rationales of the Black Arts Movement—unthinkable without Cruse's intellectual contributions—epitomized his championing of an unapologetically black public sphere as a cornerstone to continued democratic striving. Functioning as the aesthetic wing of the era's pronounced black nationalism and Black Power causes, the Black Arts Movement established itself throughout urban America in the mid- to late 1960s. As Cruse had imagined, the movement witnessed the African American founding of underground literary journals such as *Liberator* and *Umbra Poetry Journal,* the elaboration of agitprop street performances and public poetry readings as pivotal expressive practices, and the establishment of black-owned performance venues such as the Black Arts Repertory Theatre and School in Harlem. In short, figures such as Baraka, Cruse, Charles Fuller, Nikki Giovanni, and Ed Bullins asserted that black artists could play a prominent role in political transformation as members of a revolutionary public sphere that might provide an actual voice to African American urban dwellers, rather than depending upon white liberals within the Democratic Party or upon official organizations such as the NAACP to relay the voice of justice and change on their behalf. Consistent with Cruse's theorization of a fiercely independent black public sphere, artists and intellectuals associated with the Black Arts Movement attempted to foment an aesthetic of social upheaval throughout U.S. urban centers, daring to conceive of cultural forums in which the conversations and overall representation of black society would no longer be confined to the middle-class aspirations of figures such as Hansberry and what Cruse identified as white liberal admiration. The Black Arts Movement's collective hope was the establishment of an alternative public arena organized by issues (such as the immediate elimination of urban poverty) they viewed as painfully absent from the platforms of the mainstream Civil Rights Movement and media coverage of race-based political issues, which focused predominantly on the integration of public spaces (such as Southern lunch counters) and the shoring up of voting rights.

The rise of the Black Arts Movement, and of Black Power in general, occurred at the confluence of two historical processes—one domestic and one international in scope. The domestic front in this perfect historical storm, which Robin D. G. Kelley identifies as the conventional (and seemingly recalcitrant) narrative of U.S. historians, gathers its momentum from events such as the turning away of the Mississippi Free Democratic Party from the 1964 Democratic Convention and the subsequent assassination of Malcolm X, resulting, by 1966, in a pronounced Black Power stance whose adherents "were tired of and impatient with the slow pace of the civil rights establishment, and a new attitude overtook the movement [toward racial justice]: no more compromise, no more 'deals' with white liberals, no more subordinating the struggle to the needs of the Democratic Party. Out of bitter disappointment rose a new black revolution."[53] This now-pronounced revolutionary stance, which Cruse, fresh upon his Cuban experience and still stinging with his realizations regarding Village race relations had begun formulating prior to the 1964 convention, became for a time completely unhinged from conventional alliances (that is, with white liberals and the Democratic Party) within the political sphere of the U.S. nation-state, and invigorated by intellectual support of decolonizing movements throughout the world. Or as Cruse, writing in *Crisis*, explained in relation to his Cuban experience: "a new revolutionary wave in the world at large . . . had lifted us out of the anonymity of lonely struggle in the U.S."[54] Inspired by revolutions in not only Cuba, but throughout Asia and Africa, many intellectuals and artists involved in the domestic black freedom struggle became less interested in gradualist and integrationist reform and more interested in political movements throughout the globe, as seen in the Black Panthers' overt support of Castro, Mao Tse-Tung, and the North Vietnamese, along with the Black Arts Movement's efforts at facilitating what some of its figures saw as an "Africanist" urban style (of dashikis and "la mode au naturel" hairstyles). This widened perspective is also seen in Cruse's dismissive exclamation that "it is in the Federal government that the integrationists . . . place their ultimate faith."[55]

Perhaps the most famous statement in this regard remains Malcolm X's "The Ballot or the Bullet?" in which he decried legislative gradualism, the mainstream Civil Rights Movement, and future coalition-building with white liberals. X, who along with Baraka and Ginsberg had hosted Castro on his 1960 visit to the United Nations (when Castro famously decided to stay at the Hotel Theresa in Harlem), made the further argument that the black freedom struggle needed to forge "new friendships" and "new alliances" with global decolonizing movements (including the Cuban Revolution) and that the terrain of political struggle needed to shift from the precincts of the U.S. nation-state to the United Nations.[56] Such declarations catapulted black politics into new and increasingly expansive directions, and thus represented a more general attempt at imagining political arenas and forms of political expression beyond the narrowed institutional geography and official public culture of the nation-state—a direction that was also undoubtedly influenced by Cruse's understanding of Castro and his revolution.

It should be said, in fairness to Martin Luther King, Jr. who often absorbed much of the rhetorical scorn of figures such as X and Cruse, that his appeal and dexterity as a thinker and leader was often misrepresented—as was the actual power and appeal of the Black Church as a public political forum that was not only historically invested in social justice and liberation theology, but capable of producing a figure such as King. Indeed, I would go so far as to suggest that King and the movement he spearheaded had been conveniently cast at times as the rhetorical scarecrow of black nationalist arguments that denied the complexity of his political thought in unwarranted ways. It is particularly notable that in the final year of his life King himself had publicly advocated for many of the economic and foreign policy causes championed by the advocates of Black Power, positions that materialized in his support of the Memphis sanitation workers, the Poor People's Campaign, and his 1967 "Beyond Vietnam" address at Riverside Church. Yet despite Cruse's rhetorical excesses in this regard, his writings help illuminate the extent to which global political events of the Cold War era, and especially the Cuban Revolution, affected the course of African American political, literary, intellectual, and artistic culture in some fairly significant ways—providing heroic political models and a language of engagement for those unconvinced by either the limited rationales of Cold War liberalism or the achievements of the mainstream Civil Rights Movement (momentous as they may seem to us now). As would be the case with Cruse's fellow Village resident, Amiri Baraka, the Cuban Revolution performed a myriad of roles in the evolution of Cruse's work, allowing him to reflect upon and actively generate the nascent concerns of the black liberation movement, while shedding light on the discursive preconditions of public political expression and nationalistic pieties during the Cold War era. It might also be said that many of Cruse's trepidations—which included concerns over racialized forms of economic disparity, substandard urban education and housing, and charges of police brutality/profiling against people of color—continue to be on the table in the post–Civil Rights United States, suggesting that we have yet to find effective ways to deliberate over and solve these problems, while continuing to identify the primary threat to our national security/interests with vaguely defined, though confidently pronounced, external threats to the American way of life.

# 3

# Unsettling the Democratic Score

Music and Urban Insurgency

As Cruse mentions in *Crisis of the Negro Intellectual*, Amiri Baraka played an integral role in the Beat orbit and the Greenwich Village art scene of the 1950s. As one of the only African American writers associated with the Beat Movement—at a moment when it dwelt in close proximity to a more extensive network of artists and writers comprising the New York School—Baraka viewed himself as a "colleague of the spirit" who empathized with the movement's "young white boys and girls in their pronouncement of disillusion with and 'removal' from society as being related to the black experience."[1] Indeed, Baraka's characterization goes a long way toward validating Cruse's initial idealism regarding the New Bohemia, and Baraka was so committed to the Beats during his formative years as a poet that he wrote one of movement's most elegant defenses—a 1958 letter to their detractors in the *Partisan Review* defiantly explaining the aesthetic and cultural significance of Kerouac and his peers. As we shall see, however, Baraka's Cuban experience—first captured in his *Evergreen Review* essay "Cuba Libre" while he was still writing as LeRoi Jones—notably altered his relationship to his Beat "colleagues," facilitating a shift in perspective notable in his artistic and critical output over the course of the 1960s, a period in which Baraka's work often resituated conventional Beat subject matter and aesthetic practices within an increasingly pronounced framework of social, political, and cultural activism elaborated (as was the case with Cruse) within the precincts of global anticolonialism and the gathering storm of black nationalism.

Baraka's experiences in Cuba ultimately convinced him that the "implied rebellion" he originally celebrated in the Beat aesthetic was not rebellious or revolutionary enough—especially, as it turns out, in relation to racial injustice. Both Van Gosse and Timothy Tyson have already argued as much, asserting that Baraka underwent a political and cultural epiphany in Havana that sent him on a new intellectual and activist course for years to come, including his eventual name change from Jones to Baraka, his role in the formation of the Black Arts Movement and the Black Arts Repertory Theatre and School, and his involvements in various forms of Third World Marxism. To a large extent, "Cuba Libre" represents Baraka's parting shot to the Beat Generation as he became increasingly interested in mobilizing the political capacities of African American musical and expressive culture, and in the process he extended and deepened the concerns of Cruse. As was the case with Ferlinghetti and Mills, his portrayal of Castro's revolution—and his attendant valorization of African American expressive practices—embodied a telling critique of the U.S. public sphere and its relationship to conventional or procedural politics, including the official liberalism of the Cold War Democratic Party and the mainstream Civil Rights Movement. It is on this last point that he departs markedly from the concerns of Ferlinghetti and Mills, as Baraka's Cubalogue—along with his writings on jazz and blues from the period—explicitly engage with U.S. racial history, paying particular attention to what he saw as the long-standing failures of mainstream reform efforts over a protracted historical arc.

## Cuba "Moves"

Baraka visited Cuba—along with Cruse—in July of 1960 as a member of an FPCC Tour composed of African American artists and intellectuals. Near the outset of his original version of "Cuba Libre," which appeared in the November/December 1960 issue of *Evergreen Review,* Baraka admits that he arrived in Cuba with virtually no interest in explicitly political affairs—that his political outlook, if he could be said to have had one, was based solely on a bohemian rejection of 1950s social mores. His attitude toward politics, however, began to shift significantly on a train ride to the Sierra Maestra, where Castro and others were gathering to speak on the current state of the revolution and during which he was confronted by members of the Latin American Youth Congress (LAYC) regarding his lack of explicitly political commitments. A female member of the LAYC, whom Baraka does not name, assailed him with a trenchant critique of U.S. foreign policy in which "[e]veryone in the world . . . has to be communist or anti-communist. And if they're anti-communist, no matter what kind of foul person they are, you people accept them as your allies. Do you really think this hopeless little island in the middle of the sea is China? That is irrational."[2] At one fell swoop, the young activist from LAYC inverted the allegedly rational paradigms of the Cold War public sphere, which tended to voice unconditional support for the "foul" Batistas of the world, despite their well-documented political misdeeds and human rights violations. The United States, she assured Baraka, was in fact the embodiment of political irrationality, while warning him that if he continued to ignore this fact in his intellectual and artistic work, he would amount to nothing more than just another "bourgeois coward."[3] She was soon joined in her consternation by the Mexican poet, Jaime Augusto Shelley, who chastised Baraka for wanting to "cultivate his soul in the midst of ugliness," while imploring the American poet to embark on a more politically aware poetics.[4]

As was the case in Cruse's recollections, an inter-American summit of sorts transpires on the train ride into the Sierra Maestra—a heated conversation between activists and artists from throughout the American hemisphere who had been brought together under the auspices of Cuba's budding revolutionary culture. This conversation, however, markedly contradicts the political sobriety and pragmatic deliberation advocated by Cold War U.S. liberals, as upon entering the train Baraka is immediately handed a rum drink; the revolutionary exchange of ideas, according to Baraka's narrative, takes place within a largely festive environment, as people dance, scream, and shout their way through the train, balancing their political commitments with an ecstatic sense of slightly drunken revelry, which resonates with Kerouac's portrayal of Beat "kicks" in works such as *On the Road* and *Visions of Cody* while going a long way toward explaining Baraka's decision to name his essay after a Cuban rum cocktail. Caught up in the carnivalesque atmosphere unfolding around him, Baraka finds himself equally "moved" by the Cuban people he meets along the way. The train makes several stops on the way to the Sierra Maestra, and at Matanzas and Colon the intellectuals and artists aboard the train are swept up by the Caribbean and Afro-Cuban music of the local populations awaiting them on the platform. Reflecting on the swirling masses, partaking in a form of political carnival, Baraka wonders: "What was it, a circus? Could there be that much excitement generated through all the people?"[5] Overwhelmed by the "People moving, being moved," Baraka witnesses something he "had never seen before, exploding around me," sending the train "rock[ing] wildly across and into the interior" as its reveling passengers begin singing a cha-cha for Castro and Guevara.[6] Baraka later recounts the spontaneous calypso dancing and "Mardi Gras scene" following upon Castro's address in the Sierra Maestra with a similar sense of excitement and awe.

Baraka's focus on musical and political rapture at once resituated the ecstatic

Latin American wanderings of figures such as Kerouac within a political movement culture. Kerouac's identification of jazz as one manifestation of the "world beat" pulsing through the "equatorial belly of the world" in the Caribbean, India, Mexico, and Morocco, valorized non-Western music as the sonic expression of anti-civilization and anti-intellectualism; the real value of the "world beat," as Kerouac dubbed it, was that it lacked any real political value or sophistication, and thus provided an (undoubtedly primitivist) escape from Western cultural mores and the dictates of rationality.[7] But upon journeying to Cuba, Baraka found himself physically *and* politically moved, as stock features of Kerouacian fiction—such as the cross-country train ride and aural epiphany—took on new roles in an inter-American political drama. And just as Ferlinghetti criticized Kerouac's political apathy in "Poet's Notes on Cuba," Baraka closes "Cuba Libre" complaining that young rebels in the United States merely "grow beards" without becoming politically engaged, constituting a "bland revolt. Drugs, juvenile delinquency, complete isolation from the vapid mores of the country—a few current ways out. But name an alternative here. Something not inextricably bound up in a lie."[8] Addressing several Beat stereotypes at once, Baraka dismisses the bohemian milieu he had left behind in Greenwich Village as severely limited and naive in its political and social vision.

Baraka's Cuba visit also altered his understanding of "revolution" and, by extension, the possibilities of mainstream political reform within the United States. Confronted with the revolutionary movements of "the Cubans, and other emergent peoples (in Asia, Africa, South America)," he admitted that the "new ideas" emanating from what Mills termed the "hungry-nation bloc" had revealed his own provincialism.[9] Prior to his Cuban experience, Baraka understood revolution as a "romantic" and "hopeless" idea that North Americans "have been taught since public school to hold up to the cold light of 'reason.'"[10] According to Baraka's revised thinking, though, the originating dynamism of U.S. political traditions had atrophied into a state of paralysis over time. Or as Baraka claims in his reflection on the dancing Cuban masses: "Damn, that people still *can* move. Not us, but people."[11] Again, while addressing the lack of appealing political alternatives in the essay's closing paragraphs, he exclaims: "It's much too late. We are an *old* people already."[12] The U.S. citizenry, in other words, had become far too removed in Baraka's estimation from their revolutionary heritage—or their original "movement" cultures—unlike the "new peoples" of the decolonizing world attempting to create their political systems and cultural lives anew.

Sounding much like Mills, Baraka asserts that the collective outlook on "revolution" in the United States had been bracketed within a limited vision of the possible, which equated social progress with voting and piecemeal reform rather than the sudden or spontaneous overhaul of systems of injustice; what he is reflecting on, in a sense, are the limits of doing politics within the national public sphere—and through official governmental channels—where the preservation of the national community and dominative ideas (such as the free market) set a prediscursive horizon on the discussion of social problems through appeals to pragmatism or the politically "reasonable." In one of the essay's most compelling passages, Baraka reminds his readers that appeals to reason are not appeals to universal, neutral forms of rationality, but that the boundaries of the politically "reasonable" (or of Fisher's "rational world paradigm") are always the historical manifestation of politically interested justifications that "our usurious 'ruling class' had paid their journalists to disseminate."[13] The weight of these justifications and rationales, Baraka warns his readers "has settled on all our lives. . . . That thin crust of lie we cannot even detect in our own thinking. That rotting of the mind which has enabled us to think about Hiroshima as if someone else had done it, or to believe vaguely that the 'counterrevolution' in Guatemala [against Arbenz] was an 'internal' affair."[14] Furthermore, Americans had become incapable of standing up to the willed corruption of public dialogue because they had been taught, through the educational system and the mainstream media, to rely on voting and official legislative channels as the proper agents of political and social change. As Baraka puts it, the case for the politically reasonable, or for remaining pragmatic in one's political expectations "allows that voting, in a country where the parties are exactly the same, can be made to assume the gravity of actual moral engagement."[15] Baraka's statements in this regard attempt to illuminate the ways in which we take the teleological capacities of our basic constitutional structure for granted, as somehow overly capable of securing democracy and social justice in some ideal and future instant. But relying upon proceduralism, or waiting for state and federal legislatures to redress injustices through their officially sanctioned measures, might actually constitute a temporal roadblock to democratic striving—especially in those instances, such as racially motivated violence and oppression, in which the situation calls for the immediate or instantaneous rectification of injustice or imperial overreach.

Sounding much like Ferlinghetti and Mills, Baraka offers Cuban revolutionary culture as an inclusive and vibrant alternative to the well-reasoned public arena that vilified Cuba at home and whose ossified patterns of political perception had been so aptly diagnosed by the female member of the LAYC. In turn, his experience of the spontaneous and musical aspects of the Cuban Revolution inspired a marked change in his own aesthetic and political commitments as Baraka began to sever himself from the Beat Movement in order to celebrate African American musical forms as an alternative political history—or alternative public sphere—that might reinvigorate U.S. political culture, or compel it to *move*, in a fashion similar to the way in which the world's new peoples were reinvigorating their political institutions and life-worlds. Castro personally implored Baraka to take the revolution home with him, and he certainly did, as his work thereafter forged a cultural connection between the Cuban Revolution and emergent expressions of black nationalism—a connection catalyzed by his experience of Cuba's singing and dancing masses.[16] To some extent, this was a startling development, as Baraka's first version of "Cuba Libre" had very little to say about race relations in the United States, though his subsequent rewriting of "Cuba Libre," discussed below, more pointedly stressed the racial aspects of his experience as the political upheavals of the 1960s headed toward their advanced stages. We might say, in other words, that Baraka indeed took the revolution home with him, but in a way that Castro had not necessarily imagined, as his now-pronounced interest in the political propensities of musical forms led him into an extensive artistic and critical engagement with jazz and blues, which in turn separated him politically from both his white "colleagues of the spirit" in the Beat Movement *and* the mainstream Civil Rights Movement, which was starting to kick into high gear.

## Newark Moves

As Iain Anderson has noted, Baraka's interest in writing about jazz and blues coincided with a suddenly pronounced concern for racial politics and for theorizing a more explicit political aesthetic, as figures such as Augusto Shelly challenged him to do.[17] Along these lines, Baraka's critical and historical work in *Blues People* (1963) and *Black Music* (1968) hailed black musical forms as the embodiment of a protracted democratic struggle traceable to the diasporic dislocations fomented by the Atlantic slave trade, reconstructing, in the process, a politically heroic narrative of black musical practices whose insights predate Paul Gilroy's own influential treatment of the topic in *There Ain't No Black in the Union Jack* (1991) and *The Black Atlantic* (1993). In both works, Gilroy made a stunning contribution to postcolonial theory by arguing for an approach to Afro-diasporic musical culture as a breeding ground for alternative political rationalities necessitated by the political shortsightedness of Enlightenment democracy, which had formulated its ideals of freedom at the exclusion of the enslaved populations embedded within its circuitry. Laura Doyle has usefully referred to the resultant contradictions as the "racialization of freedom" based on the realization that "in Atlantic modernity, freedom [was] a race myth" in which the white architects of modern democracy monopolized the capacity for liberation and democratic agency through a racialized "interproduction of freedom and bondage" originally traceable to the discourse of Anglo-Saxon rights that emerged just prior to the English Revolution and subsequently provided the foundational coordinates for the racial ferocity of the Atlantic slave trade and violent encounters with America's first peoples.[18] Confronted by the mass and systematic denial of the conventional forms of political participation emerging within the main drift of Atlantic modernity, Gilroy makes the accompanying claim that Afro-diasporic peoples discovered in music "a substitute for the formal political freedoms they were denied under the plantation regime," transforming the aesthetic or cultural realm into a site for making social and political claims.[19] In other words, upon being legally denied conventional literacy and citizenship rights within Atlantic democracy—which amounted to an inability to enter the dominative public arena of the nation-state as sovereign participants—Afro-diasporic music came to represent an "extra-linguistic" communicative act that provided shape to concerns endlessly deferred by means of wide-scale oppression and consciously planned dehumanization.[20]

Throughout *Blues People* and *Black Music,* Baraka similarly insisted that black musical culture served as a repository for the repressed political desires of Afro-diasporic peoples collectively shut out of participating in the print-based public sphere (of Benedict Anderson's "imagined" national communities) by the race-based denial of literacy.[21] Black music had always constituted, Baraka contended, an alternative public history of diaspora and forced servitude, allowing a counterpublic of "Blues People" to voice their political desires and own the movements of their otherwise enslaved and oppressed bodies on the margins of mainstream political conversation and its journalistic mediums.[22] Shortly after his visit to revolutionary Cuba, Baraka began ambitiously reconstructing this heroic history of black music, which he then employed to reflect critically on the assimilationist strategies of the mainstream Civil Rights Movement, led by organizations such as the NAACP and figures such as Martin Luther King, Jr. In turn, jazz and blues were recast as revolutionary mediums engaged in an African American class drama that privileged black populism and the immediate, spontaneous overhaul of systems of oppression to the integrationist efforts— or what Baraka saw as the gradual reform policies—of the official Civil Rights Movement. Though historically vilified as "devil music" by the Black Church, which was at the forefront of the postwar struggle for Civil Rights, Baraka contended that jazz and the blues held the key to forms of black cultural awareness and world-making more in keeping with the movements of "new peoples" throughout the decolonizing world.

Baraka's "Jazz and the White Critic," which first appeared in *Downbeat* in 1963 (and was later collected in 1968's *Black Music*), represents the budding cultural historian's initial statement in this regard. Baraka criticized white jazz writers for being overly concerned with aesthetic appreciation of the music (especially in regards to technique and rhythm) at the cost of its socio-cultural aspects, thereby catering to the tastes of white audiences and a black middle class interested in cultural and socio-political integration via a celebration of "America's classical music." He asserted, in turn, that the musicians "who were responsible for the best of the music, were always aware of their identities as black Americans and really did not, themselves, desire to become vague, featureless, Americans as is usually the case with the Negro middle class."[23] Jazz and blues were encoded, Baraka argued, with the legacy of slavery, for musicians "played jazz . . . as they had shouted and hollered in those anonymous fields, because it was one of the few areas of human expression available to them."[24] Denied access to print-based literacy over an extended historical arc—and thus from the mainstream expression of political opinion in the national public sphere—musical forms served as the repository for African American history and knowledge, a history that white critics often ignored and from which the black middle class of the 1950s and 1960s had done its best, in Baraka's estimation, to distance itself. African American music was, that is to say, the public discourse for a nation within a nation "and its sources were *secret* as far as the rest of America was concerned."[25] Moreover, Baraka asserted that jazz and blues comprised a "stance" or "attitude" that viewed American political, social, and cultural life from its long-vilified margins, and avant-garde performers such as John Coltrane were the most recent carriers of this tradition: "The catalysts and necessity of Coltrane's music must be understood as they exist even before they are expressed as music. The music is the result of the attitude, the stance. Just as Negroes made blues and other people did not because of the Negro's peculiar way of looking at the world."[26] The Jazz avant-garde of the 1950s and 1960s, according to Baraka's cultural history, was only the latest manifestation of a "constantly evolving social philosophy" that highlighted spontaneity, ceaseless creativity, and the often cacophonic expression of social alienation (rather than the acceptance of political silence) as means of survival in a hostile environment that had denied its adherents true connections to the official avenues of national belonging.[27]

*Blues People* (1963) elaborated upon the ideas Baraka first auditioned in "Jazz and the White Critic" in a more substantial fashion. In the book's opening chapter, "The Negro as Non-American: Some Backgrounds . . . ," Baraka explored the extent to which the conditions of U.S. citizenship had been historically grounded in a series of race-based exclusions (stretching from the founding Constitutional documents through Jim Crow). According to Baraka, African Americans had consistently been denied a "genuine niche in the mainstream of [U.S.] society in which to function as a *citizen*," and this repudiation constituted (over and over again) the racial boundaries of citizen-formation in general.[28]

If, Baraka suggested, "there was always a border [in U.S. society] beyond which the Negro could not go. . . . And it was this boundary, this *no man's land*, that provided the logic and beauty of his music," then black musical forms registered the denial of rewarding nationality, which could be traced, in its first instance, to the Atlantic slave trade.[29] The evolution of these forms in turn registered the ongoing struggle of Afro-diasporic peoples in the United States and served as a collective form of communication for a counter-public constituted of "Blues People." Black music, in other words, comprised a cultural history that embodied, according to Baraka's logic, the marginal status of an internal colony as it became tangibly altered over the course of historical time. Modern Blues styles, for instance, emerged during Reconstruction and post-Reconstruction and expressed the woe and dejection of political defeat alongside danceable song structures, capturing both the agony and joy of partially freed bodies.[30] Baraka told a similar story of the Great Migration and the emergence of race records. As black populations migrated from the agricultural South to various points in the industrial North, they became a modern and unified people through the consumption of a common culture.[31] Race records registered the continued separation of black culture from the general American public, while solidifying a set of musical conventions no longer constrained within regional geographies. Time constraints, four stanza blues, the stride piano technique of players such as James P. Johnson, all became stock features of "the music" as listeners and musicians separated by vast geographical distances began to codify a shared sense of musical style and structure.[32]

But not everyone embraced the new, modern styles of America's Blues People. The Black Church, according to Baraka, consistently dubbed these musical forms as "devil's music," capable of releasing unseemly passions and sinful forms of behavior. The dismissal of the "people's music" corresponded, in Baraka's estimation, with black middle-class striving largely traceable to the Great Migration, which had created an economic cleavage in African American society even as it had provided new forms of solidarity and collective identity. The Black Church and its middle-class denizens had proven adept at business and saving money in the industrialized North, and their rejection of black musical heritage corresponded with their willful embrace of the "White Man's God" and an integrationist strategy which consistently pushed "for the complete assimilation of the Negro into white America"—a strategy Baraka saw embodied in his times by Martin Luther King, Jr. and the modern Civil Rights Movement.[33] Baraka argued, in turn, that middle-class integrationists were not true Blues People; echoing his earlier critique in "Jazz and the White Critic," Baraka asserted that the black middle class "has formed almost exclusively around the proposition that it is better not to be black in a country where being black is a liability. All the main roads into America have always been fashioned by the members of the black middle class (not as products of a separate culture, but as vague, featureless Americans)."[34] Baraka closed *Blues People* by arguing that this history of "featureless" integration has spawned two corresponding cultural movements: the emergence of the noisy, "screaming" avant-garde of the 1950s and 1960s and the increased attraction of black nationalist groups such as the Nation of Islam at the very moment in which African Americans were supposedly taking vital steps (largely through the leadership of the Black Church) toward a long-denied national inclusion.[35] The emergence of this new avant-garde—marked by atonality and a rejection of conventional melodic and harmonic structures—alongside the growing appeal of alternative political groups, signaled, for Baraka, a more extensive disenchantment with the politics of integration.

Baraka provided a more detailed sketching of the contours of his evolving cultural and political beliefs in the 1964 short story, "The Screamers." Set in Newark, New Jersey—where Baraka was born and raised—"The Screamers" is a semi-autobiographical tale that recasts the "moving" Cuban peasantry as the working class and impoverished denizens of Graham's Jazz Club. The unnamed narrator (based on Baraka himself) rejects the promises of middle-class integration for the politically alluring tenor saxophone player, Lynn Hope, an "ethnic historian" whose screaming horn provides aesthetic shape to the legacy of U.S. racial oppression.[36] As the narrator explains, the crowd in Graham's "hated the popular song," preferring the noisy style of Lynn, based as it was upon the "repeated rhythmic figure, a screamed riff, pushed in its insistence past music. It was hatred and frustration, secrecy and despair. . . . There was no compromise, no dreary sophistication, only the elegance of something that is too ugly to be described, and is diluted only at the agent's peril. . . . That stance spread like fire thru the cabarets and joints of the black cities, so that the sound itself became the basis for thought, and the innovators searched for uglier modes."[37] Hope's playing epitomizes the rhythmic honking and jagged screaming that characterized the avant-garde horn players of the period (such as Eric Dolphy, Ornette Coleman, John Coltrane, and Pharaoh Sanders, along with late Bop players such as Illinois Jacquet). For Baraka, these styles echoed the "screams" and "shouts" of slavery's fields, just as the U.S. congress was on the verge of passing the Civil Rights Act of 1964, which forbade discrimination by state and federal agencies, along with outlawing segregation in most public places (including, of course, public educational facilities). The horn screams—rather than singing joyously or melodically—of "hatred" and "frustration" presenting listeners with a "basis for thought" unwilling, Baraka writes, to accept "compromise" just as one of great legislative significance was being offered. Horns screaming "thru the cabarets and joints of the black cities" seemingly speak to a brewing disillusionment and militancy even as African Americans were realizing these much-needed legislative strides. Or we might say that the screaming horns stand in metonymically for a set of concerns left out of mainstream reform efforts—that the screaming represents a sublimated rage and frustration over that which was not being expressed in mainstream political channels, carrying the additional weight of a forcibly silenced past.

As in *Blues People,* Baraka's short story contrasts the musical tradition of Hope with what he understood as the cultural prejudices of the Black Church. His narrator, who has been raised in a Christian household by his postal worker father and social worker mother, attends Graham's rather than religious services. Indeed, the events of the story unfold on a Sunday evening, the narrator informs us, just as "the Baptists were still praying in their 'fabulous' churches."[38] Lynn, instead, becomes the narrator's "priest" as he further admits that "God never had a chance."[39] True black culture and history, Baraka asserts once again, might be best discovered in the underground currents of the music—in the dive club rather than the church—as he equates rejecting the church for Graham's to leaving "America on the first fast boat," seeing as the Black Church was the spiritual and political home of the black middle class and its dreams of melting into what he had described as a "featureless" America.[40] Its members listened to the watered-down swing of white vocalist Jo Stafford and attempted, Baraka mockingly explains, to solve political problems by joining the Urban League and other mainstream reform organizations such as the NAACP. Baraka's narrator has an utterly different political approach in mind, an outlook anchored in the young writer's experience of the "moved" and "moving" revolution of Castro's Havana. "Lynn," the young narrator tells us, "was trying to *move* us," and his honking rhythm accomplishes just that purpose as the impoverished and working class patrons of Graham's—or "all the Biggers who would not be bent"—become overwhelmed with riotous energy and the unseemly passions feared by the Black Church, dancing their way into Newark's streets where they violently clash with the city's white police force.[41] In the concluding pages of the story, jazz spontaneity is reconfigured as a key feature of emergent black nationalism, as Graham's patrons form a revolutionary conga line behind the screaming horn of Hope and attempt to "destroy the ghetto" while ridding Newark's streets of racist policing in the most immediate way.[42]

"The Screamers" politicized a more extensive Beat interest in jazz, reframing musical expression as a public medium for black political demands, and laying the philosophical groundwork for the decisive role that Baraka would come to play within the Black Arts Movement. One of the movement's guiding notions was that black urban residents were perfectly capable of redefining the spaces in which they lived according to their own terms. When Baraka's "screamers" rush into the street, following Lynn, who has crossed the proscenium, they spontaneously reinvent a public space for collective cultural expression—a space that then must fight for its right to exist against the symbols of white authority, the urban police force whose principal occupation has long been the maintenance of order, while securing the borders of ghettoized urban space. Jon Panish's characterization of "The Screamers," and the ways in which it differs from Kerouacian treatments of jazz aesthetics, brings the socio-political stakes of Baraka's narrative even clearer into view. As Panish explains, "The Screamers," "unfolds like an extended jazz solo with its energetic first person narrative, accentuated rhythm, vivid images, colloquial language, and alternating high- and pop-culture references. Although there are also significant differences, [Jones's] story resembles Jack Kerouac's jazz-influenced, first person writings in these formal elements."[43] The differences, however, are the story here. While Baraka may focus serious attention on cultural and class distinctions within African American communities, his story ultimately identifies black music as a communal, democratic activity based on a deeply felt connection between performers and their audiences, who have tended to view black musical culture as "a potentially emancipating response to oppression."[44] This portrayal is a far cry—or "scream," I suppose—from Kerouac's embrace of jazz aesthetics in documents such as "Elements of Spontaneous Prose," in which he lionizes jazz "blowing" as deeply introspective and privatized, a personal act of intuitive genius that might momentarily liberate the artist (and the creative act) from the trappings of Cold War mass culture, all the while privileging individual creativity and the personal imperatives of improvisation over the traditionally communal aspects of jazz and blues.[45] Kerouac, that is to say, celebrated the personal aspects of jazz aesthetics in a way that resonated with the "white critic" whom Baraka had dismissed in his 1963 *Downbeat* essay.

Lynn's music functions as a participatory, discursive glue that allows the crowd at Graham's to occupy their bodies as an oppositional collective, or to see themselves, in the words of the narrator, as a "clear image of [what] we should always be. Ecstatic, completed, involved in a secret communal expression . . . [and] the sweetest revolution."[46] At the height of the mainstream Civil Rights Movement, Baraka's short story rejects gradualist politics (enacted patiently through the legislative apparatus) and mainstream assimilationist strategies in the name of an insurrectionary and violent clash with Newark's legacy of racialized policing—or we may say it strikes the initial chords of separatism (over-against assimilation) in Baraka's work, anticipating many of the animating concerns of Black Power and the Black Arts Movement to come. In terms of the Black Panther Party, for instance, Nikhil Pal Singh has explained that "the Panthers were effective in producing themselves as [black anti-citizens] because they refused the terms of black inclusion and citizenship in the American polity at precisely the point of their greatest augmentation and reform since the Civil War and Reconstruction, as a result of the Civil Rights Act of 1964, the Voting Rights Act of 1965, and Johnson's War on Poverty programs. It may have been the offer of state-aided integration into civil society and the public sphere that gave such a powerful charge to the Panther's refusals and contestations."[47] That is to say, the Panthers, like many of the various Black Power Movements of the mid-1960s to early 1970s, were animated by serious apprehensions regarding the conditions of political inclusion. Civil Rights legislation, these groups collectively argued, might not ultimately go far enough toward correcting and alleviating the effects of protracted U.S. racism, especially in terms of providing for the economic reconstruction or revitalization of America's racial enclaves (via progressive forms of economic redistribution). Merely asserting liberal-democratic forms of political universality (such as protecting the right to vote) could never reach down far enough into the culture, so the argument goes, to reconstruct historically sedimented economic and social inequities. The rise of black nationalism and separatism, in other words, spoke to the ongoing frustration of urban communities in the very midst of Civil Rights reform, a frustration that would express itself most forcefully in the race rioting that occurred throughout major U.S. cities (including Newark) during 1967—a series of events foreshadowed by the fictional patrons of Graham's in 1964. Moreover, in terms of what was actually achieved during the peak years of the Civil Rights era, Baraka's insights dovetail with Michael Denning's assertion that "African-American civil rights were the result not of a long and patient working through the political system, but of brief insurrectionary moments, not of social movement alliances with sectors of the [political] elite," but of civil disobedience and rioting, which came to a head between 1963 and 1967—or during the very period in which Baraka was composing "The Screamers"—and which forced the hand of mainstream politicians within the U.S.[48]

Ihab Hassan's characterization of the aesthetic rationales of the Black Arts Movement also remains particularly apt in terms of discussing the movement's hostile and uncompromising relationship to the dominative public arena and the political mainstream. In Hassan's estimation, Baraka's plays from the period just after "The Screamers" and *Blues People*—such as *The Toilet* (1963), *The Dead Lecturer* (1964), and *The Slave* (1964)—firmly ensconced the young playwright as the central voice of a new black nationalist aesthetic that was both "revolutionary" and "communal, gravid with the sense of a black destiny," which it took "loudly to the streets," attempting to create an alternative public arena via community art projects and street performances aimed at galvanizing black urban dwellers into a more militant wing of the black freedom struggle.[49] Hassan's treatment of Baraka also remains instructive in regards to Cruse's dismissal of Hansberry in the early 1960s, as Hassan asserts that Baraka's plays, along with his founding of the Black Arts Repertory Theatre in Harlem, represented a theatrical alternative to Hansberry's attempts at employing black family drama as a window into the "universality of suffering" on both sides of the color line.[50] Operating from "the other pole of Black drama"—or what Cruse referred to as "the nationalist strain"—Baraka employed "theater mainly as a political weapon, [as] an extension of Black Power," hoping to conjure a "total theater" capable of rallying black urban audiences into a more forceful movement for immediate equality, while simultaneously giving voice to the concerns of the street (as did the saxophone of Hope).[51]

## Theoretical Interlude: Democracy Unbound

At the height of the mainstream Civil Rights Movement, "The Screamers" rejected gradualist politics—enacted through the legislative apparatus at the behest of civil organizations such the NAACP and the Black Church in collaboration with the Democratic Party—in the name of a sudden and insurrectionary confrontation with injustice, wedding Baraka's perception of spontaneous and organic revolution in Cuba with the nascent concerns of black nationalism and the Black Arts Movement through the trope of participatory musical forms.[52] "The Screamers," in other words, stressed black music as a meeting ground for a particular *demos* or constituency; in turn, it dramatized a recurrent conflict within Western democratic philosophy against the more immediate historical background of the modern Civil Rights era and the global anticolonialism Baraka had located in Cuba and elsewhere. Italian political philosopher Antonio Negri has helpfully described this conflict as an ongoing struggle between *constituent* and *constituted* power. According to Negri's schema—which owes much to the political thought of Baruch Spinoza—the *constituted* state (or constitutional nation-state) continually (re)emerges as a control barrier fencing in the oppositional propensities of a fully unleashed popular sovereignty. The specter of Spinoza's unleashed "multitude" necessitates the consolidation of state power itself, which then attempts to contain the energies and demands of *constituent power* within circumscribed "political space—the agencies and courts of government which channel it in certain directions," facilitating the reproduction of the prevailing state form in a way that poses little threat to the status quo.[53] Put differently, the constitutional state and its official procedures always represent a compromise with more threatening or revolutionary social ruptures, as they pose institutional limits on the hopes and dreams of the *demos*, represented in "The Screamers" by the dancing and riotous audience at Graham's and more generally by the talk of revolution (rather than reform) and take-it-to-the-streets insurgency that came to animate New Left liberation movements over the decade to come.

According to Negri, the dialectical struggle between constituent and constituted power represents modernity's central political drama, though the philosophical traditions anchoring this conflict significantly predate the modern period. Ellen Meiksins Wood has helpfully identified Plato's *Protagoras* as the founding text of what she calls the tradition of *anti-democratic democracy* in the West, a political and philosophical tradition in which the official claims of democracy have been consistently antithetical to the desires of the *demos*.[54] The title character of the *Protagoras* argues that true democracy—the foundation of the political good—requires that common laborers be granted the right to directly address the Greek assembly in matters of the state. Rather than extolling the virtues of representative governance as the core feature of democracy, Protagoras builds his definition of democracy upon a radically open discursive foundation that supports the popular and direct address of governing bodies in public arenas. The rest of Plato's intellectual life, Wood argues, was spent refuting Protagoras' claims, an effort which reached its apotheosis in *The Republic*. The Protagoran-Platonic debate finds its fulcrum in the belief that "ordinary people" possess the mental capacities to identify their needs and actively determine the conditions of governance (the Protagoran position) countered by the assertion that the general populace lacks the mental gifts necessary to engage in self-rule and should instead be subject to censor and the will of philosopher kings (the Platonic position).

Protagoran arguments foreground laboring classes and commoners (or "the people" in the populist sense) as *unconstrained public subjects* with direct input into the workings of the assembly and its policies. But the Enlightened revolutions—in their *constituted* outcomes—ensured the ability of propertied classes to check *and* access the benefits of rule once preserved by monarchies. Wood concludes, in other words, that the origin of modern constitutional principles was Platonic to the extent that it "displaced the social implications of 'rule by the demos'—such as the balance of power between rich and poor—as the central criterion of democracy."[55] The modern nation-states of the West were invested from their outset in preserving the status of moneyed aristocracies against the entreaties of the constituent mass. As Wood further explains, "the assertion of aristocratic privilege against encroaching monarchies produced the tradition of 'popular sovereignty' from which the modern conception of democracy derives; yet the 'people' in question was not the *demos* but a privileged stratum constituting an exclusive political nation situated in a public realm between the monarch and the multitude."[56] The logic of this new, aristocratic democracy displaced demands for open discursivity and economic equality through the figure of the mediating state and a limited (or "exclusive") vision of the public political arena. In terms of American political philosophy, the Platonic position found its earliest expression in James Madison's "Federalist No. 10" and Alexander Hamilton's "Federalist No. 35," both of which posited electoral representatives from the educated and propertied classes as a protective barrier against the unruly demands of the revolutionary *demos*. In Federalist formulations of democracy, Protagoran forms of open discursivity were displaced by more benign forms of "freedom of speech." By means of this displacement, "civil liberties" thus became anchored in liberal-democratic conceptions of citizenship that supplanted the notion of direct and uninhibited public address with a *non-interventionist right* to complain or voice one's "opinion" about political decisions in an often inconsequential way (the "blogosphere" has seemingly emerged as the most recent medium for non-interventionist complaint, a digitized safety valve).

The work of Jurgen Habermas is also particularly useful here, especially his definition of "constitutional patriotism" in which proper political argumentation occurs solely in reference to the constitutionally approved institutions of the nation-state. Under the conditions of constitutional patriotism, the preservation of national unity and the presupposed institutional integrity of the legislative apparatus effectively bracket out any "irrational" political demands which endanger them; that is to say, constitutional patriotism operates within a pragmatically limited public arena in which the rationality (to return once again to the vocabulary of Walter Fisher) of demands and protestations is judged according to their constitutional propensity—or their ability to be enacted through the existent channels of legislature and governance. But as Craig Calhoun has pointed out: "The concept of [constitutional patriotism] suggests both limits to political loyalty and loyalty to the legally enacted constitution as such . . . [in which] the constitution provides both a referent for public discussion and a set of procedural norms to organize it and orient it to justifiable ends."[57] Put in yet another way, constitutional patriotism holds legislative proceduralism sacrosanct, as the central or animating feature of a democratic civic religion (hailed by Richard Rorty) that most often measures the patriotism of its constituents through their willingness to confine their political concerns within the institutional procedures of the nation-state, which basically adds up to voting regularly and writing or petitioning their elected politicians whenever they deem it necessary. That is to say, rather than confront the state and its institutions in a purely antithetical fashion, political discourse and social justice claims must operate within preconditioned boundaries of publicness and subjecthood—or else be identified as a politically irrational threat to the national interest.

Beat concerns with Cold War political expression and deliberation—including those of Baraka—might come more clearly into view when discussed in relation to the thoughts of Deliberative Democrats, who have been working through these issues since the 1960s and thus represent an intellectual peer group of sorts. Deliberative Democracy refers to a rhetoric-based subfield within political science whose practitioners have included Habermas, along with figures such as John Rawls and Seyla Benhabib. Benedetto Fontana, Cary Nederman, and Gary Remer have defined the concerns of their field as follows: "Deliberative democrats . . . have sought to uncover the principles justifying a stronger and more robust conception of democracy than is on display today in democratic societies. In particular, the theory of deliberative democracy, as often conceptualized, has placed a premium on the role of political expression—public speech, discourse, reasoned debate—as the key to democratic politics."[58] The primary focus of Deliberative Democrats has been on the relationship between politics as a language-based activity and politics as a technical or procedural activity, attempting to tease out the complex relationship between the rhetorical conditions of political argumentation in the public sphere and the formation of governmental policy through congressional and juridical initiative. An abiding interest of thinkers within this field has been the extent to which the arenas of public expression (such as the mass media) help legitimate state power and its intentions, and by extension the ways in which the intentions and rationale of the nation-state in a given historical moment might circumscribe or limit public deliberation over foreign and domestic policy in ways that remain non-threatening to the prevailing interest structure and those entrusted with its maintenance.

In turn, one of the most pressing questions for Deliberative Democrats has been how we might make the conditions of deliberation more truly participatory, displacing the power elite's ability and ongoing willingness to set the fields of political discussion according to their own interests—interests that are most often universalized as the "national interest" or the "public good" despite the actual public's general inability to actively participate in or lend its voices to the conceptualization of such interests or notions of the good. Especially since the 1960s, Deliberative Democrats have actively inquired "into the conditions . . . necessary for the emergence and expansion of public/political space," seemingly taking their cues (as was the case with so many academic disciplines) from the social movements of the period, interested as they were in a similar expansion of democratic expression and practice.[59] But for deliberative democrats such as Rawls, Habermas, and Benhabib, the expansion of public political spaces and venues must always favor "speech and language informed by reason and argument; [such thinkers] relegate all other forms of talk . . . to the extrarational or nonrational sphere. Moreover, deliberative democrats consider . . . other forms of public action such as displays and performances ill-suited to public deliberation and exclude them as well from the sphere of rational activity."[60] It is on this point that they differ critically from the Beats and other figures treated here, who not only participated in politically motivated ways in a variety of media and cultural forms, but saw such efforts as critical to revealing the extent to which the rational claims of mainstream political argumentation during the Cold War era (and one might argue, any era) could never be purely rational or reasonable—that the "rational world paradigm" and its grounding terms, such as rationality and reason, are always historically and politically loaded and tend to compromise, through their imposition, a fuller diversity of political conversation. Baraka himself attempts to get at this fact in his indictment of U.S. notions of the "cold light of [political] reason" as intertwined with the historical interests of a "usurious 'ruling class.'" He also, in his representation of black musical forms as an alternative sphere of political expression and rationality, rejects the devaluation, on the part of Deliberative Democrats, of aesthetic and cultural forms as somehow inadequate in their attempts at political argumentation. As with Fisher's thoughts on the narrative paradigm—or the argumentative capacity of storytelling—Baraka's writings on the carnivalesque qualities of the Cuban revolution, along with his subsequent writings on jazz and blues, imply that political argumentation can be discovered in all sorts of symbolic action. Indeed, the aesthetic realm might oftentimes become the place where beliefs and issues judged as politically unspeakable—or "extrarational"—actually find their niche.

What is ultimately at stake in these debates over the defining qualities and animating conditions of political discourse are the ways in which the official institutions of democratic life—including the spheres of public expression that support them—might at times forestall the realization of more substantial forms of economic, social, and cultural democratization. Civil disobedience and insurgency, to extend this idea a bit further, discover their shape where the official channels of civic engagement hit their dead end on the thoroughfare of the status quo. Those are the times when democracy, if it is to remain true to its professed beliefs, necessarily gets messy and begins to spill into the streets. This publicly enacted antagonism, in which people occupy their bodies rather than their voting rights as instruments of democratic redress or demand, might be attributable to the fact that elected representatives—or even the leaders of mainstream social movements—are often incapable of speaking for all of the concerns and proclivities of those they have been appointed to represent. Or we might say that each new movement toward democratic life, secured through the mainstream legislature and judiciary, actually exacerbates some lingering limit on democratic participation—some "scream" of discontent or dissension yet to be fully articulated, an inscrutable excess given shape by the (oftentimes well-intended) institutionalization of social change. That is to say, the occasional appearance of a suddenly agonistic *demos* or constituency might be inescapably programmed into constitutional democracy, as new legislation and reform designed to heal social inequity often creates fresh antagonisms or highlights protracted contradictions still waiting to be rectified. This seems quite obviously to have been the case with the upsurge of Black Power in the midst of the nation's most significant period of legislative Civil Rights reform—an upsurge anticipated in Baraka's "The Screamers."

## "Cuba Libre" Redux

Baraka's second version of "Cuba Libre" deals with these issues even more explicitly, especially through his treatment of Robert Williams. The revised version of Baraka's Cubalogue, published in his 1965 political autobiography *Home: Social Essays,* displays the writer's evolving racial consciousness in far more candid terms; the *Evergreen Review* version is primarily race neutral, as it largely embodied a general indictment of what Baraka viewed as the rhetorical limits of U.S. media and governmental practices in relation to foreign policy—practices that Ferlinghetti and Mills identified as a Cold War cognitive block in their own respective Cubalogues. By 1965, however, as the Civil Rights Movement was reaching a crescendo—and following upon Baraka's reassessment of his experience of the revolution through the historical, theoretical, and fictional work he had done on the role of black music as an alternative sphere of discursive and political struggle—those earlier concerns became more directly focused on U.S. race relations, further widening the intellectual and political gaps between Baraka and his white compatriots in the Beat Movement while announcing his newfound admiration for the proto–Black Power activist Williams.

If the first version of "Cuba Libre" represents a political coming-of-age, the second version functions as a conversion narrative more certain of its political direction, with Williams emerging as a guide through the ambivalence and frustration expressed in Baraka's first attempt at his Cubalogue. In the closing paragraphs of the original "Cuba Libre," Baraka conveys his dismay over the political culture of his day, dismissing both the New Bohemianism and U.S. foreign policy as imperfect and unattractive alternatives to what he viewed as an increasingly troubled domestic and world situation. Exasperated by the contradictions of Cold War America—and especially its hypocritical political rhetoric—Baraka finally implores the reader to "name an alternative here," some other form of social and cultural affiliation on which he might pin his newly awakened political desires.[61] In the 1965 version, that "alternative" becomes embodied in the figure of Robert Williams, who received only the slightest of attention in Baraka's *Evergreen Review* essay. This is not a minor omission, as it was Williams who was largely responsible for getting Baraka invited to Cuba in the first place. Williams had initially visited Cuba early in 1960 at which point, as Timothy Tyson explains, he "helped to put together a special issue of the weekly Cuban literary magazine *Lunes de Revolución*, on 'Los Negros en USA,' which featured work by James Baldwin, Langston Hughes, Harold Cruse, LeRoi Jones [Amiri Baraka], John Hendrick Clarke, and Alice Childress."[62] The subsequent 1960 FPCC tour, which Baraka attended alongside Williams and Cruse, was in fact designed to showcase the writers Williams had featured in his guest-edited version of *Lunes*, though Baldwin, Hughes, and Childress could not make the trip for various reasons.[63]

Williams's stormy history within the NAACP and his years of asylum within Castro's Cuba go a long way toward explaining his expanded role in the 1965 version of "Cuba Libre," especially given the trajectory of Baraka's political and cultural development since his own 1960 visit to the island. Williams himself would eventually expatriate to Cuba in 1961, fleeing the American South at the tail end of a series of events recounted in *Negroes with Guns*, a proto-text of the budding Black Power Movement. Published by Marzani & Munsell Press in 1961, *Negroes with Guns* relates Williams's armed struggle against white supremacy as a member of the Monroe, North Carolina, chapter of the NAACP. His confrontation with local authorities—documented weekly in Williams's own small press publication *The Crusader*—culminated in his eventual flight to Cuba in 1961 to avoid prosecution on a questionable kidnapping charge that placed him atop the FBI's most wanted list. Contrary to the pacifistic aims of the national office of the NAACP, Williams had secured a National Rifle Association charter permitting him to arm the Monroe branch as a rifle club. From then on, Williams and others attended protests with their weapons in full view and protected the homes of the branch's prominent figures with around-the-clock armed surveillance. The Monroe branch actually had some initial success in integrating the facilities of the city's public library. But when they attempted to integrate other public facilities, such as the Monroe swimming pool, both the Ku Klux Klan and the local police responded in full strength, escalating the situation into a series of violent clashes which eventually led to Williams's protracted stay in Cuba (where Castro had offered him political asylum) beginning in 1961. As tempers flared and riots began to rage in response to the Monroe chapter's attempt at integrating the public swimming pool by force, Williams petitioned the U.S. Justice Department for their support, and perhaps armed protection.

His request was immediately rebuked by Robert F. Kennedy, who dismissed the situation as a concern for local authorities.[64] Over the course of the ensuing hostilities an elderly white couple, Bruce and Mabel Stegall, whom Williams's supporters identified as principal figures of the local Klan culture, were seized by rioters in Williams's neighborhood and brought to his home. The Stegalls later claimed that Williams took them hostage in order to use them as a bargaining chip with local authorities. Williams in turn claimed that he confined them to his home in order to protect them from a gun-toting crowd of roughly two hundred people who were chanting outside for the Stegalls to be killed.[65] After being tipped off that national guardsmen were on the way to his house in order to seize him, Williams fled with his family, an escape that eventually landed them all in Cuba. As he was preparing to flee his home, however, Martin Luther King, Jr. placed a telephone call to Williams which he refused to accept, exclaiming: "What the hell does he want? I don't have time for that shit now. He [King] was supposed to have been here last week" to aid in the public pool protest.[66] In the days that followed, Williams was charged with kidnapping the Stegalls, a charge which Robert F. Kennedy subsequently upheld as just, taking the side of Monroe Mayor Fred Wilson over Williams.[67] Williams's troubled relationship with both Kennedy and King—highlighted in the events leading up to his Cuban exile—speaks volumes on his alienation from the mainstream Civil Rights Movement and its support base of liberal politicians.

Williams was undoubtedly moved by a logic and strategy that had transgressed the progressive pale in the United States. It was also during this period of intensifying conflict with the Klan and local police in which Williams began privately publishing *The Crusader*—a mimeographed newsletter documenting the Monroe struggle. He continued to publish *The Crusader* after his flight to Cuba, where Castro also provided him with access to a radio signal strong enough to reach the American South. So along with *The Crusader*, Williams regularly broadcast his views on American foreign policy and racism into southern Florida. Williams dubbed his program "Radio Free Dixie," a name that encapsulated its transnational listener territory. Named for the American South and broadcast from Cuba, Radio Free Dixie presented a technological challenge to the political boundaries of the Cold War public arena through the insurgent possibility of radio waves, which easily traversed the Straits of Florida (thus violating territorial limits on political conversation). Williams's politics, in a way that Ferlinghetti would have no doubt appreciated, were elaborated within alternative and insurgent uses of print and electronic media as Cuba provided a space in which the publicly banished and the political exile could initiate political conversations that had been ostracized as "radical" and "anti-American" within the dominative public sphere.[68]

*The Crusader*—the cultural precursor to Radio Free Dixie—was principally concerned with analyzing the economic aspects of U.S. racism, both domestically and internationally. At the local level, Williams identified rampant black unemployment in Monroe as the product of the "Klan's economic pressure" supported by the conscious passivity of local police.[69] Klan intimidations, coupled with the fact that many Klansmen were themselves local business leaders, resulted in the widespread unemployment of black workers and a racialized division of labor throughout North Carolina. The police supported Monroe's tilted economic arrangements by securing the racial boundaries between the city's neighborhoods, thereby legitimating the overall culture of economic exploitation within the everyday spatial politics of Monroe. Williams tended to view the hemisphere and the world as macrocosms of local forms of racism in which the U.S. military replaced local police forces as the custodians of racially differentiated economic power in "police actions" such as the Korean War. Sounding at times like a conventional Marxist, Williams asserts throughout *Negroes with Guns* that "the basic ill" of racism is "an economic ill."[70] "The Monroe Program" of reform, which Williams presented to the Monroe Board of Aldermen under the auspices of the NAACP, demanded that local government immediately rectify these ills. Points one and two of Williams's ten-point program requested that policies be enacted that would "Induce factories in this county to hire without discrimination" and "Induce the local employment agency to grant non-whites the same privileges given to whites."[71] Privileging economics as the site for combating racial inequity further distanced the Monroe NAACP, in Williams's mind, from the goals of the national office, which favored a milder civil liberties approach. The Monroe Program also differed from NAACP platforms of gradualist and pacifist reform, that is, working through the legislative apparatus in a procedural and integrationist spirit, in that point ten demanded that the Board of Aldermen "ACT IMMEDIATELY" or face escalated unrest and the threat of violent insurrection (as do the Newark Police in Baraka's "The Screamers").[72]

Moreover, this demand for the immediate elimination of racist practices was inspired by Williams's initial visit to Cuba in the summer of 1960. Williams reminisces that "my experiences in Monroe and with the NAACP which had resulted in launching *The Crusader* were also sharpening my awareness of the struggles of Negroes in every part of the world, how they were treated, their victories and their defeats. It was clear from the first days that Afro-Cubans were part of the Cuban Revolution on a basis of complete equality and my trips confirmed this fact. . . . To me this revolution was a real thing, not one of those phony South American palace revolutions. Beginning late in 1959 I had begun to run factual articles about Cuba in *The Crusader,* pointing up the racial equality that existed there."[73] These *Crusader* articles identified U.S. racism as a global economic practice—in which white corporate culture preyed upon neocolonial peripheries of color—and immediately raised the ire of the NAACP national office, which demanded that Williams stop publishing his opinions in so maverick a fashion. The NAACP was particularly offended by Williams's identification of black struggle in the United States as something other than "a native American problem," or within a "stranger" and more extensive geography.[74] They further warned him that his promotion of international mobilization and the immediate revolutionary reform of the race problem worldwide was taking him down the disastrous road of Paul Robeson, whose experiences Williams should learn from as an "unfortunate example" of the positions he was advocating.[75]

In a sense, Williams's confrontation with the main office resonates more with W.E.B. Du Bois's experience with the NAACP than it does with the situation of Robeson. While Du Bois had cofounded the NAACP, his long-term relationship with the organization was incredibly stormy. He first split with the NAACP at the height of the Depression, claiming that leadership had sold out the black freedom struggle through its uncritical support of the New Deal, which had failed, in Du Bois's estimation, to adequately deal with the inequities of race. The Harlem property riots of 1935, along with FDR's failure to pass an anti-lynching law as a component of New Deal reform, supported his assertion.[76] Distraught over the NAACP's collaborative approach, Du Bois advocated the creation of an independent public sphere—disengaged from organized labor, the (white) liberal New Deal, and the CPUSA—as the key feature of black political life. An extensive black public sphere had in fact been evolving since the Harlem Renaissance, animated by various transnational inflections ranging from Marcus Garvey's *Negro World* to sizeable community involvement in the Provisional Committee to Defend Ethiopia. Du Bois feared that the entrance of prominent black public figures—such as NAACP stalwarts Walter White and Ralph Bunche—into state service jeopardized the black public's ability to confront the state through an analytics of racial oppression that was not internalized within the pragmatic features of national politics.[77] In this way, Du Bois (in the role of sage) anticipated the dissatisfaction with mainstream political channels that would be revisited by Williams, Baraka, and eventually groups such as the Black Panther Party, in the very midst of modern Civil Rights reform; his prescience was not coincidental, as it spoke to a long history of integrationist failure articulated along the axes of civic nationalist or constitutionally patriotic political sensibilities.

Despite the disapproval of the main office, Williams persisted in his belief that the local and national struggles of people of color resonated with postcolonial and anti-imperialist movements in Latin America, Asia, and Africa.[78] According to Williams, the indignation of the national office could be attributed to the NAACP's cooperation with the gradualist strategies of the Democratic Party within the legislative confines of constitutional democracy; that is to say, the strategy of the national office registered an acceptance of the deliberative and reconciliatory capacities of the mainstream public arena and approved forms of civic participation in which Cold War liberals such as Arthur Schlesinger, Jr. had encased racial struggle in *The Vital Center*—held by many to be the bible of Cold War liberal thought (alongside Daniel Bell's *The End of Ideology*). *The Vital Center* captures a political moment in which race-based and class-based demands for economic and social justice become channeled through the regulative imaginary of Cold War civic nationalism as essential components of the global promotion of liberal democracy. That is to say, the pervasive anti-leftism of the time helped solidify the constitutional nation-state as the proper terrain for political conflict, assuaged through legislative initiative, presidential declarations, and court decisions that would formally secure political universality for those previously excluded from the full benefits of citizenship. Consider Schlesinger's approach to racial justice in the United States, rendered, as it was, within the calculus of global competition. One of Schlesinger's chief concerns was: "How can we prevent the loss of Asia and Africa to the Soviet Union?"[79] He then responded to his own question in a twofold fashion. First, the United States must reject the imperialist strategies of the Soviet Union and instead "encourage [and] strengthen . . . democratic-minded native governments"; loans and investments should be extended to these areas only in exchange for the installation of constitutionally democratic regimes.[80] Truman's Point Four Program, which achieved congressional approval in 1950, would attempt to walk Schlesinger's talk into the real world, as it aimed at protecting foreign markets from Soviet aggression by educating underdeveloped nations in the technologies of U.S. production and constitutional politics. The second part of Schlesinger's answer was discovered in the racial inequities still plaguing U.S. society. He declared, not without genuine concern, that "the shocking racial cruelties in the United States . . . compare unfavorably with the Soviet nationalities policy . . . and with the long Russian traditions of racial assimilation."[81] If Soviet racial policies proved attractive to emerging nationalisms or "new peoples" in Asia, Africa, and Latin America, they would pose a significant threat to U.S. world-ordering ambition. In turn, Schlesinger argued that establishing a more secure foothold in the decolonizing world would require the reformation of "our own racial practices . . . [and the demonstration of] a deep and effective concern with the racial inequities within the United States."[82] Because it was a global embarrassment, racism had become a national embarrassment.[83]

Liberal democracy could prove its superiority to Communism, in the estimation of Schlesinger and other Cold War liberals, by enacting a civil rights program that assured the rest of the world of the U.S. commitment to economic and social universality. Or put slightly differently, the legislative apparatuses of U.S.-style democracy already held the potential of eliminating racial inequity through law—despite the long delay of U.S. racial history to that point.[84] Melani McAlister nicely sums up Schlesinger's position in her assertion that the "gains of the civil rights movement [starting] in the 1950s were fueled by the developing sense, among most white liberals and some conservatives, that segregation at home was viewed as incompatible with U.S. 'leadership' and alliance building in the decolonizing world."[85] But, as McAlister further explains, it was not only white liberals such as Schlesinger who had helped transform domestic struggles for civil rights into a global public relations campaign. This attitude was also shared by black liberals such as UN delegate Edith Sampson and executive secretary of the NAACP Walter White, who "traveled abroad as representatives of the United States and tempered their criticism of domestic racial policy, while supporting the Cold War paradigm of U.S. policy."[86]

It was the cooperative or gradualist mindset of figures such as White and Sampson, Williams contended, that acted in complicity with racial violence by advocating that the victims of such violence continue to take one on the chin in the name of a greater democratic dream constantly deferred. Sounding much like his contemporary, Frantz Fanon, Williams argued that the militant "does not introduce violence into a racist social system—the violence is already there. . . . It is precisely this unchallenged violence that allows a racist social system to perpetuate itself. . . . We have shown in Monroe that with violence working *both* ways *constituted law* will be more inclined to keep the peace."[87] Williams was guided in part by a certain U.S. mythology of violence, informed by the American Revolutionaries and Abolitionists such as John Brown. The first revolutionaries and figures like Brown privileged armed conflict as the ethical response to injustice; when the representatives of the law (such as the police or armed forces) act in accord with racist business interests, Williams argued, armed conflict is not only justified but profoundly American. While Williams's stance on violence was connected to a real need for self-defense against continued white brutality in the South—which had accelerated alongside the increased intensity of the black freedom struggle—I would like to suggest that violence also functions as a theoretical trope in *Negroes with Guns*. Approaching violence *as political theory* (rather than as its antithesis) allows us to situate Williams's ideas within the context of long-standing theoretical debates regarding the meaning of American democracy, while elucidating why Williams found the American Revolutionaries and figures such as John Brown so compelling. Approached in a theoretical vein, Williams's position on violence bears important similarities to what Negri calls *constituent power*—or the dancing *demos* that Jones attempted to represent in "The Screamers." Williams's text romanticizes the Revolutionary period and Brown's raid on Harper's Ferry as telling moments of violent—or constituent—struggle against a firmly entrenched and undemocratic foe. In Negri's writings on constituent power, he argues that in the case of U.S. revolutionary history, the "real revolution" happened prior to the founding governmental documents. The truly revolutionary moments occurred in slave uprisings, piracy, food rioting, and the taking up of arms against colonial empire—a claim that is repeated in Williams's defense of his American right to revolutionary violence.[88] Williams was also intrigued by the Abolitionist tradition of Brown and William Lloyd Garrison, for both had railed against the dangers of political gradualism in their own time—as had the more pacifistic Henry David Thoreau. Ultimately, *Negroes with Guns* attempted to put these political traditions into the service of contemporary racial and economic struggle in the United States.

My main point here is that people involved in social movements advocate violence out of intense frustration with the officially sanctioned arenas of political debate and action. Advocating violence—as with the case with advocating civil disobedience—might be attributed to temporal frustration, or the feeling that pressing issues have not been rectified with the appropriate sense of urgency. For a thinker such as Williams, violence goes hand in hand with the politics of immediacy—or the call to ACT IMMEDIATELY. In this way, figures such as Brown and Thoreau, whose methods for dealing with injustice seem opposed, are actually kindred thinkers in a sense, consistently out of step with mainstream reform movements that attempt to carve out a space for themselves in the public arena without shaking the foundations of national civic life too vigorously. As far as the political culture of the early 1960s was concerned, however, Williams's demands for immediate economic relief and equality as a central plank in any worthy Civil Rights program was seen as irreconcilable with the nonviolent reforms-based approach of the NAACP and figures such as King, marginalizing Williams on the outskirts of Civil Rights discourse and necessitating his formation of alternative media outlets such as *The Crusader* and Radio Free Dixie. Baraka openly admits in 1965 that Williams's refutation of mainstream Civil Rights strategies made him an attractive figure for not only Baraka himself, but for Castro's revolutionary movement whose leading figures carried out their political duties with their own firearms in plain sight, usually hanging from a waist holster—a fact that Baraka makes a point of documenting on more than one occasion in his 1965 Cubalogue.[89] In terms of Williams, Baraka clearly admires him for rejecting the strategies of "passive resistance" formalized by King and for his assertion that Southern racism be answered with the threat of retaliatory violence.[90] Moreover, on account of Williams's public stance on violence and Southern racism, the mainstream press within the United States had rebuffed him at various times as a Communist, a Muslim, and an anti-American, dismissing his concerns as illegitimate through over-generalized and inaccurate ad hominem attacks within the public sphere, all of which Williams denied vehemently, if unsuccessfully.[91]

While Williams was denied a legitimate or officially sanctioned voice in U.S. public culture, Baraka explains in the 1965 version of "Cuba Libre" that the Monroe native was embraced by the Cuban media and that there "were many pictures of Williams in Cuban newspapers," and that he was regularly interviewed on Cuban television.[92] Despite the rebuke of "NAACP people and other 'official' Negroes" and being "castigated by whatever portion of the American press" had actually seen fit to report on the Montgomery struggle, Williams's ideas had found a home in Cuba's revolutionary public sphere, which welcomed his critiques of U.S. foreign policy and race relations—and seemingly his comfort with firearms—in a way in which his home nation was ultimately unable to do.[93] As was the case with Ferlinghetti and Mills, then, Baraka stresses the extent to which early revolutionary culture was actually more complex and accommodating than the U.S. media culture, which had dismissed the revolution as reactionary and even totalitarian. Indeed, as Tyson has revealed, the greatest degree of acrimony that Williams experienced in Cuba came from the visiting U.S. press, and on one occasion Williams almost came to blows with a U.S. reporter who chastised him for talking publicly about the U.S. race problem on Cuban television.[94]

To flesh this point out a bit more, Baraka's second Cubalogue hails Williams as the American Castro, who had also, by this time, been overwhelmingly vilified by the U.S. press according to a similar rationale. Returning to the indictment of constitutional proceduralism first articulated near the end of his initial Cubalogue, Baraka claims in 1965 that "Revolution in [the United States] of 'due process of law' would be literally impossible," and Williams's approach to racial injustice, based as it was on immediacy and direct democracy, represented a counterweight to officialized process, as did Castro's revolutionary program.[95] What had so frightened commentators and politicians in the United States, Baraka explained, was Castro's own professed distrust of gradual reform in favor of the "radical" and immediate reconstruction of Cuban society—a view shared by both Baraka and Williams in relation to U.S. racial relations. The early (and premature, in Baraka's eyes) indictment of Castro as a Communist and anti-American had stemmed from those who believed that Castro's radical approach to political and social reconstruction made him a pronounced threat to the "'free world' of bankers, political pawns, grasping industrialists and liars."[96] Ultimately, Baraka asked his audience to consider the extent to which the critique of political impracticality in the Cold War United States—or of political rashness that operates in excess to the limits inherent within constitutional proceduralism—had extended to the vilification of Castro and Williams equally (or we might say, to their rhetorical conflation), illuminating the ways in which the boundaries of the dominative public sphere were secured according to a similar discursive logic against both internal and external threats to the status quo and the inherent rightness of American-style constitutional democracy being promoted, by liberal theorists such as Schlesinger, as the U.S. plan for the world. It should be further pointed out that by the time of the "Cuba Libre" revision in 1965, U.S.-Cuban relations had totally deteriorated amid Castro's rise within the U.S. rosters of Cold War villainy. Baraka was simultaneously cresting into the black nationalist political and cultural positions he would assume through the early 1970s, and fittingly his revised Cubalogue valorizes both Castro and Williams in a far more pronounced way: as uncompromising revolutionaries transnationally aligned against what they viewed as the egregious and over-reaching policies of the United States (which, as we shall see in the following chapter, Schlesinger helped formalize as a member of John F. Kennedy's cabinet).

Secure in its admiration of Williams and Castro, Baraka's second Cubalogue cannot resist taking one more parting shot at Beat attitudes toward Latin America, especially the fantastical Mexico of Kerouac's *On the Road* and Burroughs's *Junky,* which had become a fashionable refuge where the New Bohemia could "make their scene, . . . [without] realizing that there are students there getting murdered and beaten because they are protesting against the fraudulent one-party regime that controls the country, which is backed to the hilt by our 'well-meaning' government."[97]

In virtually the same breath, Baraka criticizes his Beat and bohemian friends for their simplistic attitudes toward Cuba, which he again attributes to faulty media reporting and mass disinformation. Baraka struggles throughout both Cubalogues with what he identifies as highly homogenized thinking—or groupthink—in the United States, especially in regards to the supposed ruthlessness and violence of Castro and his revolutionary movement.[98] Moreover, many of his Beat and bohemian friends within the Greenwich Village scene, Baraka admits, had also swallowed the bait regarding Castro and had gone so far as to warn him of the dangers of visiting Cuba.[99] Baraka finds this extremely offensive, largely because it is the role of the artist and intellectual to generate "thought that is alien to cliché, completely foreign to the well-digested particle of moral engagement."[100] While in the late 1950s Baraka had served as one of the Beat Movement's most vociferous early defenders, he now doubted whether the New Bohemia would ever generate "any kind of [alternative] direction or purpose" to the shortcomings of U.S. domestic life and the global imperatives of the nation's foreign policy.

Between 1960 and 1965, Baraka had discovered his own sense of political direction and purpose through his experience of the Cuban Revolution and his affiliation with figures such as Williams, marking out the first major episode in what Ronald Sukenick has so aptly referred to as Baraka's "history of quick-change ethno-political ferocity," in which he ultimately pried himself loose from the Beat milieu and the Greenwich Village scene in order to follow the path of an increasingly pronounced black nationalism, highly identified with anticolonial movements (or "new people" movements) throughout the world.[101] Baraka would realize these political and cultural commitments more explicitly as a foundational member of the Black Arts Movement, shortly after his visit to Castro's Cuba and his subsequent composition of *Blues People* and "The Screamers."

# 4

# Beat Publics and the "Middle-Aged" Left

Harold Cruse was initially inspired by the Cuban Revolution on account of the pronounced cleavage he experienced between Old and New Bohemia in Greenwich Village—a generational divide separating the aging white liberals of the Cold War era from what he viewed as the more audacious and racially mixed Beat Generation. As an ardent spokesperson of that generation, Baraka's lionization of Castro's revolution and his subsequent commitments to Black Power go a long way toward validating Van Gosse's narrative of the Beat experience in Cuba, as Gosse has persuasively argued that intellectual and cultural contact with the early revolution represented a pivotal moment in the emergence of the New Lefts, a historical shift in which the Beats played a critical (if underappreciated) role. In Gosse's version of events, Cuba provided a momentary safety valve from the "U.S. Left's shrunken ghetto" through which a vast coalition of U.S. intellectuals and activists—including the figures treated herein—were able to imagine a politics of public expression and social justice momentarily unhinged from the "ghettoizing" tendencies of Cold War liberalism, which had bound ultra-patriotic appeals to procedural democracy and corporatist consensus within a hawkish embrace of postwar world-ordering ambition.[1]

Fleeing the liberalism of buzz cuts, flannel business suits, and atomic diplomacy, sojourners in Cuba availed themselves of the revolution's early improvisational qualities as a newly emergent left spectrum that might further enable them to conceptualize political modalities set free from both the triumphalism of Cold War liberalism *and* Soviet celebrations of the proletariat as the quintessential revolutionary subject. This shift in perspective was most clearly registered in C. Wright Mills's "Letter to the New Left," in which he famously encouraged young activists to view political power in more *ambient* terms—or as grounded in exceedingly diverse and farther-reaching political issues than could be represented by the industrial working classes laboring within (and thus materially reliant upon) the productive centers of the capitalist world, a suggestion equivalent to Robert Duncan's call for a politics of "stranger relations," articulated across the axes of nationality, sexuality, and race at the height of the Korean War. Mills also stressed, in a way that resonates with all of the figures treated thus far, that increased critical attention be paid to the cultural apparatus's role in the production of mass consent and cognitive/perceptual incapacity, an exhortation that added nuance to orthodox Marxism's overemphasis on the means and relations of production as the primary sites of revolutionary upheaval (or that switched the emphasis of radical critique more decidedly from the "base" to the "superstructure").

The insights of Mills and others eventually led to the mobilization, according to Gosse, of "a cadre of student activists [who] came to the fore at a handful of campuses like Berkeley and Madison, many of whom in the next decade [would] play leading roles in the antiwar movement and the revival of the intellectual Left."[2] The emergence and consolidation of New Left sympathies around Cuba is also at the forefront of Marc Schleifer's epilogue to Robert Williams's *Negroes with Guns,* though Schleifer (unlike Gosse or even Mills) appears to have been equally interested in articulating an intellectual and activist continuum between the Old and New Left against the backdrop of what was unfolding in Cuba—a continuum in which he and his Beat companions (such as Ferlinghetti and Baraka) played an integral role. Indeed, the work Schleifer produced during the early years of the revolution—including his own Cubalogue, "Cuban Notebook," published in a special 1961 Cuba edition of the *Monthly Review*—sheds a revealing light on the extent to which figures associated with the Beat Movement had begun articulating their ideas, over-against the pieties of patriotic Cold War liberalism, within a "stranger" counterpublic inhabited by stalwart supporters of the Old labor-based Left such as Carl Marzani and Paul Sweezy. As we have seen, the Beats had been dismissed and derided by Cold War liberal writers (especially those associated with *Partisan Review*) and Schleifer's conception of what was unfolding in Cuba and in U.S. culture at large provides an impetus for understanding Beat reactions to the early revolution in relation to a protracted institutional history spanning back to the 1930s and the wartime intellectual culture of the Office of Strategic Services. For two decades, Marzani and Sweezy, through their roles as writers and publishers, had been documenting and analyzing the rationales of Cold War liberalism (or the enabling conditions of what Gosse later referred to as the "shrunken ghetto" of left thought) in fairly significant ways; events in Cuba helped clarify these critiques while consolidating a new print-based contact zone, home to an anti-liberal and cross-generational counterpublic spanning "Old" and "New" in a reinvigorated and politically complex critique of Arthur Schlesinger, Jr., and the events leading to the Bay of Pigs invasion.

### The "Middle-Aged" Left

Schleifer edited *Negroes with Guns* for Marzani and Munsell Press in 1961, shortly after a Fair Play tour of Cuba had enabled him to meet with Williams for several days in Havana. Over the course of those initial meetings the expatriated Williams dictated much of what would become *Negroes with Guns* into Schleifer's tape recorder; other portions of the book were composed of reprinted articles that Williams had originally composed for his own alternative periodical, *The Crusader.* During his stay in Havana, Schleifer also assembled the observations that eventually became his own Cubalogue, "Cuban Notebook," published in a special 1961 edition of the independent socialist publication *Monthly Review,* edited by Sweezy and Leo Huberman. When Schleifer, whom I would identify as a "Beat journalist," made his initial trip to Cuba he was serving as the editor of the New York based arts and literary journal *Kulchur,* a chief publishing venue of the East Coast Beats and other members of the New York and Black Mountain Schools. Schleifer had also been an early contributor to the *Village Voice,* penning a short article dealing with the meaning of Beat, "The Beat Debated—Is It or Is It Not?" in the November 19, 1958, edition. Financed by Lita Hornick, Schleifer founded *Kulchur* in 1960 and edited the first three issues (through the summer of 1962), at which point, as Hornick recalls, "he took off [once again] for Cuba without telling me where he was going or how long he would be gone," leaving Hornick to become the managing editor for the next two years.[3] Over the course of its history, *Kulchur* was closely affiliated with the Baraka-edited journals *Yugen* and *Floating Bear,* and employed not only Baraka, but Diane Di Prima, Frank O'Hara, Joel Oppenheimer, and Gilbert Sorrentino in a range of editorial capacities. The journal is particularly notable for publishing the first of William Burroughs's *Yage Letters,* "In Search of Yage," in its third issue (edited by Schleifer while en route to Cuba), which also contained an abridged version of Baraka's "Cuba Libre." Indeed, over the first few years of its existence, Baraka served as the journal's music editor, and auditioned many of the animating ideas of *Blues People* and *Black Music* within *Kulchur's* pages.[4]

Schleifer returned briefly to the United States following the summer of 1962, after which, as Hettie Jones recalls, he left for Cuba once again, this time with the photographer Leroy McLucas, whose own Cubalogue, "Letters from Cuba," shall be discussed in my final chapter.[5] Following his second trip to Cuba— where he spent his time holed up in the Hotel Presidente with McLucas, writing letters to Jones and others—Schleifer departed for the Middle East, where he became a foreign news correspondent for CBS and eventually converted to Sufi Islam, taking the name of Suleimann Abdallah.[6] Interestingly enough, Schleifer, who now goes by S. Abdallah Schleifer, went on to become a pivotal figure in the development of mass media ethics in the Middle East, having founded the Kamal Adham Center for Journalism Training and Research at the American University of Cairo (where he continues to hold emeritus status). The Center Schleifer founded stresses cross-cultural literacy and cultural tolerance, along with freedom of speech and the right to dissent from the dominant opinions of one's society or government, qualities which, as we shall see, Schleifer found to be sorely missing within the public arena of the Cold War United States.

Over the course of his life, Schleifer has obviously entertained a number of intellectual, scholarly and political interests, and his epilogue to *Negroes with Guns* quite fittingly refuses to be doctrinaire in its reading of U.S. intellectual and activist history. While others, such as Mills and Gosse, were interested in stressing the historical fissures between the Old and New Left, Schleifer attempted to provide the history of leftist political commitments with a more pronounced sense of continuity across the Truman-McCarthyite divide—that historical lacuna in which the patriotic liberalism of the Cold War era had flourished, supposedly separating Old from New modes of leftist thought over the second half of the twentieth century. Centered primarily on Robert Williams, Schleifer's epilogue relates, on one hand, what an appealing figure Williams had become for young black activists, politically restless students, and the members of his own Beat Generation, constituencies that he does in fact identify at the core of a new progressivism emerging within U.S. political culture. On the other hand, Schleifer asserts that Williams would have been warmly embraced by legendary architects of Old Left insurgency such as Eugene Debs and Bill Haywood, and had in fact been embraced by W.E.B. Du Bois and others from an earlier generation of activists and political thinkers.

Hoping to mend what seems to be a recurrent fracturing of left histories and social movements within the United States—the type of historical caesuras, for example, which bracket twentieth-century U.S. protest traditions within the 1910s, the 1930s, and the 1960s—Schleifer openly calls "categories by chronology" into question, gesturing toward an alternative historiography of the U.S. Left from his hotel room in Havana.[7] The traditions of U.S. leftism, he insists, have been animated by historically extensive trajectories of thought and action consisting of ongoing commitments to social and political equality (including within the registers of race), anti-expansionism, anti-capitalism/corporatism, and anti-poverty. In turn, the positing of Old and New as temporal categories obfuscates this long-standing tradition and quite tangible structures of thought and feeling that span an unstable chronological divide, conventionally (and wrongly) conceptualized through superficial appeals to generational conflict and fracturing; that is to say, the distinction between Old and New is largely determined by supposed failures in cross-generational communication, incomplete historical perspective (in regards to the concerns of previous social movements), and discontinuities of motive and impulse, though generally speaking, for Schleifer, the underlying motivations for political activism and social movements maintain some level of congruence across the middle of the twentieth century (blind as he seems, at least in his epilogue, to the saliency of feminist movements across the same historical arc).

For those still interested in identifying the emergence of "new" forms of political thought within a chronological framework, Schleifer suggests that they employ the category of "Middle-Aged Left," rather than "Old Left," in order to characterize the genealogical break represented by the unfolding events of the 1950s and early 1960s. The historical fracturing that occurred within U.S. progressivism, that is to say, was due to the ascendency of Cold War liberalism—as Mills, Cruse, and later Gosse surmised to varying degrees—a fracturing that never materialized into a full break within the true radical or protest traditions of the twentieth-century United States. According to Schleifer's schema, the "Middle-Aged Left" represents those individuals who continually romanticized the New Deal as the apotheosis of America's anti-Communist progressivism and the democratic propensities of pragmatic gradualism—or Cold War liberals, in other words.[8] It is that period of the Left (if one can even refer to it as such), Schleifer implies, that *actually presents us with a historical anomaly* in U.S. intellectual history, though its architects had successfully foisted the weight of anomalous and dangerously "anti-American" political action on the 1930s U.S. Left and would attempt do so once again in relation to the nascent Lefts of the 1960s—rather infamously, in the case of Schlesinger, against the backdrop of the Bay of Pigs invasion. In any case, Schleifer was correct in noting that a resurgent moment of Left intellectualism was making itself felt within the United States (and abroad) in reaction to Cold War liberalism, or in pronounced opposition to a "Middle-Aged Left" burdened by the era's hawkish consensus and subsequently venerated by figures such as Richard Rorty.

Schleifer's work from this period, supported as it was by both Marzani & Munsell Press and *Monthly Review,* stands within the very historical continuum he hoped to elucidate, a new site of political communion in which Beat ideas became embedded within—and ultimately helped enrich—the guiding concerns of a more protracted intellectual history. Put somewhat differently, it is not at all surprising to discover Schleifer's left revisionism, and its attempt at muddying the Old-New divide, articulated in a Marzani & Munsell publication. To a large extent, the history of Marzani & Munsell, along with the personal history of its founder, Carl Marzani, call such chronologies into question as both reveal the extent to which opposed reactions to Castro's revolution within the halls of U.S. progressivism were in part traceable to the New Deal era and the institutional histories of Marzani, Sweezy, and Schlesinger—the last of whom was serving as a special advisor within the Kennedy cabinet during the Bay of Pigs invasion and the Cuban Missile Crisis. Marzani and Sweezy both located their nemesis or bête noire—as would the Cubalogue writers—in the Cold War liberalism conceptualized by figures such as Schlesinger, and Cuban events forced their long-standing disagreements to a head. The disclosure of this history in the details that follow has been a long time coming, and helps situate the scope of this project—and the deeply rooted stakes of early Beat reactions to the Cuban revolution—within a more extensive and revealing historical context.

## OSS Legacies in Cuba

State Department employee Carl Marzani was one of the first victims of postwar anti-Communist crusading, indicted for perjury and Communist subversion in 1947. The federal indictments against Marzani, handed down six weeks *after* he had resigned from the State Department, charged him with infiltrating the Office of Strategic Services (and later the State Department) on behalf of the Communist Party, and thereby attempting to teach the "corruptive" principles of Communism to fellow members of the military and foreign policy establishment.[9] Some are lucky in their enemies, but Carl Marzani never was, stretching back to his days in the Office of Strategic Services (OSS) beginning in 1942. Created by Franklin Roosevelt, the OSS was a wartime intelligence agency responsible for psychological warfare, intelligence gathering, and covert operations. Headed by General William Donovan, the agency answered directly to FDR and the Joint Chiefs of Staff. From the outset, the OSS was marked by a high degree of intellectual flexibility and freedom. The heterogeneous qualities of OSS intellectual culture can be credited to three factors: first, Donovan himself viewed intelligence work as a crude form of intellectual labor, consisting of the objective analysis of raw intelligence data; second, the pressures for military victory against the Axis powers rendered ideological considerations momentarily less relevant; third, the anti-fascist sentiments of the Popular Front made it temporarily acceptable for activists and thinkers occupying the left reaches of the U.S. political spectrum to align themselves unapologetically with the state's war aims.[10] On account of these factors, and the expanded importance of intellectual labor to modern warfare, the OSS recruited heavily among university professors and various other writers and artists, most of who staffed its Research & Analysis Divisions (R&A) or the Presentation Division. These civilian recruits comprised an ideologically diverse intellectual culture that counted Schlesinger, Jr., Gregory Bateson, John Ford, Garson Kanin, Herbert Marcuse, Ralph Bunche, Perry Miller, Paul Sweezy, Ernest Hemingway, and television chef Julia Child among its members. Ho Chi Minh, who led the Viet Minh resistance against the Japanese occupation of Indochina during World War II, also served as a secret agent for the OSS. OSS agents and employees were stationed in branches throughout the world, and engaged in information exchange with other state intelligence agencies such as the British SOE (Special Operations Executive) and the Soviet Narodnyy Komissariat Vnutrennikh Del (NKVD), the precursor to the KGB.[11] After turning down a professorship in economics at New York University, Marzani was first hired into the War Department's Coordinator of Information (COI), which became the OSS in 1942.

Marzani had worked as a street-level organizer for New York's Communist Party from August 1939 until August 1941, a period in which he was assigned to the Lower East Side. When questioned regarding his affiliation with the CP during his initial interviews, he rightly denied current membership in the party, which he had hastily departed after expressing his disagreement with Israel Amter's Soviet orthodoxy.[12] In both 1942 and 1943, Marzani was called before the Civil Service Commission to further explain some of his answers. But General Donovan, who was well-aware of Marzani's past political affiliations, sent him to the hearings accompanied by Robert Thrun, Donovan's personal attorney. In any case, as World War II was kicking into high gear, the Civil Service Commission cleared Marzani for employment within the Presentation Division, which was responsible for presenting abstracted versions of intelligence reports to high-ranking officers. Film was the preferred medium of the division, and Marzani's exposure to film production marked the initial stages of his development as a documentarian, a career he briefly and infamously pursued in the twilight of his State Department employment through his founding of Union Films—a radical New York–based film collective whose works, such as 1947's *Deadline for Action,* identified the postwar United States as an imperialist nation embarked on a course of expansionist overreach.[13] The important point here is that Marzani's aesthetic and political views evolved as a result of his artistic and intellectual pursuits within the military bureaucracy—rather than in contradiction to it, as his federal indictments later suggested.

Even more important, in terms of the present inquiry, is the extent to which the inner dynamics of OSS intellectual culture elaborated upon the ideological breaks within New Deal alliances that were occurring as the war was still at its height—breaks most clearly seen in the personal and intellectual relationships between Marzani, Sweezy, and Schlesinger, Jr. That is to say, the ideological positions staked out by these thinkers compel us into a deeper understanding of Cold War liberalism and the rationales of Kennedy's Cuba policy within the crucible of the wartime state. Marzani first became acquainted with Sweezy—a well-known socialist economist who taught at Harvard until 1942—on an OSS mission to London in 1944, when they shared a rented townhouse. At the time of their meeting, Sweezy was editing the top-secret intelligence monthly, *European Political Report*. Sweezy's editorial tenure is particularly illuminating, for *European Political Report* was at the center of intellectual feuding between OSS Paris and OSS London over Soviet issues, with many of the Paris intellectuals vehemently opposed to maintaining a cooperative relationship with the Soviet Union at war's end. Schlesinger, whom Marzani derisively refers to as an "anti-Soviet historian," was stationed at Paris and, according to Marzani's recollections, was at the forefront of anti-Soviet opinion.[14]

Schlesinger's own memoirs confirm Marzani's characterization. Immediately upon his admission to the OSS in 1943, he composed a series of internal memos calling for more ideological coherence within wartime intelligence and especially within the R&A divisions. Schlesinger argued that the agency should solve the problem of "chronic internal disagreement" by engaging in a policy of "enforced agreement," the imposition of an "intellectual unity," which he saw as key to the agency's maintenance of any real political influence.[15] As the editor of (the frighteningly named) *Psychological Warfare Weekly*, Schlesinger considered it his duty to impose ideological coherence on the journal by rejecting outright those articles he personally considered Communistic, a stance that prefigured the argumentative prescriptions he applies to the U.S. public arena in his masterwork, *The Vital Center* (1949). In January of 1944, Schlesinger lamented to S. Everett Gleason—Mediaeval History Professor at Harvard who would later become the first secretariat of the National Security Council—that "the qualities of . . . passionate partisanship, special pleading and plain lack of good judgment too often displayed by the divisions cannot be easily harmonized into a coherent, sober and honest whole unless someone outside the divisions is charged with the authority to do so."[16] Especially troubling to Schlesinger's sense of ideological "harmony" was the outspoken position of Maurice Halperin and the Latin American Division of the OSS on the Bolivian Revolution of 1943. According to Schlesinger, Halperin and the rest of the Latin American division of R&A supported the revolution because they were dogmatic, party-line Communists, who were also engaged in propagating political untruths in the agency's journals. Schlesinger openly admits that as editor of *PW Weekly* he frequently "clashed with the Stalinist views of the Latin-American section."[17] Moreover, this admission importantly signals an early fear of Latin American political movements, which manifests once again in Schlesinger's involvement in the Bay of Pigs invasion as a special adviser to Kennedy. In the more immediate historical context, Halperin was eventually tried in 1953 (a full eight years after the OSS had been disbanded) for exchanging information with the Soviet NKVD, despite the fact that the OSS was actively engaged in exchanging intelligence with the Soviets during the war.

Seeing as the OSS, from General Donovan on down, was staffed with thinkers and writers from across the complex political spectrum of the 1930s, Schlesinger's attempt at imposing intellectual unity upon the ideas of his peers appears heavy-handed. Furthermore, his political agenda within the OSS opens up some important questions concerning the orientations of postwar liberalism. Schlesinger admits, for instance, that his tenure within the OSS was spent writing anti-Communist letters home to his friends and parents, stressing that "proper liberals" reject any form of cooperation with socialists or Communists; liberals, as he would once again assert in *The Vital Center,* were the true heirs of a distinctly pragmatic American radicalism, unlike Communists who espoused inherently anti-American political values (especially in regards to the socialization of industry).[18] Schlesinger's anti-Communism was extended personally to Marzani, whom the young Harvard professor labeled a "Stalinist" and identified as his "OSS antagonist."[19] In language which mirrors Marzani's claims about OSS Paris, Schlesinger complains that OSS London was "too Soviet friendly."[20] Prior to his Paris assignment, Schlesinger, Jr. worked briefly for R&A in London and also roomed with Sweezy at the London townhouse (prior to Marzani's arrival), at which time they briefly coedited *European Political Report.* According to Schlesinger's account, the coeditorship was rough going, for he vehemently disagreed with Sweezy over the possibilities of a postwar U.S.-Soviet alliance and was even more disturbed by Sweezy's continued assertion that the goal of U.S. war involvement was "hegemonic economic power" over the globe.[21] In addition, Schlesinger tells us that most members of "R&A London believed in the vital importance of preserving the Grand Alliance after the war for the sake of world peace. They feared that premature suspicion of Communist purposes would revive Soviet mistrust and undermine the hope of postwar amity. There were also those in Gen. William Donovan's ecumenical organization who had a Marxist faith in the benevolence of the Soviet Union and in the desirability of communist revolution."[22] Schlesinger further admits that he "was less hopeful about postwar felicities" and "did not believe that the OSS should go out of its way to strengthen the Communist position in Western Europe."[23] Obviously, Schlesinger embraced his OSS service as an early opportunity to eradicate leftist thinking from the ranks of American progressivism, while doing his part to determine the fate of Cold War geopolitical divisions even as the Soviet Union remained a critical U.S. ally.

The engines of political and intellectual loyalty impelling so much of Cold War intellectual culture originate in these debates within the OSS, where they had already gained considerable rhetorical torque and momentum. Evidently, the intellectual and aesthetic culture of the wartime state was never fully unified and reflected the unstable amalgam of liberalism and socialist thinking bonded momentarily during the previous decade by New Deal populism, whose rhetorical mobilization of the "common people" (epitomized by John Ford's adaptation of John Steinbeck's *Grapes of Wrath*) carried over into a wartime visual culture inhabited by Rosie the Riveter, the war photography of Dorothea Lange, and Frank Capra's *Why We Fight* series. Nevertheless, in agencies such as the OSS, artists and intellectuals were deeply divided by competitive definitions of New Deal patriotism and the sort of international alliances for which it ultimately allowed. These institutional divisions spilled over into mainstream culture in the years following the war, contributing greatly to the atmosphere of Truman-McCarthyism, bolstered as it was by liberal pronouncements concerning proper American progressivism—by thinkers such as Schlesinger—against the rhetorical backdrop of vilified Soviet Communism. Principally at stake, in other words, was the "true meaning" of the New Deal, argued across the divide of liberal and socialist political philosophies, an impassioned division that was ultimately settled by the new period of liberal moderation and hawkishness that accompanied the intertwining discourses of anti-Communism and world-ordering ambition (or the rhetoric of Schleifer's "Middle-Aged Left").

Following upon the conclusion of the war, the functions of the OSS were briefly absorbed into the State Department, from which they eventually re-emerged as the Central Intelligence Agency (brought into existence by Harry Truman in July 1947). In his *Prison Notebooks,* Marzani explains that the OSS was disbanded three weeks after the Japanese surrender by Truman's Committee of Agency Liquidation.[24] Executive Order 9621 then transferred R&A and the Presentation Division into the State Department. The transfer of R&A and Presentation employees corresponded with a massive restructuring of the State Department itself, headed by Truman's newly appointed Secretary of State, James Byrnes. What Marzani was ostensibly mapping out in *Prison Notebooks* was the initial stages of state re-bureaucratization that culminated in the National Security Act of 1947. The *Prison Notebooks* document a nascent administrative universe in which acceptable positions within the state structure swung radically toward the wartime positions of figures such as Schlesinger and were inseparable from the U.S. project of global realignment during the war and in the immediate postwar period. Marzani explains that "During the war, as the U.S. moved to a position of primary world importance, many functions of foreign policy had been handed out to war agencies such as the Board of Economic Warfare . . . the Office of War Information, the Office of Strategic Services. . . . With the end of the war these agencies were abolished and their functions went back to State, together with part of their personnel. As a result State went up from a strength of some three thousand people in 1939 to over twenty thousand in 1946, an expansion that was sudden, chaotic, and exacerbated by a fierce bureaucratic struggle."[25] The expanded State Department moved to monopolize competencies and duties that had been dispersed over a number of agencies (such as the OSS), and to concentrate them under a new sense of symbolic authority and "ideological coherence" produced by the latest historical manifestation of the Communist threat. The reorganization or re-bureaucratization of the State Department, along with the creation of the CIA in 1947, was undergirded (as Sweezy had anticipated during the war) by postwar global ambition, and has had lasting effects on state intellectual culture in the United States.

When the OSS was absorbed into the State Department, Marzani was immediately questioned regarding his political affiliations by Byrnes himself, and was informed afterward by the Office of Intelligence, "that a resignation would be in [his] best interest."[26] It is worth stressing here that the charges eventually brought against Marzani were not only a form of scapegoating or an American version of political show trials, but also part of a literal and concerted reconstruction of state structures along more pronounced ideological lines; while the trials of figures such as Alger Hiss and Marzani fulfilled a need for anti-Communist political spectacles that was essential to the attempted narrowing of U.S. political culture within the postwar period, these trials were also necessitated by a substantial shift in the organizational orientations of the state according to the militarized anti-leftism espoused by figures like Schlesinger. Indeed, the political maneuvering that Marzani identified in his *Prison Notebooks* as a "fierce bureaucratic struggle" was solemnized in *The Vital Center* as the long overdue ascendancy of liberal ideas within Byrnes's restructured State Department, an ascendancy Schlesinger had been hoping for since his entrance into the OSS.[27] This newly solidified liberal influence required the elimination of certain elements, "hacks" as Schlesinger calls them, from the State Department as part of the new "necessities of foreign policy—the growing necessity of checking Communism by developing some constructive alternative—[which] *speeded the clarification of liberal ideas* in 1947 and 1948."[28]

Marzani's imprisonment was largely attributable to this "elimination" or purge—though the time he spent in federal prison did not calm his tendencies toward activism and dissent. During and after his incarceration he remained an active participant in alternative political culture as a novelist, historian, and publisher, producing and supporting work (such as *Negroes with Guns* and Waldo Frank's *Cuba: Prophetic Island*) that consistently rubbed against the grain of U.S. foreign policy and liberal entanglements in the Cold War consensus. In 1958 he became the controlling owner of Cameron Associates Publishing, which was soon renamed Marzani & Munsell Press, the printing house through which he published the Schleifer-edited *Negroes With Guns*. Interestingly enough, Marzani's first project as senior editor of Marzani & Munsell happened to be a paperback edition of C. Wright Mills's *The Power Elite*.

Moreover, Marzani's longstanding disagreements with Schlesinger's vision of U.S. progressive traditions and the rationales of foreign policy were mobilized in a notable way by early events in Castro's Cuba, as Schlesinger helped to significantly shape the Kennedy Administration's Cuba policy.

During his own Cuban visit of 1960, Marzani had spent a sizeable amount of time meeting with revolutionary leaders. An old contact from the OSS, Eddie Boorstein, was working as the chief economist on Che Guevara's staff and arranged an hour-long meeting between Marzani and Guevara, during which they openly discussed military strategy. Aware of Marzani's history within the OSS and the anarchist Durruti Column during the Spanish Civil War, Guevara solicited Marzani's opinion in planning for a U.S. invasion. Despite his knowledge of military strategy, Marzani missed the mark with his prediction at the time, assuming that an intervention would arrive in the form of a massive landing of U.S. marine divisions preceded by a protracted and sustained air assault— though I suppose it may be argued that following Marzani's plan would have proven more successful than what actually occurred at the Bay of Pigs.[29] Marzani also met several times with Carlos Rafael Rodriguez, a socialist economist and close advisor to Castro. In fact, Rodriguez went so far as to authorize Marzani to contact the White House on the Cuban government's behalf in order to explain the positive possibilities of U.S.-Cuban diplomacy and trade in the wake of the revolution. Marzani also hoped his communiqué, which he addressed directly to Schlesinger, would help spare Cuba from a U.S. invasion. Schlesinger responded to Marzani's concerns with lukewarm thanks, assuring his former OSS antagonist that the White House had more reliable information on the Cuban situation than he did.[30]

The highly influential intellectual historian Christopher Lasch argued that Schlesinger's position on Cuba was attributable to his membership in the "cult" of the "hard-boiled anti-Communist Left," a cult that Schlesinger had helped conjure into being since his days within the OSS. In *The New Radicalism in America* (1965), Lasch identified Schlesinger as the "representative spokesman of the new liberal orthodoxy," a discursive mélange of revisionist history, hawkish propaganda, centrist polemics, and self-serving publicity that aligned "proper" progressive thought with "the 'tough-minded' tradition of American pragmatism" against the "un-American" and "soft-minded" strains of "utopianism" running through an accompanying socialist-inflected intellectual history that had supposedly reached its peak during the turbulent decades heading up to the Second World War.[31] Schlesinger viewed his service in the Kennedy cabinet, as the president's special assistant and "court historian," as his opportunity to once again convert his political outlooks into official governmental policy, contributing mightily to "the cult of the New Frontier," an ideological contribution that included his direct involvement in the Cuban events at the heart of Kennedy's presidency.[32]

This involvement is most clearly registered in the events leading up the Bay of Pigs invasion. Schlesinger's white paper on Cuba, published in the April 4, 1961, edition of the *New York Times*, contended that Castro's young government had clearly become part of the Soviet sphere, and on account of the island's close proximity to the United States, Castro should be immediately removed from power. A day later Schlesinger followed up on his white paper with a memo to the president, reiterating his support for a "quiet infiltration of anti-Castro exiles into Cuba and subsequent [U.S. military] support through air drops."[33] But a sense of timidity also marked Schlesinger's April 5 memo, a hesitancy fueled by concerns over public and world opinion. Schlesinger cautioned Kennedy that the world community would never accept a U.S. denial of involvement as truth. He further warned the president that "the situation is made to order for the Communist agitprop apparatus. José Martí Brigades and no doubt Abraham Lincoln Brigades will be recruited to support Castro, not just from beyond the Iron Curtain, but in Western Europe, Africa, Asia and Latin America. There will be demonstrations and riots around the world on the model of the movement for Loyalist Spain in the late Thirties."[34] Schlesinger's fear—a fear that had been animating his institutional and intellectual behavior since his time within the OSS—was that the international specter of 1930s radicalism (so important to Marzani and Sweezy) would once again wield its motley head in a global protest movement against U.S. hemispheric policy.

## "New Lincoln Brigades"

Schlesinger's fear turned out to be well-founded, as hostilities and disagreements that had not been completely exhausted by Truman-McCarthyism and the attendant liberal ascendency of the 1950s soon resurfaced in a public and international manner.

Marzani's own *Cuba VS. the CIA*, co-written with Robert Light of *National Guardian*, documents the emergence of what Schlesinger identified as "New Lincoln Brigades" in telling detail. Indeed, in the weeks leading up to the Bay of Pigs invasion, Light's regular column in Cedric Belfrage's *National Guardian* had documented Washington's support for Miami-based counterrevolutionary groups such as the Cuban National Army and People's Revolutionary Movement.[35] The *National Guardian*, an alternative political journal that shared contributors with publications such as *Liberation* and *Monthly Review*, had openly celebrated the revolution since its inception as an important democratic and anti-imperialist event, regularly reprinting excerpts from Castro's notoriously long public addresses. The centerpiece of the January 12, 1959, issue was a photo essay, "A handful of men fired Cuba to topple Batista," retelling the history of Castro's insurgency in a positive and populist light that resonated with FPCC rhetoric and "Rebels of the Sierra Maestra." *National Guardian* had also been unwavering in its criticism of Fulgencio Batista. On February 9, 1959, the weekly published an article by Ernest Galarza—former director of Labor and Economic Affairs for Latin America/Pan American Union—exposing the State Department's long relationship with the Batista regime. Galarza's article, "The Batista terror never disturbed Washington," criticized the United States for providing the fallen dictator with the military equipment and armaments that enabled his long reign of terror. Throughout 1959, the *National Guardian* embodied the spirit of an increasingly mobilized global Left or protest culture, as Cuban articles by Light and Galarza regularly appeared alongside articles dealing with Kwame Nkrumah's Ghana and other African nationalist movements, exposés on South African apartheid, laudatory pieces on China's challenge to U.S. influence in East Asia, ceaseless coverage on the Civil Rights and anti-lynching movement that was gaining considerable momentum in the U.S., and a series of articles on Robert Williams's failed mayoral bid in Monroe.[36]

*Cuba VS. the CIA* elucidates the extent to which this swelling global Left— composed of figures from both Marzani's and Schleifer's generation—had reacted to the covert U.S. "police action" known as the Bay of Pigs. In a chapter titled "World-Wide Condemnation," Light and Marzani provided a detailed sketching of this global protest culture—or a "strangely-related" transnational counterpublic—drawn together in the wake of the United States' proxy invasion. To a large extent, the chapter in question was a revised version of a Light article, "World reaction to Cuba invasion hits Yankee imperialism," which had appeared in the May 1 edition of *National Guardian*, and had meticulously documented the consolidation of a global protest culture operating in New York,

Berkeley, Seattle, Philadelphia, and Detroit, as well as in Mexico City, Venezuela, Brazil, Moscow, Warsaw, Paris, Rome, Tokyo, Beijing, and Cairo.[37] Indeed, Light's article contained a photo of Mexican students burning an effigy of Uncle Sam in what has since become a stock feature of world political theatrics and social activist stagecraft. It is worth mentioning that the May 1 edition also contained an article by Belfrage himself, "Eyewitness in Cuba: It took 66 hours to smash invasion," which gleefully ruminated on the destruction of U.S.-sponsored counterrevolutionary forces. Belfrage had been composing weekly articles from Cuba since January of 1961, attacking the U.S. trade embargo, holding up the revolution as a signal event for all of Latin America, and routinely criticizing the U.S. media for its long complicity with U.S. world-ordering ambition. Moreover, his May 1 article also quotes a telegram from an incensed C. Wright Mills, exclaiming that because "Schlesinger and company have disgraced us intellectually and morally," Mills would willingly take up arms with Castro.[38]

As Schlesinger had warned Kennedy in his April 5 memo, the failed invasion had indeed galvanized a transnational protest movement in reaction to U.S. militarism and hemispheric ambition. In fact, Schlesinger's fear of a revised Popular Front—expressed in that same memo to Kennedy—proved to be quite on target, as the outbreak of protests recalled earlier movements against fascism in both Spain and Ethiopia, leaving Van Gosse to declare that as much as Schlesinger detested the idea of a nascent or New Left, he read the signs of its historical emergence better than many of his contemporary historians and cultural commentators.[39] Protestors uniformly identified the Bay of Pigs invasion as an act of hemispheric imperialism, while supporting the right of Cuba to a self-determination they viewed as long-denied. Protests in the United States, as Marzani and Light explained, included a week-long gathering in front of the United Nations, a three-thousand-person demonstration at New York's Union Square (organized by the Fair Play for Cuba Committee), and a raucous gathering of one thousand at the gates of the White House. Foreshadowing the antiwar movement to come, huge student protests took place at UC, Berkeley and at the federal building in San Francisco. Mexico City was unsettled by three days of protest; twenty-five thousand protestors showed up at the U.S. embassy, while fifteen thousand students gathered at Mexican National University (where they set their Uncle Sam ceremoniously on fire). Students also burned flags throughout Venezuela, as protests soon spilled over the boundaries of the American hemisphere to embrace constituencies gathered at U.S. embassies in virtually every NATO capital, along with Moscow, Prague, Tokyo, Beijing, and Cairo.

Aside from documenting this galvanized protest movement, Light and Marzani's text importantly documented the print culture that had helped call it into being. *Cuba VS. the CIA* includes numerous political cartoons from Rome,

Mexico, Germany, and even *Revolución* (the official journal of Cuba's revolution), which appeared in the wake of the invasion. In this way, their book on Cuba gave textual shape to a nascent counterpublic spanning both national and generational divides, as did the intellectual work of their peers from this period. That is to say, all of the Cuban-based works I have been discussing thus far attempted to intervene in the misrepresentations of the Cuban situation within the mainstream U.S. media and the ranks of patriotic liberalism—misrepresentations symptomatic of the dominative public arena of the Cold War era and what many of these figures viewed as an intellectually compromised political culture prone to both conservative and liberal chest-thumping. But at the same time these publications issued forth from cultural spaces and associative networks that exceeded (or perhaps worked on a lower frequency than) the political pieties of the national public sphere. The global formulation of Cold War power, in other words, helped solidify a national cultural formation in which a highly restricted mode of public debate attempted to regulate democratic political imagination— even in its liberal registers. The emergence of an alternative public arena around issues of U.S. global policy modeled "stranger" forms of political solidarity that exceeded the discursive preconditions of the national public sphere and entrenched divisions of Cold War geopolitical posturing across the U.S.-Soviet divide—both of which had been ardently supported by Schlesinger and other liberal intellectuals across the same historical moment.

As should be fairly obvious by this point, the contours of this alternative public arena—or transnational counterpublic—were also recognizable in the international exchange of ideas taking place in Havana during this period, an exchange that included Marzani protégé and Beat journalist/editor Marc Schleifer. Schleifer's "Cuban Notebook" was published in 1961, appearing alongside articles by Paul Baran, Fidel Castro, and Che Guevara in a special Cuba edition of the Sweezy- and Huberman-edited *Monthly Review*. Ruminating upon recent portrayals of the revolution within the U.S. media, Schleifer begins his "Cuban Notebook" by asserting that Cuba "survives and grows without reference to the Fantasy Cuba of terror and imminent collapse, created these last two years by those minds directing our public policy and public opinion."[40]The U.S. public sphere, Schleifer asserts, has been sown with the "seeds of misconception" about the revolution, which have been chiefly challenged by "the obscure radical press . . . and a few of the literary quarterlies."[41] Schleifer later applies some names to his "obscure" intellectual realm, explaining that it was peopled by figures such as Baran, Sweezy, Huberman, Mills, Ferlinghetti, and Baraka, whose collective work in the small and alternative press (as an intellectual counterpublic of sorts) offered a journalistic corrective to the general misunderstanding of the early revolution and its aims. Schleifer's observation reveals the extent to which the political concerns of the Beat milieu (as members of the nascent New Left) had become resituated within a new set of intellectual relationships (alongside figures of the Old Left)—a set of relations embodied in Schleifer's inclusion in Sweezy and Huberman's *Monthly Review* alongside Baran, Castro, and Guevara, not to mention an extended print culture that included Marzani & Munsell Press, *National Guardian, Evergreen Review, Kulchur,* and *Liberation,* collectively invested in challenging the pronouncements of Cold War liberal intellectuals (or the "Middle-Aged Left") in journals such as *Partisan Review,* along with the centrist or "patriotic liberalism" at the heart of the public sphere, most evident in Schlesinger's ability to use the *New York Times* as his political mouthpiece.

Schleifer further addresses the discursive limits of public culture in the United States—or of Mills's cognitive or analogical bloc—through a personal anecdote regarding the *New York Post.* After returning from Havana he was contacted by a reporter at the *Post,* who asked Schleifer to compose a short article on his Cuba trip. While Schleifer enthusiastically agreed, he soon found the task "impossible" as the political limits placed on mainstream journalism made an honest portrayal inconceivable. Sounding much like Mills and Baraka, Schleifer laments that "Every reportorial 'fact' demanded a qualification if I were not to be party to further misunderstanding. What I'd stumbled upon was the problem of dealing with the faulty powers of American perception."[42] This was the same problem confronted by virtually all of the other Cubalogue writers, a problem attributable to the early revolution's ideological shiftiness, or its standing as a still-emerging event that could not be easily internalized within the rhetorical or symbolic matrices of conventional Cold War public culture. At the root of this problem, according to Schleifer's Cubalogue, was the "New Frontier" consciousness of the Kennedy administration, which encouraged Americans (as Henry Luce once had) to set the table for world democracy, while clouding, so Schleifer argues, the American perception of history and Latin American social movements via a durable (yet well-worn) nationalist mythos. Rather than recognizing the Cuban Revolution as an heir to the American Revolution, collective consciousness was prey to "New York armchair intellectuals fighting off the redskins on the New Frontier" in publications such as *Partisan Review, Commentary,* and the *New York Times.*[43] The "New Frontierism" of the Kennedy Administration (and its intellectual class of Cold War liberals like Schlesinger) tended to discuss the imperialistic tendencies of the United States in "the classic idiom of the frontier," contending that the spread of American civilization demanded pushing back the world's "redskins" in places like Cuba and Indochina.[44] The shortsightedness of U.S. political perception, Schleifer complained, was due to the fact that the federal government and its journalistic cronies had represented Cuba through the symbolic (or analogical) lens of the frontier—rather than the American revolutionary tradition. As was the case with Mills's diagnosis of the U.S. media, Schleifer asserted that miscomprehension of the revolution might be attributed to a misleading and wrongly applied analogy; it was, in turn, within this space of analogical disagreement that the revival of left activism and intellectualism that Schleifer was so interested in documenting began prying itself permanently loose from the organizing doctrines of Cold War liberalism. To be sure, one of the FPCC's standard positions was that the Cuban Revolution allowed Americans to witness a reenactment of their own revolution, a view Taber himself had advocated in his 1957 CBS documentary, "Rebels of the Sierra Maestra." Moreover, the FPCC's understanding of Cuba as an American Revolution was a fairly popular outlook when the organization was founded in 1957, but one that was soon abandoned with Castro's nationalization of industry and initiation of other socialist-oriented public policies. It was then that images of Castro as a lawless demagogue first appeared in the U.S. press, typified by documents such as Schlesinger's white paper on Cuba published in the *New York Times* on the eve of the Bay of Pigs invasion.[45]

### Beat Counterrevolutionaries?

Schleifer's Cubalogue appeared in an issue of *Monthly Review* that, again, notably lacked ideological coherence, as was the case with publications such as *Lunes* or *Liberation*. In 1948, Sweezy and Huberman had founded the *Review,* a socialist publication with tangible roots in the Old labor Left, with the financial backing of friend and literary critic (and fellow Old Leftist) F. O. Matthiessen. The special Cuba edition was notable, however, for its mosaic of viewpoints on the revolution. Guevara's contribution, "Cuba: Exceptional Case?," represents one of his most well-known essays in which he holds up the Cuban Revolution—despite its emergence out of a particular colonial economy—as a blueprint for a more general Latin American revolt against ongoing subordination to U.S. interests. In his own short article, "Indemnity for Prisoners," Castro offers to free the Bay of Pigs prisoners into U.S. custody in exchange for the tractors needed for agrarian reform. The much longer piece by the socialist economist (and proto–World Systems theorist) Baran is actually a transcript from an address he delivered on Pacifica Radio in April of 1961, criticizing what he saw as the imminent invasion of Cuba by U.S. forces. Baran's article is particularly noteworthy for its explicit criticism (once again) of Schlesinger's role in the invasion, identifying his white paper on Cuba as a "bourgeois" apologia for liberal-democracy and its approved forms of proceduralism. Baran asserted that

This paper, written in close collaboration with President Kennedy by Professor Arthur M. Schlesinger, Jr., of Harvard University, gives the reason of our policy toward Revolutionary Cuba. And this reason boils down to a very simple proposition: the United States is committed to resist by all means at its disposal any revolution in Latin America, and presumably elsewhere, which transcends the limits of a bourgeois revolution. Any revolution which goes beyond certain political reforms, . . . any revolution which goes further—toward socialism—is a revolution which the U.S. sets itself up to fight to the bitter end. Mr. Schlesinger commends certain accomplishments of the Cuban Revolution such as schools built . . . but he very carefully omits all reference to such reforms as the nationalization of factories, the formation of collective farms . . . all measures which are indispensable to genuine progress and genuine development of Cuba's economy and society.[46]

Baran goes on to argue that the State Department, through the agency of Schlesinger's white paper, "has proclaimed itself to be the supreme judge" of legitimate and illegitimate revolutionary action the world over.[47] Because it jeopardized U.S. economic interests in Cuba, Baran contended, Schlesinger rejected the nationalization of Cuban industries as an invalid form of revolt that "has not been carried out by a process of free elections. Quite an historian he who believes that revolutions are carried out by elections!"[48] But that was exactly what Schlesinger not only believed, but had been advocating for years under the rubric of what Rorty later referred to as the "American Civic Religion" of Cold War liberalism.

Nevertheless, Schleifer's "Cuban Notebook" is markedly different from these three pieces as it openly criticizes certain features of the Revolution from a Beat (and what might be identified as a more decidedly New Left) perspective. Indeed, in the contributors section of the special Cuba issue, Sweezy and Huberman describe Schleifer's article as being "in an entirely different vein" than the other articles, attributable to his standing as "a sensitive young American poet who went to Cuba last winter with few preconceptions and no political commitments."[49] This lack of a clearly defined ideological viewpoint, however, did not preclude Schleifer's article from appearing within the special Cuba issue and the editors go so far as to identify Schleifer as an important intellectual role model for young Americans, while exclaiming that "few could [probably] convey their thoughts and feelings as successfully."[50] To a great extent, then, Schleifer's inclusion was representative of the extent to which the modalities of leftist thought in the United States were changing and becoming more expansive in their focus—though this change was in part being facilitated by *Monthly Review*, as deeply entrenched in the 1930s as its roots might have been.

While Schleifer was impressed by the nationalization of industry and other economic reforms, he focuses a great deal of his attention on the plight of the Cuban sex industry as a site of economic and social inequity inadequately dealt with by the revolution to that point. So in addition to questioning U.S. media portrayals of the revolution, his narrative also begins to pose some significant questions regarding the revolution's direction, while attempting to supplement Marxist economism and Cuban revolutionary rhetoric with pronounced Beat concerns—or we might say that he attempts to compel the still-early revolution in some "stranger" directions as he elaborates more general concerns with economic justice and anti-poverty within a more extensive set of political subjectivities. "The Industry," according to Schleifer's parameters, is composed of pimps, prostitutes, "exhibition and blue movie promoters, postcard and flipbook distributors, [and] homosexual hustlers."[51] On the whole, "The Industry" is counterrevolutionary, as the ascendancy of Castro came at a high financial cost for the sexual servants of American "college boys on Christmas vacation, sailors and marines on shore leave, or adventurous salesmen."[52] The imperial extraction of sexual services by "Puritan America" puts actual flesh on Nicanor Parra's metaphor of legs spread wide for the American phallus.[53] That is to say, "The Industry" is a *sexualized class formation*—a Cuban counterpublic composed of movie producers, prostitutes, homosexual hustlers, and other pornography distributors—created by the sexual tourism that thrived during the Batista years.

Indeed, both legitimate and illegitimate U.S. business interests had flourished during Batista's reign. By 1959, as Martin Duberman has observed, U.S. corporations were into Cuba for close to one billion dollars a year, dominating virtually every sector of the Cuban economy from afar.[54] Moreover, it was when Castro launched a sweeping program of economic reform in 1959 that his troubles with the United States really began. His land transfer program nationalized all large estates and parceled them out to small farmers and peasant collectives. U.S. sugar companies operating in Cuba lost close to two million acres of land as a result of expropriation and nationalization. But the most stinging blow to U.S. interests came in October of 1960 when Castro nationalized *all* foreign enterprises operating in Cuba, including the United Fruit Company (in which CIA director, and former OSS officer, Allen Dulles was a stockholder). The sudden expropriation of U.S. corporate holdings was a far cry from the economic policies of Fulgencio Batista, whose torturous excesses were overlooked on account of his pronounced anti-Communism and appeasement of U.S. business interests.

Equally important was the fact that the U.S. Mafia had operated in Batista's Cuba with a great deal of impunity, financing casinos, the drug trade, prostitution, sex shows, and some of the island's most luxurious hotels, such as Meyer Lansky's Hotel Riviera, which housed U.S. tourists visiting the island to partake in gambling and inter-American sexual adventure. Overall, Mafia business interests in Havana helped transform the city, in the word of Tomás Fernández Robaina into "The Brothel of the Caribbean," where the prostitutes with whom Schleifer was concerned numbered in the tens of thousands.[55] Louis A. Pérez has similarly explored the extent to which the "metaphor" of "Cuba as brothel" organized a dominant strain of U.S. thought regarding the island. Especially in the decade leading up to the revolution, Cuba was viewed primarily as "a site of moral license. It was not a country to be taken seriously, hardly thought about before 1959 as anything more than a place of tropical promiscuity, illicit pleasures, and risqué amusements," a Caribbean fantasy space "in the service of the North American libido."[56] This fantasy space was largely facilitated by Batista's relationships with Mafia figures such as Lansky and Charles "Lucky" Luciano since first being promoted to the position of Colonel in the Cuban military in 1933.[57] Batista's stand against Castro's revolution was in turn partially funded by Mafia interests, and Castro himself was anti-Mafia as he viewed the wide-ranging influence of organized crime as a moral blight on Cuban life and a serious impediment to Cuban economic autonomy.[58] To a large extent, the Cuban economy just prior to the revolution was not uniformly undeveloped as much as it was in a state of uneven economic development, as both legitimate and illegitimate forms of foreign investment had transformed Havana into an island of development with a tourist and entertainment economy distinct from the peasant countryside. The distinct economy of Havana, it might be said, helped fuel revolutionary animosity, centered, as the revolution was, in the underdeveloped provinces. This distinction might also explain why the sexualized class formation of Havana's "Industry" was not adequately theorized within the populist calculus of the early revolution (centered, as it was, in the Sierra Maestra).

In any case, Schleifer's sympathies remain with those hustler classes which the Beats had canonized to the status of literary sainthood in works ranging from *On the Road* to *Junky*, though his concerns ultimately depart radically from Kerouac's and Burroughs's predatory treatment of such populations in many of their works (as explained in chapter one). In Schleifer's Cubalogue, that is to say, the long-standing Beat interest in the marginalized denizens of street economies takes on a pronounced political timbre as he faults the revolution itself for the now-dire predicament of the sex industry's sudden castoffs. He explains that of all the groups that oppose Castro in Cuba, they constitute the only group with "an honorable grievance," and he further explains that U.S. operatives have been quick to latch onto their dissatisfaction in an attempt to draft them into a counterinsurgency.[59] Prior to the revolution, the income of sexual laborers came predominantly from "Yankee dollars" and the revolution had since done nothing to recognize their post-revolutionary struggles or make any kind of financial or social amends. In short, sexual practices and the sex trade had not been as adequately politicized within the professed goals of the early revolution as much as land redistribution and the seizure of U.S. interests had been. What Schleifer was getting at here were the limits of political reform in Cuba; sexual labor had been bracketed off from the other social programs forwarded by Castro's early government, or we might say it had no place in the public culture of the revolution (open as that culture may have initially been to literary and other intellectual influences from abroad). In a sense then, Schleifer's focus balances "Old Left" interests in laboring cultures with emergent "New Left" commitments to expanding the rosters of political dissatisfaction beyond traditional renderings of the "working classes," dramatizing the general continuum of left commitments across what others had viewed as a stark chronological divide—a divide more broadly challenged by the diversity of political argumentation contained within Marzani & Munsell Press, *Monthly Review, Liberation, Kulchur,* and several of the other journals I have been discussing throughout.

So while Cuba might have helped recatalyze and reorganize the political and cultural imaginations of a broad range of U.S. intellectuals and activists during the period in question, it did not always do so in an affirmative or idyllic fashion, as shall become even more evident in the following chapter. In relation to sexual labor, Schleifer tells us, the revolution had not gone far enough. To some extent, Castro and the other revolutionary leaders agreed, especially in terms of prostitution. Beginning in late 1961, Cuba embarked on an ambitious rehabilitation program for the island's sexual workers, which included the illegalization of prostitution and the creation of educational and job-training opportunities (including free daycare) for former female prostitutes. At first, the revolutionary government had kept brothels operating with stricter health standards, which included sexual laborers being tested for sexually transmitted diseases, shortening their hours, and banning drinking and drug use in bordellos. Shortly thereafter, the government banned prostitution for good, though its efforts in this regard remain unsuccessful.[60] But it was not only prostitutes with whom Schleifer was concerned. His apprehension was more generally inspired by "The Industry," which also included the plight of Cuban homosexuals, a plight taken up once again in Allen Ginsberg's reactions to the early revolution.

# 5

# (Back) Toward a Stranger Democracy

Allen Ginsberg also experienced the sexual rigidities of Cuban Revolutionary culture firsthand, while visiting the island as part of an international writers' conference in 1965. By that point, U.S.-Cuban relations had deteriorated considerably, requiring Ginsberg to sue the U.S. State Department in order to secure the visa required to attend the conference, where he roomed with Nicanor Parra. While in Havana, Ginsberg witnessed Cuban military personnel rounding up homosexuals at a movie theater, after which those arrested were sent to a work camp.[1] Ginsberg also discovered that Cuba's Social Deviance Squad (or the Lacra Social) was known for jailing not only homosexuals, but "the Cuban version of beatniks, known as *los infermos* ('the sick')," which was shorthand for a vast number of young people engaged in artistic pursuits whose revolutionary value was not immediately apparent and who tended, like many of their Beat counterparts in the United States, to wear "tight pants" and grow "beards and long hair," for which they were endlessly persecuted (despite the appearance of Castro and Guevara).[2] In turn, Ginsberg became increasingly convinced that the only appropriate response to what he had witnessed was a public tirade. For the remainder of his stay he openly criticized Castro's "gay policy," while calling the Cuban leader's own heterosexuality into question. Castro's revolutionary government was also particularly offended by Ginsberg's suggestion that they invite the Beatles to play a national concert in Cuba, as "the Beatles had no ideology."[3] Viewed in the light of Ginsberg's overall reaction to the revolution's attitudes toward sexuality, however, his suggestion of a nationally sponsored

Beatles concert represented far more than nonideological clowning. Ginsberg held throughout the 1960s that the Beatles were themselves revolutionary on account of their androgynous style of long hair and "that high tender-voiced cry from the male. That's the really significant thing about the Beatles. . . . that tender sound that previously was barred from consciousness as being effeminate."[4] Obviously Ginsberg thought Castro's revolution could use an injection of sexual freedom and androgyny—or more fluid and accepting notions of sexual identity.

Reflecting upon Ginsberg's 1965 visit to the island, Guillermo Cabrera Infante explains that "during his visit Ginsberg said things in public that were a crime in Cuba even in private. He said that Fidel Castro must also have had homosexual experiences as a boy. 'We all have them,' Ginsberg clarified, 'why not him?' To top it all off, Ginsberg then confessed his love for Che Guevara—but it was not a proletarian love. 'I would very much like to go to bed with him,' he declared."[5] Cabrera Infante's recollections reveal the extent to which Ginsberg's commentary rubbed against the grain of the revolution's public culture. This was further confirmed when the poet Antón Arrufat, a former member of the *Lunes* editorial board who had personally invited Ginsberg to Cuba, received a written reprimand from Castro himself. At the time, Arrufat was the managing editor of *Revista Casa* (the official journal of Casa de las Americas) but was shortly thereafter removed from his post, signaling that Ginsberg's sexual politics were somehow antithetical to *Casa*'s editorial aims.[6] While Havana had undoubtedly emerged as a hub of transnational literary and political culture in the early years of the revolution, the reforms ultimately advocated by Castro's government were not as sexually daring as thinkers such as Schleifer or Ginsberg initially hoped.

While Ginsberg was openly impressed with economic reform and the island's literacy programs, he ultimately dismissed the promises of the revolution on what he identified as "humanist grounds." Indeed, his chief disappointment with Castro was that he had misled everyone when he claimed his revolution was "still a humanist revolution. If it's a humanist revolution, they cannot put down gays. Otherwise, it's doubletalk. I think it's important to support any separation out from American imperialism and conspicuous consumption, and any sort of independence from American psychological domination. But, on the other hand, the reason for doing so is to become human again and independent. If the definition of human and independent means sustaining an old, authoritarian viewpoint toward sexuality . . . then it would be better that American radicals at least realized that they're dealing with human beings in the Cuban situation rather than divine authorities."[7] Aside from disparaging the almost religious embrace of Castro and Guevara among young American radicals of the 1960s—an embrace whose rationales were explored in chapter four—Ginsberg's statement suggests that a truly humane revolution must begin to reimagine human existence across the registers of sexuality. As a result of Ginsberg's very public rebuke, Cuban authorities could not get him out of Cuba fast enough. Once Castro had had enough, Ginsberg was seized and placed on the next flight departing Havana—which happened to be headed to Prague.

## Cuba's "New Man"

What Ginsberg witnessed in Cuba could largely be attributed to the solidification of Guevara's New Man Ideology as Cuban national policy, an ideological tightening (or we might say "clarification") that reverberated throughout the island's cultural and social life over the course of 1965. As Ana Serra has so helpfully pointed out in *The "New Man" in Cuba* (2007), Guevara's "Socialism and Man in Cuba" helped "coalesce" the process of revolutionary "identity construction" which began in 1961 with the "banning of the movie *P.M.* by Sabá Cabrera Infante and Orlando Jiménez Leal and the closing of *Lunes de Revolución*."[8] Those events marked a transition away from the cultural attitudes of "the first few years of the Revolution . . . when writers generally displayed more enthusiasm and the ability to express themselves with relative freedom"—or what we might simply call the *Lunes* period—and toward a call for explicitly socialist "political commitment in the arts" signaled in Castro's "A True Social Revolution Produces a Cultural Revolution" (1961) and more fully formalized by Guevara's "Socialism and Man in Cuba." Published in 1965—first in the radical Uruguayan weekly *Marcha,* then in *Verde Olivo,* the official journal of Cuba's armed forces—Guevara's statement on Cuban aesthetics argued that the revolution's authentic culture would be produced by young, still-emerging voices (rather than the established voices grouped around *Lunes*). Guevara's principal claim was this: once Cubans have been liberated from their "alienation" and come to own the products of their labor more directly, art and culture will cease serving an escapist, bourgeois function (offering only momentary solace from the sphere of alienated activity or laboring potential) and become instead a celebration of Communistic life rendered by Cuba's young artists and writers. These "new men" will discover their ambitions and aspirations in the values of the revolution itself, rather than in the romance and illusions of commodity capitalism, and shall thereafter bear the responsibility of reeducating the masses in the new Communistic values of Cuba, playing a vanguard role within the conscious conversion of all of Cuban society "into a gigantic school," and thus releasing the island at long last from the clinging remains of "bourgeois" subjectivity inherited through years of cultural, economic, and political contact with the United States.[9]

Interestingly enough, Guevara admits that revolutionary Cuba underwent an unanticipated cultural renaissance in its earliest years—it just was not the type of renaissance that the Communistic Guevara could condone. At the outset of the revolution, Guevara admits, "Artistic inquiry experienced a new impulse. The paths, however, had already been more or less laid out and the escapist concept hid itself behind the word 'freedom.' This attitude was often found even among the revolutionaries themselves, a reflection in their consciousness of bourgeois idealism."[10] As far as Guevara was concerned, the new spirit of artistic "freedom" and intellectual autonomy embodied in early revolutionary publications such as *Lunes* discovered its commitments more in literary escapism and aesthetic avant-gardism than it did in actual revolutionary values, mostly because of the influence of a previously established literary generation (peopled by figures such as Cabrera Infante and Arrufat) incapable of shaking the allures of artistic cosmopolitanism and experimentation for experimentation's sake. Guevara warns throughout his essay that the culture of the early revolution had "relapsed into the decadence of the twentieth century," primarily because Cuba's artists and intellectuals were "not truly revolutionaries."[11] Guevara in turn placed his curative hopes in a new generation of artists who would reach maturity alongside the values of the revolution, and thus learn "to sing the song of the new man in the true voice of the people."[12] When creative activity finds itself subordinated to highly prescriptive political motivations (that is, as merely a component of a predetermined vanguard or reactionary agenda), the results are typically paradoxical; in this case, Guevara claims that the new Cuban artist will not serve as "the docile servant of official thought" but the willing servant of official revolutionary policy, which he will come to love of his own volition— or through the conscious embrace of emergent socialism's self-evident superiority as theorized from above by the revolution's leaders, yet somehow organically recognized and rendered by a new class of artists emerging from the liberated masses. The "new men," in other words, will recognize the clarity of their artistic vision if and when Guevara and others validate their vision, a dialectical inevitability that somehow bypasses (or leapfrogs) the conditions of docile intellectual servitude. Indeed, we might say that Guevara's essay ultimately posits a fantastical vision of organic revolutionary culture (as historically inevitable *yet in need of ideological prodding from above*) in the place of the *actually organic* revolutionary culture that emerged over the course of 1959–1961, embodied in journals such as *Lunes* and works such as *P.M.*

Visiting Cuba in 1965, Ginsberg touched down in an ideologically charged environment whose dictates of revolutionary masculinity reverberated throughout the whole of Cuban public life. In "Socialism and man in Cuba," Guevara proclaimed that "in the attitude of our fighters could be glimpsed the man of the future," an attitude that figures such as Reinaldo Arenas held culpable for the spike in homosexual persecution during the first years of the New Man period. Arenas's well-known memoir, *Before Night Falls*, proffers a telling indictment of the activities of the Lacra Social during the early 1960s, asserting that "the persecutions started and concentration camps were opened . . . while the 'New Man' was being proclaimed and masculinity exalted."[13] The insights of Arenas, who suffered and witnessed these injustices firsthand, support Serra's assertion that the New Man period ultimately legitimated heteronormativity as a professed quality of revolutionary literature, banning "effeminate behavior as counter-revolutionary" and lacking in properly masculine valor.[14] Guevara's notion of the New Man, that is to say, was encoded with both aesthetic and heteronormative preconditions, advocating a hyper-masculine revolutionary machismo which Ginsberg intuited fairly quickly during his 1965 visit.

## Pa'Lante

It would actually be more accurate to say that Ginsberg intuited the revolution's intertwined aesthetic and sexual reactionaryism as early as 1962's "Prose Contribution to Cuban Revolution," published in the one-issue journal *Pa'Lante*. As we shall see in what follows, Ginsberg's essay and the journal in which it appeared were already refuting the ideology of the New Man on several fronts—while attempting to preserve the legacy of *Lunes de Revolución*—before Castro and Guevara's paradigm of revolutionary culture had fully coalesced. As Serra explains in great historical detail, the meaning of the New Man has shifted according to the revolution's needs in various moments of its evolution. In its earliest years however—and despite the fact that both Castro (in his "Words to the Intellectuals" address) and Guevara had decried socialist realism as a style—both nevertheless asserted that "the 'content' of creative work must remain within the limits of what was [now] considered revolutionary," and journals such as *Revista Casa*, so integral to Cuban and Latin American self-definition since its founding in 1959, supported Castro and Guevara's assertions by publishing "numerous articles on Marxist aesthetics, many of which defended the ideas of Marx and Lenin as the only possible foundation for Cuban letters."[15]

Generally speaking, the periodicals and literary magazines that rose to state-sponsored prominence in the wake of the *Lunes* affair, such as *Revista Casa*, *Unión,* and *Mundo Nuevo,* consistently forwarded "the idea of 'revolutionary literature' to mean 'consistent with the official discourse of the Revolution,'" unlike *Lunes,* which had "espoused a vision of the intellectual as a *provocateur* and a critic" without "specific political allegiance."[16] Owing to the fact that *Lunes*, in the words of William Luis, had been committed to broadly conceived notions of anti-imperialism while incorporating "the latest literary and artistic currents of the time," the journal helped foster the less constrained worldliness or cosmopolitanism of figures such as Jorge Luis Borges, Julio Cortázar, and perhaps most importantly its chief editor, Guillermo Cabrera Infante, all of whom typically contextualized their work within wide-ranging traditions of world art and literature, including the U.S. and European Modernists and the French Existentialists.[17] It might be further said, then, that *Lunes*'s professed commitment to what Luis has termed the values of "modernity" anticipated the emergence of the Latin American Boom, as the journal's interest in avant-garde aesthetics and High Modernist commitments to the esoteric as integral revolutionary values dovetailed with the pronounced textual experimentation characteristic of Boom writing and more specifically of writers such as Borges, Cortázar, and Cabrera Infante who appeared within its pages. The formal experimentation of the Boom, characterized by stream of consciousness, interior monologue, the blurred boundary between poetry and narrative prose, and the surrealist (or magically real) fictional worlds of figures such as Cortázar and Gabriel Garcia Márquez was not completely out of step with the goals of Beat writing, especially the latter's interest in improvised/spontaneous prose and genre-blurring jazz prosody. *Lunes*'s aesthetic commitments in this regard support Serra's statement that while the early Cuban revolution might not have been "directly responsible" for what soon became known as the Latin American Boom, "both phenomena" undoubtedly "influenced each other" in the years prior to the solidification of Guevara's "New Man." Indeed, this has been the primary tension through which people have conventionally viewed what was at stake in the consolidation of the New Man ideology, epitomized by Emir Rodríguez Monegal's seminal work in *El Boom de la novela latinoamericana* (1972).[18]

According to such accounts, *Lunes de Revolución* generated a more robust (or "stranger") conception of revolutionary culture than that which came to dominate Cuban letters through the ascendency of Casa de las Américas, a trajectory which corresponds markedly with the coalescence of the New Man as national policy. As Serra has indicated, since its inception the highly coveted Casa de las Américas prize "was of necessity awarded to works that were supportive of the Revolution's mission."[19] Casa leaned heavily toward a literature fully aligned with explicit political engagement and revolutionary literary commitment throughout the Americas, a position that Roberto Fernández Retamar, who remains the president of Casa de las Américas, had fully formalized in 1971's *Caliban* (codifying a set of ideas he had been auditioning in *La Gaceta de Cuba* and *Revista Casa* over the course of the 1960s). In Retamar's theoretical schema,

Caliban's resistance of Prospero in Shakespeare's *The Tempest* was elevated to a blueprint for all of Latin American and Caribbean literature that, in order to obtain the correct tone of opposition and postcolonial empowerment must, following Caliban's lead, reveal and refute the imperialistic and colonizing tendencies of U.S. and European culture (or the American hemisphere's Prosperean strain) in favor of an unapologetic ethos of cultural self-definition, which José Martí famously captured in his assertion of "Our America" (over-against the value system of the United States). The "Calibanesque" position, then, represents what Retamar (echoing Guevara) considered the necessary refutation of the colonial/imperial attempt to dictate cultural standards and "proper" conceptions of aesthetic form and activity on the subjugated "others" of the American hemisphere, who, in the words of José David Saldivar, have been historically exposed to a form of "Prosperean . . . mind control."[20] Retamar's formulation was undoubtedly Manichaean, based as it was on an opposition of pure and rigid contrasts that Saldivar rightly attributes to the legacy of Atlantic anticolonialism as articulated in the work of figures such as Aimé Césaire (especially his 1969 revisionist play, *A Tempest,* which recasts Caliban as an advocate of Afro-Diasporic Nationalism), a tendency that Saldivar sees further reflected in the literature of Austin Clarke (Barbados), Edward Kamu Brathwaite (Barbados), and Reina María Rodriguez (Cuba), all of whom won the Casa de las Américas prize during Retamar's tenure.

The political and cultural allure of the Calibanesque is certainly understandable and its emergence as an aesthetic program does not lack for justification, especially given the long history of U.S. and European colonial/neocolonial domination of Latin America and the Caribbean. Moreover, Retamar's thoughts resonate notably with those of Baraka and Cruse, registering a shared structure of feeling across Atlantic anticolonial thought—inclusive of black cultural nationalism within the United States—while illuminating the extent to which revolutionary reforms catalyzed the reactions of the Cubalogue writers in contradictory ways (often according to the political experiences they carried into their contact with the revolution). My goal, in other words, is not to dismiss what I see as the well-grounded concerns of Retamar and others, but to point out that this contemporary manifestation of the Calibanic strain (previously rehearsed in the Atlantic *Négritude* of figures such as Césaire and Léopold Senghor) emerged largely within the cultural vacuum created by the forced dissolution of the *Lunes* collective and in many ways ran counter to the cosmopolitan leanings of the Boom writers and the "stranger" politics of figures such as Ginsberg (that is, the "cosmopolist" tendency which Castro, as Guillermo Infante indicated, eventually came to see as counterrevolutionary and Guevara understood as a dangerous remnant of Western bourgeois thought). While the principal Boom writers undoubtedly entertained leftist sympathies of varying shades, they tended on the whole to embrace formal innovation as a political gesture, guided by an interest in expanding human consciousness itself— an outlook they inherited in part from the High Modernists and existential philosophy (along with earlier figures within the Latin American avant-garde such as Borges and Mário de Andrade), and that, as we shall see, they importantly shared with Ginsberg. Serra has pointed out that Retamar's own assertion of Cuban revolutionary values as the only principles "capable of ending social injustice" throughout Latin America, was essentially an angry response to Carlos Fuentes's declaration that the "new literature" of the Boom was itself revolutionary precisely because it "attempted to subvert traditional literature and reified notions of reality."[21] Fuentes's argument in this regard dovetails notably with Cortázar's belief that "art's task is to disrupt and renew [aesthetic] forms so that man might find himself again. Sympathetic with the world's revolutions, . . . [Cortázar] often found himself at odds with revolutionaries who [theorized and privileged] simple, familiar [aesthetic] forms accessible to 'the people'" and who thus attempted to forward the aims of leftist revolution by appealing to monolithic conceptions and/or renderings of revolutionary content.[22] In a pronounced way, then, the outlooks of Fuentes and Cortázar reveal the extent to which the Boom writers had embraced the High Modernist dictate that narrative experimentation that disrupts (or alienates) the reader's preconceived notions of order and rationality might in turn broaden the ways in which people comprehend the origins of thought, creativity, and desire.

*Lunes*, as Rodríguez Monegal, Luis, and Serra have all pointed out, never embraced monolithic political or aesthetic conceptions, but instead fomented a tradition of provocation that eschewed identifiable dogma in the name of cultural and political diversity, all the while supporting Cuban economic independence from the United States. Appearing in May of 1962—nearly a year following Castro's "Words to the Intellectuals" address, which set in process the cultural tightening that took *Lunes* under and cleared the necessary ideological space for Guevara's impending philosophy of the New Man—the one-issue journal *Pa'Lante* paid homage to the lost cultural moment embodied by *Lunes* in some fairly obvious ways. Published in New York by the League of Militant Poets, *Pa'Lante* featured the prose and poetry of the Beats—including Ginsberg's prescient "Prose Contribution to Cuban Revolution"—alongside pieces by members of the *Lunes* editorial collective, such as Guillermo Cabrera Infante and Pablo Armando Fernández, and a number of other notable U.S. and Cuban writers, some of whom remained overwhelmingly positive in their assessments of the revolution. To a large extent, then, *Pa'Lante* continued to function (if quite briefly) as the type of open discursive space celebrated in the Cubalogues of Mills and Ferlinghetti, as its contributors persisted in the debate regarding the revolution's cultural direction. That is to say, while the League of Militant Poets claimed to believe in socialism as an economic concept, they did not employ any particular mode of socialist thought as a precondition for culture; indeed, they concluded their opening editorial statement claiming to have been inspired by the "dream of Whitman."[23] Announcing their allegiance to Whitman's epic roll call of the voluminous aggregate, the pieces collected in *Pa'Lante* represented a variety of cultural and political outlooks, including essays, short fiction, and poetry by Ginsberg, Guillermo Infante, and Armando Fernández, which was both explicitly and implicitly critical of Cuba's cultural turn toward a pronounced political aesthetic grounded in the stated goals of the revolution. Interestingly enough, the closing pages of *Pa'Lante* contained an advertisement for the special Cuba issue of the *Monthly Review*, which I discussed in the last chapter, cementing its place within the emergent left print culture that Schleifer so usefully elucidated.

Luis has argued that *Lunes* was "modernist" in the sense of being future-oriented, an editorial mission that resonated within the name of the journal itself, as *Pa'Lante* is a syncopated slang term for *para adelante* (to move forward or advance); the closest we might come to a contemporary English translation can be found in "let's roll" (originally part of U.S. hip-hop vernacular). Along those same lines, the editors claimed that they were "devoted to the American renaissance and the writing of a new world . . . the world of the future."[24] As was the case with *Lunes*, the *Pa'Lante* editors conceived of their journal as "a meeting place" for Latin American and U.S. writers—with a pronounced Beat presence—unified only in their concern for creating a new "communal" aesthetic of "love" and "beauty" in the Americas.[25] As facile as this aesthetic philosophy might sound, it went hand in hand with pacifistic and anti-imperialist commitments that echoed the rationales of the Waldport Fine Arts Project and Ferlinghetti's subsequent founding of City Lights Books, where the outlooks of the Waldport group exerted a profound influence on the political outlooks of the pocket poetry series—including the Rexroth-edited volume *Thirty Spanish Poems of Love and Exile* and Ginsberg's *Howl and Other Poems*. In a way that recalls the principled anti-nationalism of the Waldport artists at an advanced and perilous moment in Cold War geopolitics, the *Pa'Lante* editors proposed building a world of "peaceful coexistence" within the American hemisphere and imploring the United States to "Put your bombs away. Don't waste blood fighting history in Vietnam, Laos, Cuba."[26] Indeed, to return to one of the central points of the last chapter, the reference to Vietnam and Laos reveals how the antiwar movement to come was already rooted to some extent in reactions to the Cuban Revolution and the resultant posturing of U.S. foreign policy.

In all of these ways, *Pa'Lante* might be seen as the culminating document of the Beat experience in early revolutionary Havana, as well as a testament (intentional or not) to the longer political and cultural histories that helped frame that experience for all of the figures treated thus far. Thus, while *Pa'Lante* claimed to be forward-looking, it was not seeking its inter-American future solely within the cultural landscape of the New Man, constrained as it was by Guevara's deterministic notions of revolutionary history from which cultural forms of the proper political hue would inevitably proliferate through what can only be seen as a forced organicism—an argument represented in *Pa'Lante* only once, in José Antonio Portuondo's essay "A New Art for Cuba," which asserted the Cuban masses as the proper subject matter of a new art that would grow out of the asserted values of the revolution over time.[27] That is to say, both Castro's and Guevara's visions of the future had become predetermined, highly sutured to the official values of the revolutionary state (even if still emergent) in a way that unconditionally dismissed or denigrated the enemy's interpretations or aesthetic renderings of the world and human experience (that is, the artistic traditions of the capitalist or bourgeois West in Guevara's schema). Or as Castro himself explained in his 1961 "A True Social Revolution Produces a Cultural Revolution" address, all cultural content would thereafter be permitted, but only within the context of the revolution. These preconditions—as future-oriented as they might claim to be—violate Charles Taylor's assertion that the democratic propensities of public culture rest in its ability to confront the state as its antithesis when necessary, the very qualities that figures such as Ferlinghetti and Mills hoped to discover in Cuban public culture (over-against what they saw as the deracination and cooptation of the U.S. public sphere). They also rub noticeably against the grain of the aesthetic avant-gardism that Castro and Guevara so vociferously dismiss, based as it so often is on an ethos of protracted antagonism. That is to say, while both political vanguardism and aesthetic avant-gardism share futurist aspirations, the avant-garde, as Renato Poggioli has famously explained, tends to valorize "action for action's sake," grounding its justifications and experimentations in open-ended modes of agitation and provocation (or an ethics of opposing the status quo without end).[28] As proponents of the avant-garde—ranging from the Surrealists to Cabrera Infante and other Boom writers—tend to view pure antagonism and agonism as virtues in themselves, they also tend to argue that truly liberated societies need to vigilantly maintain spaces for both (or surrender their claims of freedom).[29]

As a result of *Pa'Lante*'s stated goals and the heterodox outlooks of the writers included in its sole issue, the journal's collective perception of the Cuban situation was highly nuanced, implying that the contents of the cultural sphere should be permitted to exceed the dictates of political, and in this case revolutionary, praxis. On one hand, the journal was decidedly critical of U.S. policy toward Cuba and defended the revolution's right to exist—and even contained Portuondo's essay, which anticipated Guevara's claims in "Socialism and Man in Cuba." On the other hand, however, contributors such as Ginsberg and Armando Fernández were equally critical of the revolution's own evolving rationales and policies, especially the sense of ideological constriction first introduced into the revolution's public culture beginning in June of 1961—setting off the series of events that cost Armando Fernández and Cabrera Infante their editorship of *Lunes*. One of the most interesting editorial choices in this regard was the inclusion of a fragment from Sergei Eisenstein's screenplay from *Ivan the Terrible Part III*, featured as *Pa'Lante*'s concluding piece. The motivations regarding that choice can be gleaned from the editors' introductory comments on the selection, especially their observation that "Because of government criticism of [*Ivan the Terrible*] *Part II* and Eisenstein's death in 1948, what would have been *Part III* was never completed."[30] That criticism can largely be attributed to Joseph Stalin, who had championed Eisenstein's work for many years only to eventually turn his back on the director for dogmatic political reasons—or on account of an ideological conflict that prefigured, in a sense, Castro's treatment of the *Lunes* intellectuals and his own condemnation of the experimental film *P.M.*

Despite Eisenstein's sizeable contribution to film narrative, most notably in regards to his theories and use of montage, many continue to view his oeuvre as the ideal filmic accompaniment to the Stalinist era, as works such as *Strike* (1924) and *The Battleship Potemkin* (1925) are typically considered faithful ideological renderings of that era's political orthodoxies. But in the final years of Eisenstein's life his aesthetic undoubtedly parted ways with the prevailing attitudes of the Stalinist regime, an intellectual and artistic split epitomized in the controversies surrounding his *Ivan the Terrible* project, a planned trilogy of which only the first part (*Ivan the Terrible Part I* or *Ivan Grozny*) ever made it to the movie houses of Stalin's Soviet Union. *Part II* (also known as *The Boyars' Plot*) would not see the screen until the Soviet "thaw" of 1958, while *Part III* (or *The Battles of Ivan*) was never fully completed. Begun in 1941 in the spirit of pronounced wartime nationalism—a time Eisenstein viewed as particularly suited to an historical treatment of Ivan Grozny's sixteenth-century unification of Russia—the trilogy's full realization was derailed by Stalin and other Soviet officials who viewed *Part II* as a not-so-veiled critique of their own dictatorial and violent tendencies. Or as Ronald Bergan has explained, "the Tsar's acts of cruelty in the name of a unified Russia came uncomfortably close to home" for Stalin and other high-ranking members of the Soviet brain trust.[31] Additionally offensive to Stalin, as he revealed in a personal conversation with Eisenstein in

February of 1947, was the indecisiveness or "Hamlet-like qualities" of Ivan—or we might say his ideological incoherence or uncertainty—which made it appear as if his actions against foreign influence in Russian affairs, violent as they may have been, were not truly his own but the product of "everyone tell[ing] him what he ought to do."[32]

*Ivan the Terrible Part III* conflicted with the entrenched ideological positions of Soviet state power in ways that the *Lunes* editorial board—and especially Guillermo Cabrera Infante—would have no doubt appreciated. True to Stalin's critique, the excerpted scene published in *Pa'Lante* features an almost whimsical Ivan, who leaves the fighting during a critical battle for Old Livonia (now Estonia and Latvia) in order to assure that his first in command, Malyuta Skuratov, may be granted his dying wish of seeing the Baltic Sea. The whimsy of Ivan's actions finds an appropriate match in the poetic aspects of Eisenstein's loosely structured and expressionistic script, which reads like the free verse favored by the Beats and is possessed by operatic qualities in which soldiers are said to "dance and prance" into battle—not at all unlike Baraka's "Screamers" or the Cuban peasants he witnessed commemorating the revolution in the Sierra Maestra.[33] The inclusion of this fragment takes on further significance when considered against the fact that Cabrera Infante deeply admired Eisenstein's films and had published reviews—under the pseudonym of G. Cain—of nearly all of the director's major works in the Cuban magazine *Carteles* (over the course of the mid- to late 1950s). Indeed, Cabrera Infante's work as a film historian and critic had led to great renown in the years prior to the revolution. At *Carteles,* he regularly reviewed (often in retrospect) what he considered to be the central filmic accomplishments of American and European auteurs such as Orson Welles, François Truffaut, and Eisenstein, as well as compiling a fairly comprehensive critical oeuvre spanning U.S. genre films. Importantly, his criticism knew no ideological bounds as he displayed a shared reverence for the aesthetic accomplishments of directors operating in a number of national cinemas under equally diverse political assumptions, along with a quite evident regard for films that explored new formal possibilities—a critical aspiration reflective of the auteur school's tendency to sanctify a director's personal vision or individual genius above all else. Cabrera Infante's reviews were always delivered with a level of erudition and critical sophistication that echoed the writing style of *Cahiers du Cinéma* (which he adored) and the highly literate criticism of James Agee and Dwight Macdonald. Significantly, then, G. Cain's passion for world cinema, along with his commitment to the auteur approach (of *Cahiers*), telegraphed the "cosmopolist" and "avant-gardist" philosophies of *Lunes,* a development that the revolution's leaders should have no doubt anticipated.[34]

## Beat Cuba (Revisited)

*Pa'Lante* also included a fair amount of Beat writing, including Michael Mc-
Clure's "Fidelio," which reads largely as a romantic restatement of Lawrence
Ferlinghetti's concerns in "One Thousand Fearful Words for Fidel Castro." Long
active in the Bay Area's theater scene and a faithful proponent of public poetry
performance, McClure's poem champions Castro's speaking style—or what the
Beats would have referred to as his poetics of performance—exclaiming that
Castro's "tongue is ruby meat and vibrates a new melody / of new virtue to
the starving and poor."[35] Overall, "Fidelio," written with McClure's characteristic brio, suggests that Castro's revolution has carried the "hopes of freedom"
throughout the world, though McClure warns the young revolutionary to "BE-
WARE OF THE EAGLE WITH WHITE HEAD!"[36] "Fidelio," then, recalls earlier
sympathetic renderings of Castro while attempting, through the appeal to Castro's public speaking style, to assert the revolutionary leader's "Beatness" or to
reaffirm his standing within the inter-American Beat orbit. Leroy McLucas's
cover photograph of Che Guevara seems to have been similarly motivated, as
it features Guevara leaning against a coffee bar and sipping an espresso, hair in
slight (but requisite) disarray as his Colt pistol rests exposed on his right hip. In
his own brief discussion of *Pa'Lante*, Van Gosse refers to McLucas's photo of Che
as "jarring" and "glamorous," likening it to "publicity shots of James Dean."[37]
Guevara looks quite "Beat" in other words, as McLucas captures Che's undeniable sense of "cool," a politics of style that had undoubtedly influenced Beat
assessments of the Cuba situation in the years before Ginsberg witnessed the
Lacra Social cracking down on the island's young Beats and bohemians (identified as *los infermos*).

   *Pa'Lante* also featured an epistolary essay by McLucas, "Letters from Cuba,"
which is the closest the journal came to revisiting the genre of the Cubalogue.
In fact, "Letters from Cuba" was composed by McLucas as he was residing at the
Hotel Presidente with Marc Schleifer throughout the winter of 1961, a period in
which they were both writing (unpublished) letters to LeRoi and Hettie Jones
back in New York.

   In commenting on Cuban newspapers, McLucas admits that their most interesting feature—or the thing he "dug" the most—was *Lunes de Revolución*.[38] But
in what can only be read as a striking departure from the other Cubalogues—
and especially from Schleifer's concerns regarding the denial of social justice
to the Cuban sex industry—McLucas spends an inordinate amount of time lamenting his inability, on account of his English-Spanish language barrier, to
meet Cuban women willing to have sex with him, and further admits that he
has resorted to soliciting prostitutes as a solution to his sexual dilemma.[39] In-

deed, his enthusiastic description of Cuban brothels is more aligned with Kerouac's and Burroughs's treatment of Latin America than with the reportage of Ferlinghetti and others, though in his closing paragraphs McLucas presents an indictment—in undeniable Beat argot—of the U.S. public sphere more in keeping with one of the central concerns of the Cubalogues: "I dig things up in the Big Apple are getting sort of rough for those who turn on, fight for freedom, anti-bomb shelter, or those who just don't dig that fucking system anymore. Now/tell me mr. hearst, why do you want everyone to ride in the same hearst, can we not have a choice. And you, mr. new york time, you tell some of the truth some/time, but most of your time is full of shit-time and i wonder sometime if your time is not part of the luce time. Oh mr. life, can you tell of a better life, will life get richer and longer."[40] In the end, McLucas counters his indictment of the U.S. popular press with a positive rendering of a "free" Cuba, "free with feeling, free with truth, free with theory, even the waves of the sea that surrounds her exist freely"—though by the time of the essay's appearance the *Lunes* McLucas so "dug" no longer existed.[41]

Alongside these pieces by McClure and McLucas—both of which recall the early Beat exuberance for the revolution in their own ways—were selections by Pablo Armando Fernández and Cabrera Infante, each of whom had documentable relationships to the U.S. Beat Movement and notably troubled relationships to the Cuban government by 1962. As Serra has observed, Fernández has had a historically complex relationship with Castro's Cuba, and his contribution to *Pa'Lante*, "The Poet to His Dead Mother," captures this complexity in its foundational moments. While on one hand, Fernández was named Cuba's Poet Laureate after Nicolas Guillen and went on to receive the island's National Prize for Literature in 1996, he was, on the other hand, exiled to London during the fallout from the suppression of *Lunes,* and upon being forced to return to the island remained a political untouchable (branded as a "counterrevolutionary") until the early 1970s.[42] While Fernández remains a public supporter of the revolution, Serra argues that that was not always the case, even in terms of his 1968 novel *Los niños se despiden (The children say good-bye)*, which, despite its concluding celebration of revolutionary utopia, advances "the controversial idea that utopia cannot be built until revolutionary identity or the New Man is deconstructed."[43] This insight into the possible limitations of the island's coalescing cultural ideology animates, to some extent, Fernández's contribution to *Pa'Lante*, which appeared during his London exile (and is included as a "fragment of a work in progress"). "The Poet to His Dead Mother" is after all a first-person elegy, written in a nostalgic mode out of touch with what will eventually become Guevara's call for the "New Man." Fernández's elegy relates the poet's search for his dead mother, who died in November of 1959 (the year in which the revolution began to fully realize itself) and in lines such as "I am looking for my mother who didn't want to die / who didn't die," the mother figure seemingly represents a composite of Fernández's actual mother and prerevolutionary Cuba—the Cuba of Fernández's childhood recalled fondly throughout as "a magic land" where he was "safe / from stories about the coming of men who lived through / war, plague, the many beliefs of this century."[44] Childhood is valorized as "safe from history" and devoid of ideological certainty or determinism, granting the poem a level of nuance that Serra has identified in *Los niños se despiden*. That is to say, in the case of "The Poet to His Dead Mother," Fernández, so it seems, is highly invested in carving out and celebrating a more ideologically free space (as was *Lunes*) through the backward and strategic glance of personal nostalgia—the implication being that a certain degree of cultural openness had ultimately been lost in Cuba (the hard facts of which had led to his London exile). On another level, then, the elegiac mode functions as a reminder to the revolutionary leaders that people possess very real attachments to their most immediate past, or that a new revolutionary man or society, conjured simply through the supposed gravity of cultural policy and suppression, may be met with hesitancy on the part of those now required to fit into its imposed contours of being and duty.

Guillermo Cabrera Infante's selection, "She Only Sang Boleros," deals with the allure of the immediate past even more explicitly—within the confines of 1950s Havana nightlife which had served as the inspiration for *P.M.* Written in a free-form style reminiscent of Kerouac's and Baraka's "bop" or "jazz prosody," "She Only Sang Boleros" was later included in Cabrera Infante's most famous work, the 1967 novel *Tres Tristes Tigres* (mistranslated into English as *Three Trapped Tigers*), still considered one of the most representative works of the Latin American Boom and written over a four-year period of exile in Brussels, Madrid, and finally London. "She Only Sang Boleros" celebrates prerevolutionary nightlife in Havana in a way that resonates with both *P.M.* and Beat portrayals of drunken revelry in U.S. jazz clubs; moreover, the novel that came to contain it, *Tres Tristes Tigres*, echoes the Beat fascination with car culture and movement as it evolves around characters driving from one location to the next, reveling in the nocturnal Cuba of the 1950s. The fragment contained in *Pa'Lante* consists of the narrated reflections of a newspaper photographer who becomes briefly infatuated with a corpulent Afro-Cuban woman, Estrella Rodríguez—a bolero-singing nighthawk based on Cuban singer Fredesvinda García, famous for performing a cappella in prerevolutionary Havana's well-known "artists' bar" or Bohemian hangout, the Celeste. Sounding much like Kerouac's description of his bohemian friends in *The Subterraneans* (1958), which detailed Kerouac's own interracial love affair with Alene Lee (fictionalized as Mardou Fox), Cabrera Infante explains that Estrella was a central member of the "chowcito," "a group of people who got together to get lost in the bar around the jukebox after the last show, and who getting lost refused to recognize that outside it was day and all the world was working or going to work, all the world except this world of people who submerged themselves in night and swam around in the declivities of darkness, artificial world of the frog-men of night."[45] The "chowcito," in other words, were 1950s Cuba's version of the Beats—renamed *los infermos* by 1965—with a pronounced disinterest in revolutionary work ethic or in forging any kind of new revolutionary subjectivity (rendered by Cabrera Infante's story in retrospect). In her discussion of *P.M.* Serra has noted that the film was declared "obscene" because it showed Cubans dancing and partying "rather than working for the revolution," a celebratory treatment of Havana's nocturnal underground, which also holds the center of Guillermo Cabrera Infante's contribution to *Pa'Lante*.[46]

The puritanism that Ginsberg attributed to Castro and his revolutionary circle, witnessed early on in Fidel's declarations regarding the moral blight represented by Mafia-controlled Havana, paradoxically sent the Cabrera Infantes (though early supporters of the revolution) fleeing into nostalgic renderings of pre-Castro Havana, which, despite its connections to the debilitating and predatory nature of U.S. economic influence, might have encouraged a greater degree of personal license; or we might say that, as lurid and deplorable as it might have been on so many levels, Batista's Havana nevertheless encapsulated a more expansive sense of human need and desire, an urban environment whose proclivities and attractions were not dogmatically set by economism or the precepts of revolutionary manhood. Memories of pre-Castro Havana—which continue to serve as a political dividing line for expatriated or exiled Cuban-Americans—become refashioned, in the case of the Cabrera Infantes, as critiques of the revolution's strictures on personal freedom and libido, which ultimately posited laboring potential as the most important of human activities. As was the case with the selection by Fernández, nostalgia was subversively offered as an antidote to the willed futurity of the New Man ethos—or we might say that a more expansive and just future, for the figures in question, would in part require a searching glance over the shoulder.

Whereas both Fernández and Cabrera Infante contributed works that implicitly criticized the crystallization of revolutionary values contributing to their exile from the island, Ginsberg's "Prose Contribution to Cuban Revolution" posed some quite explicit and pointed questions regarding the direction of Cuban revolutionary society—questions whose relevance would only be reinforced by what he eventually witnessed during his 1965 visit. "Prose Contribution" is a political bildungsroman whose reflections are inspired by Cuban events but directed toward different rhetorical ends than the earlier Cubalogues, as Ginsberg throws much of the initial enthusiasm of Ferlinghetti, Baraka, and others into a state of doubt. Unlike the Cuba writings of his Beat peers and fellow travelers, "Prose Contribution" was the product of a nearly two-year stay outside of the American hemisphere, in which the perpetually controversial poet had also sojourned through Tangier, India (where he composed the *Indian Notebooks*), Bangkok, Vietnam, and Greece. The chief thread of his essay is autobiographical, as Ginsberg recounts his early years at Columbia University and his dreams of becoming a labor attorney. During his initial years as a student, Ginsberg admits viewing himself as a "labor leader people's hero," imbued with messianic dreams of leading a worker's revolution—dreams that were shattered by his subsequent encounters with New York City's working classes in the cafeterias of Harlem, Times Square, and Morningside Heights.[47] From those encounters, he came to realize, in a way that recalls Mills critique of the "labor metaphysic," that the proletarians he hoped to save were "imaginary masses," a Marxist theoretical construct that bore little resemblance to the variety of U.S. class formations on the ground. The working classes he encountered, Ginsberg recollects, also frightened him with their "roughness," bookish as he had been for most of his life.[48]

Disabused of his messianic dreams of becoming a labor leader, Ginsberg fell in with Kerouac, Burroughs, and Herbert Hunke (a Times Square hustler who served as an early Beat muse or prototype for the New York writers, an imaginative position later taken up by Neal Cassady). Operating against the backdrop of Cold War America, the other New York Beats had taught Ginsberg to think beyond his conventional proletarian notions (as rebellious or oppositional as they seemed to him at the time) and to instead value a "sense of personal genius and acceptance of all strangeness in people as their nobility; staying *out* of conflict and politics, staying with sort of Dostoyevskian-Shakespearean *know* [ . . . ] of things as mortal, tearful, transient, sacred—not to join one side or other for an Idea, however serious, realizing the relativity and limitation of all judgments and discriminations."[49] Ginsberg goes on to suggest, in other words, that he reached political maturity only when he moved beyond the dream of proletarian struggles enacted in conventionally formulated political terrains, in order to embrace the outlooks of the New York Beats as a deconstructive political stance—outlooks that, according to Ginsberg's framing of the problem, favored an ethics of unconditional tolerance and principled skepticism as the starting points for democratic practice, or for the realization of truly revolutionary justice. The "acceptance of all strangeness," Ginsberg asserts—in a fashion quite similar to Robert Duncan at the tail end of World War II—would be key to resisting what he viewed as the increasingly suicidal forms of mass nationalism and identity constriction that had come to exemplify the Cold War period.

Moreover, he began to apply these realizations to Castro's Cuba, suggesting that the revolution itself had failed to mature from its own immediate economic concerns (as he once had in the worker cafeterias of New York) toward a "stranger" politics, and had thus ultimately failed to embrace the potential of "hitherto unrecognized areas of awareness" or "unrecognizable or undiscovered areas of being."[50] To a large extent, the problems Ginsberg identifies within Cuban revolutionary society resonate with Mills's admonition that the still emergent New Left formulate an activist politics not confined to the "labor metaphysic" of traditional Marxism and the Old Left, while at the same time echoing Fuentes's avant-gardist claim that revolutionary forms of culture should unsettle our "reified notions of reality," or come to celebrate ways of being that might challenge the apparent stability of the dominant and binary discourses (that is, divided "one side or other for an Idea") structuring so much of Cold War political life.

A revolution—according to Ginsberg's pronounced existential outlook—could only be truly revolutionary when it allowed human beings to radically reconsider the parameters of being and social belonging, or to reimagine conventional and (in Ginsberg's mind) stultifying political encampments. Ginsberg was chiefly concerned with the ongoing facilitation of Cold War nationalism through mass cultural and new communication technologies that had imprisoned or ossified human identity within nationalistic models of loyalty and duty, thus sacrificing "undiscovered," vilified, and creatively evolving approaches to existing in the world. Indeed, a similar critique runs through Mills, Ferlinghetti, Baraka, and Schleifer as a collective indictment of the imaginative or discursive limits structuring the national public sphere, an indictment that dovetails with Cabrera Infante's identification of *Lunes* with the voice of "spontaneous" and "poetic being" (a tendency that Luis has since termed "modernity," or the search for new, unimpeded consciousness rather than a retreat into Caribbean prelapsarianism). Ginsberg's essay begins to suggest, however, that despite the original optimism of these other figures—based as it was on the collective hope that Cuba might become home to a political culture and public sphere resistant to the binary logic of Cold War geopolitics—Castro and the other revolutionary leaders were beginning to take the country in some well-worn political and cultural directions. That is to say, Ginsberg asserts that in the cultural events that unfolded in the wake of the Bay of Pigs, Castro was guilty of asserting the same set of ideological limits that had been embraced by his political peers within the United States, Russia, and China, where governments operated "within rules of [political] identity" based in "an outmoded means of consciousness" or the "present day 2-dimensional political consciousness" that had overrun global political life since the end of World War II.[51] Or perhaps even more succinctly, Ginsberg suggests that official restrictions on social identity and political expression, articulated across increasingly rigid and "outmoded" axes of national collectivity and supported by each nation's media apparatus, had "brought all governments to edge of world destruction. No government, not even the most Marxian revolutionary and well-intended like Cuba presumably, is guiltless in the general world mess, no one can afford to be righteous anymore. Righteous and right and wrong are still fakes of the old suicidal identity."[52]

## Cold War Censorship and the Heteronormative Nation-State

To a large extent, Ginsberg's thoughts in "Prose Contribution" echoed the committed anti-nationalism of the Waldport Fine Arts Project, under the auspices of which his own father, Louis Ginsberg, had once presented his own wartime poetry in a public exhibition. This "cosmopolite" ethic (so detested by Castro and others) favored principled open-endedness and vigilant contrarianism as foundational elements of an idealized democracy *always as yet to be achieved* (that is, a proliferate and critical discursive practice without foreseeable exhaustion), an ethic that resounds through the multiplicitous viewpoints assembled in *Pa'Lante* and, to a larger extent, the aesthetic commitments of Latin American Boom writers such as Cabrera Infante. As far as the political and cultural commitments of Ginsberg were concerned, this ethic finds its most tangible enunciation in his thoughts regarding censorship and sexuality, which had been forged above the hearth of Cold War nationalism and geopolitics. Within the closing pages of "Prose Contribution," for instance, Ginsberg declares that Cuba's revolutionary leadership must help facilitate "real technical revolution in [Cuban] Poesy" by actively avoiding "any, meaning ANY, mediocre bureaucratic attempt to censor language, diction or direction of psychic exploration" as they would be partaking in "the same old mistake made in all the idiot academies of Russia and America."[53] In terms of the United States, Ginsberg's credentials in this regard were well-established by the censorship trials surrounding *Howl and Other Poems,* which had wedded Cold War national security concerns with officially sanctioned heteronormativity in a way that prefigured Ginsberg's eventual misgivings over the ideological leanings of revolutionary Cuba.

The initial reception and seizure of Ginsberg's *Howl and Other Poems* as obscene must be situated within the sexual politics of the Cold War era. More pointedly, the seizure of *Howl and Other Poems* as obscene should be viewed within the context of governmental efforts to suppress homosexual behavior and an emergent queer social movement in the Bay Area, with San Francisco's North Beach serving as one of the chief sites of conflict. Much of what transpired in the Bay Area and throughout U.S. culture during the 1950s can be traced to World War II, which helped facilitate an extensive coming-out of homosexual culture in the urban and industrial United States. Citing the influential work of John D'Emilio, Roderick Ferguson has explained that "World War II was a 'nationwide coming out experience.' The war took place after the Great Depression, which had seen a drop in marriage and birth rates. Moreover, the war uprooted millions of young men and women from their families and placed them in non-familial and sex-segregated contexts; it encouraged civilians in rural areas to leave their communities and families and to migrate to urban areas in the North in search of jobs. Those civilians now were beyond the watchful eyes of family and neighbors."[54] This new sense of uprootedness and possibility—largely inspired by the promises of wartime production in national urban centers—corresponded with a new rise in public homosexual spaces such as the gay bar.[55] Nevertheless, the Cold War seemingly authorized the federal government and cultural industries to reenforce heterosexuality as a patriotic norm. According to Ferguson, this recalibration of sexual norms was directly related to U.S. global ambition, which proffered the "virile, tough guy" (for example, John Wayne, the new union man) as the normative mode of masculinity against the specter of Soviet geopolitical competition.[56]

The federal government played a major role in explicitly establishing heterosexuality as a national defense policy. In 1950, a U.S. Senate subcommittee determined that male homosexuals posed a notable national security risk and were therefore unfit for government service. Multiple reasons were given for this finding. Homosexuals were said to lack the emotional stability needed to perform work in the national interest. They also, according to the Senate subcommittee, lacked "moral fiber" and were thus more likely to participate in treason.[57] Possessed by an inordinate degree of narcissism, the report continued, homosexuals in government would be highly "susceptible to the blandishments of foreign espionage agents."[58] Also, on account of the public stigma attached to homosexuality, the report warned that upon being found out homosexuals were more prone to blackmail by foreign agents threatening to disclose their closeted sexuality to others. Along similar lines, the subcommittee was uneasy about the strategies that homosexuals had developed to pass in the straight world; while dissimulation was particularly useful in the fields of espionage, it was nevertheless argued that homosexuals could not be trusted to consistently reveal their true intentions to their supervisors. But most troubling to the Senate subcommittee was the threat of "stranger relations" attached to homosexuality. Their argument, in all of its crudeness, went something like this: a man capable of having sex with other men is more capable of loving the enemy and betraying his nation.[59]

While there had been official military policies against homosexuality in place during World War II, there is also evidence of de facto relaxation of this policy—

as long as a soldier did not publicly admit his homosexuality (as Robert Duncan had). Michael Sherry contends that commanding officers actually found it helpful to have soldiers willing to perform in drag (and presumably provide sexual services) for male soldiers separated from female contact for extended periods of time. This relaxation of wartime policy (an early version of "don't ask, don't tell") corresponded with the cultural loosening D'Emilio and Ferguson have located in the industrial and shipping centers of the time. But this momentary loosening also led to a dialectical upswing of postwar sexual repression. Wartime tolerance—limited in its existence as it may have been—was fleeting, in other words, and was quickly followed by insistent and quantitative "changes in public policy and culture, the full effects of which only emerged after the war. The military, for example, urged on by psychiatrists and other experts, formalized a pathological concept of homosexuality and applied it punitively to gays and lesbians, especially after the war. The war thus placed liberating and repressive forces on a collision course with each other."[60] In other words, World War II was partially responsible for the emergence of homosexuality as such an incendiary political issue in cities such as San Francisco, where pronounced governmental conservatism collided with proliferating queer social movements across the Cold War era.

Identifying sexual "deviance" with political deviance was a stock motif of Cold War public discourse in the United States. While Dwight Eisenhower may have been a critic of Joseph McCarthy's methods, the president and the junior senator from Wisconsin saw eye to eye when it came to the issue of homosexuality. Eisenhower's executive order 10450 (1953) codified the following "conditions" as national security risks: alcoholism, previous mental instability, documented association with Communist front organizations, and homosexuality.[61] In 1953, the president used Order 10450 to remove roughly 1,500 people from government employment. In an edition of *Meet the Press* aired soon after these mass firings, McCarthy famously linked homosexuality with Communism when he declared that 90 percent of the firings were either Communists or homosexuals and that the exact percentage of each could not be teased out, the implication being that they were imbricated categories.[62] A year earlier, McCarthy had rehashed and enthusiastically embraced the findings of the 1950 Senate subcommittee in *McCarthyism: The Fight for America* (1952), while publicly identifying the U.S. State Department "as a seething hotbed of homo-communist activity, an enclave of effete patricians."[63] McCarthy's characterization resonated with archliberal Arthur Schlesinger, Jr.'s own description of the State Department, in *The Vital Center*, as home to "effete and conventional men who adored countesses, pushed cookies and wore handkerchiefs in their sleeves," shedding light on the extent to which the Cold War consensus extended into areas other than the Soviet military threat.[64]

The politicization of homosexuality in the Bay Area had developed across a long historical arc that intersects with the history of industrialization, militarization, and reactionary politicking I have been recounting. San Francisco was established as a site of sexual permissiveness—starting with the same-sex dances of the Gold Rush era and flourishing through the Renaissance and "Hippie" periods of the 1950s and 1960s—through constant agitation and confrontation with political and police authorities over public space, most notably the sanctity and legitimacy of the gay bar.[65] While homosexuality was undoubtedly a political blind spot for the Popular and Cultural Front of the 1930s, the period was nevertheless an important time for the solidification of queer culture and its alternative public spaces. As Nan Alamilla Boyd suggests in her penetrating study of San Francisco queer culture, "San Francisco's queer history—its history of publicly visible queer cultures and communities— blossomed in 1933 with the repeal of Prohibition and the emergence of queer entertainments in the city's tourist district nightclubs, bars, and taverns."[66] But as war broke out in the following decade, the city's queer culture entered into a love-hate relationship with the militarized forces encamped throughout the Bay Area.

Following upon the attack on Pearl Harbor, the Bay Area instantly became a quasi-militarized zone, with San Francisco established as the chief point of embarkation into the Pacific Theater and a strategic stronghold that needed to be fortified against an imagined Japanese invasion. The influx of service personnel into the Bay Area tilted population demographics into a decidedly male majority, who would now need to be sexually entertained in a city lacking in female companionship. This male population boom corresponded with pronounced labor migrations to the area's newly founded defense plants which, as Ferguson and D'Emilio suggest, inspired a corresponding loosening of sexual conventionality during the period in question. The modern queer culture that had begun to emerge in the 1930s soon boomed alongside wartime production and area troop deployment, leaving city officials in a quandary as to how they were to effectively police homosexual behavior. The responsibility for regulating the city's sexual practices fell on three agencies: the California Board of Equalization (a liquor control agency), the San Francisco Police Department, and the U.S. Military Police. All three shared the responsibility of perusing the city's gay bars and securing them against explicit sexual interaction between servicemen and the city's queer population (which official discourse held in problematic contradistinction). The enabling component of this new expression of cooperative policing was the May Act of 1941, in which Congress permitted the military police to patrol recreational sites within the vicinity of military bases in an effort to eliminate prostitution and vice.[67]

But these new forms of cooperative policing also facilitated an oppositional queer culture organized around "the right to public assembly."[68] The disciplinary methods of San Francisco's trinity of sexual righteousness represented new intrusions into a queer culture that had in part grown in relation to the needs of military personnel. The end result of this disciplinary mission, however, was not the displacement of queer behavior, but the galvanization of the area's diversified queer cultures into a more unified counterpublic. Or put differently, one of the unintended consequences of militarism was the politicization of vilified—or estranged—forms of sexual behavior into a liberation movement focused upon its right to equally inhabit public space (or the public realm). The most significant accomplishment of this new resistance culture was the 1951 Supreme Court decision *Stoumen v. Reilly*. Arising from the indefinite suspension of the Black Cat's liquor license (the Cat was owned by Sol Stoumen) by the California Board of Equalization, the Court's decision affirmed that homosexuals had the right to publicly assemble.[69] Bolstered by this decision, the Bay Area's queer culture expanded in an unprecedented fashion, and a new gay and lesbian bar scene emerged with tremendous force in North Beach, an area of the city that had developed a long reputation for vice and licentiousness.[70] North Beach, of course, was also home to City Lights Books, where Ginsberg's *Howl and Other Poems* was seized in 1956 by San Francisco's version of the Lacra Social. Through the agency of San Francisco's queer cultures, homosexuality had become an explicitly public issue debated against the backdrop of the period's militarized nationalism, a fact that goes a long way toward explaining Ginsberg's reactions to the Cuban revolutionary government's suppression of homosexuals during his 1965 visit.

Returning to a point I explored in chapter one, the seizure of *Howl and Other Poems* by city vice police—who cited the book's content as a danger to the moral fiber of Bay Area children—should be understood within the context of general Cold War paranoia and a rather overt wave of anti-vice crackdowns initiated in 1956 by San Francisco's newly elected McCarthyite mayor, George Christopher. Christopher campaigned on a moralist platform typical of the time, pledging to rid San Francisco of its political pariahs and miscreant elements of various criminal stripes. Supported in his moralist endeavor by the *San Francisco Examiner*, the new mayor soon embarked on an ambitious crusade against North Beach in particular.[71] *Howl and Other Poems* was undoubtedly caught in Christopher's crosshairs, especially as Ginsberg was operating in a North Beach artistic community whose contours overlapped with the neighborhood gay and lesbian bars where he himself was a patron, and his controversial City Lights volume had indicted the inanities and dangers of Cold War militarism and materialism from the viewpoint of his openly professed homosexuality. In section II of "Howl," Ginsberg had condensed these concerns with the Cold War United States into the figure of "Moloch," the demonic embodiment of U.S. militarism, corporate imperialism, and heteronormativity whose madness has destroyed "the best minds" of Ginsberg's generation.[72] Moloch was an ancient deity worshiped by an idolatrous sect of Israelites who honored the demonic god with child sacrifice, and in "Howl," the poet conflates the bloodthirsty Moloch with postwar "boys sobbing in armies," alluding to the reinstatement of the peacetime draft in 1948.[73] Moloch is simultaneously "a cloud of sexless hydrogen," "demonic industries," "running money," "spectral nations," "monstrous bombs," "the heavy judger of men," and "the crossbone soulless jailhouse and Congress of sorrows" who had "entered [his] soul early" and "frightened [him] out of [his] natural ecstasy."[74] Moloch, as poetic symbol, condenses all those postwar phenomena that Ginsberg and the other Bay Area intellectuals and poets found so abhorrent: sexual Puritanism; rampant consumerism; atomic diplomacy; the military industrial complex; fear-based nationalism; and compulsory heterosexuality. It was against these forces and phenomena that Ginsberg trumpeted unconditional and uninhibited "ecstasies!," "visions!," "adorations!," "New loves!," and "the whole boatload of sensitive bullshit."[75]

Ginsberg realized that the pervasive anti-Communism of the time was markedly possessed by sexual consequences and the closing lines of his poem "America" directly conflate Cold War paranoia with the sexual anxieties of figures like Eisenhower, McCarthy, and Schlesinger, Jr. Ginsberg's refusal "to join the army or turn lathes / in precision parts factories," a dual condemnation of the military and its connections with the postwar industrial sector, is quickly followed by his assertion that "I'm putting my queer shoulder to the wheel."[76] Counterpoising his homosexuality or "queerness" to the militarized industrial labor of the new union man heading the Cold War nuclear family, Ginsberg was also announcing the "labor" of activism that animated the rest of his life and reached its crescendo during the liberation movements and protest cultures of the coming 1960s (for whom Ginsberg took on a cultish, almost guru persona). Moreover, the sexual connotations of the closing lines of "America" place added significance on Ginsberg's earlier admonition that America "go fuck [itself]" with its nuclear bombs—or that its bombs be used as dildos rather than weapons—a sly poetic reversal which posits a more open sense of sexuality over-against militarized nationalism and atomic imperialism. Confronting an America that had judged him and his fellow homosexuals as "psychopathic anyway," Ginsberg stands as both the historical witness to and the antithetical embodiment of those proclivities and political outlooks that the Senate subcommittee on homosexuality and figures such as McCarthy and Eisenhower had identified as a threat to national security in the years just prior to the publication of *Howl and Other Poems*.

As it turns out, homosexuality was also at the center of the cultural and political storm which took down *Lunes de Revolución*. As Cabrera Infante explains, Castro's government seems to have been particularly disturbed with the sexual orientation of the *Lunes* orbit, many of whose members were openly homosexual. Virgilio Piñera, the playwright, poet, and short story writer of poor origins, had become one of the literary patron saints of *Lunes*, and a vociferous defender of the journal during its June 1961 trial (which had transpired four months prior to the completion of "Prose Contribution"). He was soon after arrested by the Lacra Social on charges of "passive homosexuality."[77] Antón Arrufat, who was also openly homosexual, survived the *Lunes* trial to briefly become editor of *Revista Casa*, a post he was forced to resign in the wake of the 1965 Ginsberg visit. This crackdown on sexual orientation might also provide an additional optic for seeing the Cuban government's reaction to *P.M.* William Luis has questioned whether the "The festive attitude of the Afro-Cubans in the film may have been considered antithetical to the austere ideological positions that the white leaders of the Revolution wanted to impose on the rest of the population," despite Castro's professed policy of anti-racism.[78] But we might further ask whether, already disturbed by the sexual orientation of the *Lunes* circle, the same-sex camaraderie of *P.M.* may have been distressing to Cuba's cultural authorities in ways that Castro and the Comisión Revisora never openly admitted. In a sense, the subject matter of *P.M.* bears some resemblance to Robert Frank and Alfred Leslie's 1959 film *Pull My Daisy* (G-String Productions), still viewed as a hallmark of U.S. independent cinema. Based on Kerouac's early play *The Beat Generation* and narrated by Kerouac himself, the film was an exercise in vérité starring Beat figures such as Ginsberg, Gregory Corso, and Peter Orlovsky. The action unfolds in the New York apartment of Milo the train brakeman (played by the painter Larry Rivers) and much of its drama is produced by Milo's pronounced ambivalence toward his spouse (played by Delphine Seyrig) in favor of his male friends. Moreover, the film ends with Milo leaving his wife behind in their apartment as he runs into the East Village streets with his Beat compatriots. Coupled with its title, the film may easily be read as a slightly veiled study of same-sex orientation set against the heteronormativity of 1950s U.S. domesticity.

*P.M.* replicates the Beat geography of male bonding at the center of *Pull My Daisy*, and the Cuban film's codirector, Orlando Jiménez Leal, went on to shoot the short documentary, *Improper Conduct* (released in France in 1984), with Nestor Almendros, criticizing Castro's policies regarding homosexuality and exposing the concentration camps Castro had erected for sexual deviants.

Overall, the earlier backlash against Jiménez Leal and Sabá Cabrera Infante's *P.M.* suggests that the "decadent" or "cosmopolite" culture of the *Lunes* period had become equated with more licentious forms of sexuality in the mind of Cuba's revolutionary leaders, an ideological proclivity which *Pa'Lante* seemingly responds to in Ginsberg's "Prose Contribution." Evidence of this response might also be found in Amiri Baraka's contribution to *Pa'Lante*, "A Chase (Alighieri's Dream)," which later appeared within the author's surrealist roman à clef, *The System of Dante's Hell* (1965), detailing his coming-of-age within the abstract and expressionistic inferno of the industrial Northeast and the rural South. Building upon the dramatic action of "The Screamers"—which was quite obviously influenced by Baraka's experience of the early revolution—"A Chase" briefly mentions Lynn Hope accompanying Newark's social outcasts, who include young, black homosexuals, on another riotous march through the city's Belmont neighborhood (expanding, in a sense, on the official roster of Castro's revolutionary masses in a way that Ginsberg would have appreciated). Returning to *Pa'Lante*'s inclusion of the fragment from Eisenstein's screenplay, Dwight Macdonald had famously and derisively identified *Ivan the Terrible, Part II* as "an anti-Stalinist, gay fantasy" crowded with "pretty" male actors of ambiguous sexuality whom Ivan makes a point of touching as much as possible.[79] Given Eisenstein's own bisexuality, Macdonald's reading (despite its homophobic undertones) seems apt, and provides yet another way of comprehending the editorial motivations of the League of Militant Poets.

## A Final Defense of the (Dostoyevskian) Strange

In a letter composed to San Francisco poet Philip Whalen on February 2, 1961, Jack Kerouac reveals that "I wrote drunk letter to Ferling[hetti] calling him funny names like bastard, I think he took it seriously, tell him not to . . . I was calling him down on his sympathy for Cuban Firingsquad Raoul Che Guevara Murder Revolution."[80] Kerouac's contrite and apologetic tone regarding Ferlinghetti's interest in Cuban affairs finds notable contrast in a December 11, 1963, letter Kerouac wrote to John Clellon Holmes in which he complains that "Allen G. is already here, I had no time to send him to you, as a matter of fact I don't even particularly wanta see him with his pro-Castro bullshit and his long white robe Messiah shot."[81] Written while Ginsberg was visiting Kerouac in New York—a visit, which as Ann Charters notes, represents the swansong of their friendship—this latter letter reveals the incendiary role the Cuban Revolution played within the Beat community. Not only did it set off a chain of events that pried Baraka free from the Beat orbit, but it was also at the center of one of the movement's most notorious break-ups, as Kerouac rejected Ginsberg for William Buckley and the neoconservatism of figures such as Podhoretz just as Ginsberg was emerging as a political and cultural role model (or "long white robe Messiah" in Kerouac's estimation) for certain members of the ascendant New Lefts of the 1960s. Kerouac also adored John F. Kennedy (*the* Cold War Liberal president), which further explains his reaction to the Cuban events of the early 1960s, yet he nevertheless failed to realize that Ginsberg's reactions to Castro and the revolution were not only possessed by a high degree of nuance but had in fact been articulated from a viewpoint of political "strangeness," which he had attributed to Kerouac and the New York Beats. Indeed, in "Prose Contribution to Cuban Revolution" Ginsberg had begun to reframe the Beat preoccupation with social and cultural peripheries into a condemnation of Castro's revolution, a denunciation whose rationales were confirmed firsthand during his 1965 visit to the island and that prefigured the insights of the Gay Liberation Movements over the decade to come—movements that emerged, in the words of Lisa Duggan, within the context of more extensive and "innovative critiques of a widening variety of constraints on human possibility," much as Ginsberg and Mills had anticipated as early as the 1950s.[82]

In "Prose Contribution," Ginsberg suggested that future political movements would need to embrace a more expansive sense of human desires and proclivities, to the extent that they would search out political solutions in forms of being (including sexuality) excessive to the over-rationalized organization of national societies according to limited renderings of human existence and complexity—and thus limited conceptions of equality and justice. Despite the initial optimism of the FPCC and publications such as *Liberation,* Ginsberg's essay asserts that Cuba was not evolving into a democratic "third way," but another replica of the overly intrusive and sexually stultified modern nation-states of the Cold War era. Such nation-states, according to Ginsberg, violated the conditions of what he termed "Dostoyevskian-Shakespearean *know*," which valued "strangeness" and was skeptical of binary political schemas. Ginsberg's mention of Dostoyevsky as a harbinger of Beat notions of the politically strange warrants closer examination, especially as Ginsberg alluded to Dostoyevsky once again during a critical moment of his 1965 Cuban visit. When invited to the home of Yves Espin, a renowned architect and a brother-in-law of Raúl Castro, "Espin's guests asked him numerous questions, including his opinions about the revolution. Allen replied that there was still too much fear in Cuba. Artists were not truly free to express themselves—not if they had to fear being branded anti-Castro or antirevolution. 'If a big Dostoevsky, with no sense of guilt and a huge brown humor, wrote a novel about Lacra Social and a terrible in-group club and art school and everybody's sex lives and Marxist dogma and gossip, could it be published here?' Allen wondered aloud. He then answered his own question.

'Nobody here wants that kind of genius art.' Laughing, Espin agreed this was true."[83]

Like Eisenstein, Dostoyevsky had directly experienced the cruelties and vicissitudes of Russian bureaucracy (under Nicholas I) and it endowed his work with an overwhelming sense of skepticism and despair when it came to official state institutions such as, we might say, the Lacra Social and the increasingly dogmatic political class of Cuba's now pronouncedly Marxian revolution. Moreover, characters such as Dostoyevsky's Underground Man epitomize or are indicative of the extent to which Russian intellectualism and artistic culture had begun to struggle for its very existence under widespread Nicholavean censorship aimed at halting the Russian entry into Western modernity begun in earnest under Peter I during the early eighteenth century. Nicholas's tyranny was fueled by a reactionary desire to turn back the clock of Russian history to a romanticized period of cultural insularity opposed to the cosmopolitan sociability, culture and architecture embodied in St. Petersburg (which served as Russia's capital city until 1918). The Nicholavean era in which Dostoyevsky came of artistic age was characterized by the wide-scale suppression of unconventional artistic practices and the top-down engineering of public opinion; along with his love of modern bureaucracy and surveillance (facilitated by his malicious and sadistic secret police) Nicholas abhorred the notion of modern progress, or any attempt at bringing Russian society (and its expanding imperial domain) up to industrial, cultural and political speed with western Europe.[84]

Dostoyevsky's "genius art," as Ginsberg puts it, ultimately embodies an extended critique of official ideology and bureaucratic practices as mind-deadening and destructive. His own momentary flirtation with the socialist utopianism of mid-nineteenth-century Russia, as a member of the Petrashevsky Circle, had resulted in his being exiled to Siberia for four years, and his post-prison writings find Dostoyevsky increasingly dubious in regards to dyed-in-the-wool political ideologues. More specifically, in works such as *The Double* (1846) and his classic *Notes from Underground* (1864) he confronted what George Cotkin describes as "the crushing power of a faceless bureaucracy" in which the Russian bureaucrat Golyadkin and the Underground Man (himself a retired civil servant) experience the official and overly rationalized claims of governance as a form of epistemic closure (that is, a roadblock on what might be thought) always threatening to obfuscate wider vistas of human potential, and ultimately spilling over into forms of personal madness irreconcilable with the sanctioned social order.[85]

Dostoyevsky's abiding distrust of worldly authority was matched by a pronounced romance of social deviance—or of those marginalized to the Russian underground—which establishes him as an important precursor to the Beats, while illuminating his contribution to that sorrowfully patient, introspective, and poetic fatalism known as the Russian Soul. Moreover—and this seems an incredibly important point in regards to Ginsberg's assertion that the revolution had yet to embrace its Dostoyevsky—the Russian novelist's distrust of authority and overly rationalized ideology often existed in a blatantly rendered dialogical context. That is to say, in works such as *The Possessed* (1872) and *The Brothers Karamazov* (1880), characters frequently engage in extended Socratic dialogues over the meaning of human existence, probing conversations in which they stand in as representatives for the competing ideas or ideologies of the time (be they Christian, Nihilistic, Anarchistic, Socialistic, etc.). These incisive philosophical dialogues most often eschew a final, identifiable synthesis— or, in Ginsberg's words, they seem to willfully refuse the full embrace of "one side or another for an Idea." Mikhail Bahktin in turn celebrated Dostoyevsky's novels on account of what he identified as their linguistic "unfinalizability." Dostoyevsky's characteristic "unfinalizability" provided the literary muse for Bakhtin's socio-linguistic theories of polyphony or heteroglossia, an ethics of communication that situates its political strength in its democratizing resistance to "centripetal linguistic forces" that attempt "to unify and centralize the verbal-ideological world" replacing polyphony with "a unitary language [that] gives expression to forces working toward concrete verbal and ideological unification and centralization, which develop in vital connection with the processes of sociopolitical and cultural centralization."[86] Bakhtin ultimately applies the notion of centripetal linguistic forces to any bureaucratic attempt at verbal-ideological consolidation under the rubrics of a zealously asserted "authoritative discourse," as became the case with the New Man ideology during the period in question.[87]

Bahktin's thoughts on the ethical imperatives of polyphony or heteroglossia over-against the encroachments of authoritative discourse provide us with a final theoretical lens through which we might comprehend the Beat involvement in the early affairs of the Cuban Revolution—along with the disappointment eventually experienced by Ginsberg. A Bahktinian ethics of the public sphere would necessarily foreground decentralized and disunited multivocality as a grounding condition of democratic speech, facilitating the sort of public culture for which the Beats and their fellow travelers longed, first in the United States, then in Cuba. While the earlier Cubalogues had valorized Cuba's potential in this regard against the backdrop of what their writers saw as the limited political valencies offered within U.S. public culture—and most especially within the orienting notions of Cold War liberalism—figures such as Ginsberg and Guillermo Cabrera Infante had begun over the first half of the 1960s to identify analogous restrictions on public expression and ontologies of being in Cuba, bolstered by Cuban revolutionary nationalism as it evolved out of the idealistic and "strange" polyphony of its founding moments replicated one final time in *Pa'Lante*. From the viewpoint of Ginsberg and Cabrera Infante, however, Cuban officialese and its forceful assertion of the New Man ultimately triumphed, ending once and for all the Beat era of the Cuban Revolution and helping to facilitate a cultural and political legacy which the residents of Cuba and the United States are still living with today.

# Coda

A New Imaginary . . . ?

While being interviewed by Marc Schleifer for the October 15, 1958, edition of the *Village Voice*, Allen Ginsberg responded to Norman Podhoretz's infamous characterization of the Beats as "anti-intellectual" by asserting that both he and Jack Kerouac had "had the same education" as Podhoretz at Columbia University.[1] Ginsberg's brief retort reveals the extent to which differing responses to the Cuban Revolution—along with the eventual emergence of New Left intellectualism and social movements over the decade to come—might in part be traced to intellectual infighting in 1950s New York. Moreover, this infighting cast a long shadow over Podhoretz's career, explaining his decision to title one of his memoirs *Ex-Friends* (2000), a neoconservative bildungsroman documenting his contentious relationships (and eventual intellectual break-ups) with Hannah Arendt, Norman Mailer, and an extended cast of significant others. Indeed, Podhoretz's initial chapter, titled "At War with Allen Ginsberg," rehashes forty years of contentious exchanges between the former Columbia classmates over the moral and political soul of U.S. society. Ginsberg and Podhoretz had first met at Columbia in 1946, when Ginsberg published one of Podhoretz's poems in *The Columbia Review,* the undergraduate literary journal of which Ginsberg was then the editor.[2] Soon after becoming friends, Podhoretz found himself increasingly repelled by what he viewed as Ginsberg's "perversity" and his vision of an "antinomian America," and this divide, which delineated the separation between "squares" and "hipsters" in Podhoretz's conception of the 1950s, only widened in the following decades of social and political upheaval. Curiously enough, Ginsberg still held Podhoretz in high enough esteem to have sent him an advance copy of *Howl and Other Poems* in 1956, along with a request that Podhoretz compose a review. While that review never transpired, the episode served as the catalyst for Podhoretz's "Know-Nothing Bohemians" article in the *Partisan Review*, his scathing dismissal of the Beat ethos as a degenerate and lurid "assault on America," glorifying drug use and "sexual perversity" while defying the precincts of normality, discriminate taste, and sound knowledge of social and political realities.[3]

According to Podhoretz's version of events, the moral and political degeneracy espoused by the Beats fueled the emergence of what we now call the New Left, or more accurately the New Lefts. Identifying Ginsberg as "one of the leading spirits" of the "new radical movement of the 1960s"—whose rationales had been presaged in Ginsberg's poetry since "Howl"—Podhoretz admits being openly perplexed by the fact that Fidel Castro would have expelled his "de facto ally" from Cuba in 1965.[4] Podhoretz defines the "new radicalism" he so despised as a wide-ranging and diverse counterculture unified chiefly by a "fierce hatred of America," and advocating radical social upheaval over piecemeal "reform within the going political system."[5] In this way, the nascent Left of the 1960s, Podhoretz argues quite adroitly, was oftentimes more invested in denouncing the outlooks and methods of "the liberal establishment" than it was in denouncing the political right, a historical fact undoubtedly supported by the collective indictment of Cold War liberalism coursing through the Cubalogues. Despite the liberal anti-Communist zeal driving his early career as a public intellectual, Podhoretz's politics drifted ever rightward after being named editor of *Commentary* in 1960. By the end of the 1960s, his evolution into a staunch neoconservative was complete, catalyzed as it was by his open disdain for the new radicalism in its myriad manifestations. It was during this same general period that Podhoretz began to use *Commentary* to denounce "busing to achieve integration, affirmative action, homosexual rights" and any number of liberal or leftist causes.[6] He also heaped an inordinate amount of scorn on homosexual writers such as Ginsberg, James Baldwin, and Gore Vidal for weakening the American character, and forever damaging the nation's "military spirit."[7]

Marshall Berman has written that while Ginsberg and his intellectual circle were highly adept at criticizing the militaristic excesses and social shortsightedness of Cold War America, they were nevertheless unable to articulate a convincing set of social and political alternatives during the hawkish maindrift of the late 1950s. In Berman's estimation, works such as Ginsberg's *Howl and Other Poems* revealed the "spiritual poverty" of New Frontierism, expansive networks of bureaucracy, unapologetic military posturing, and the homogenizing "expressway world" of the new and vast suburbanism, without, however, offering an "affirmative vision of alternate modern lives."[8] As is usually the case with Berman, his observations regarding the Beat circle are both astute and nuanced, but we might make the further assertion that the Cuban encounter marked the place from where Ginsberg and others began to more fully articulate their alternative visions for social and cultural life; divergent as those visions might have been from each other at times, they nevertheless anticipated the political and social upheavals of the late 1960s and early 1970s (as Podhoretz, despite his disdain, so aptly diagnosed). The Cubalogues, that is to say, forecast the cultural sea change rising to the surface of American political and social life, the forceful emergence of vast waves of liberation movements whose cresting momentum had been intuited from the beachheads by Ginsberg's "Howlers" and Baraka's "Screamers."

The flourishing of New Left liberation movements over the course of the 1960s presented Cold War liberalism and the hawkish consensus with its most vociferous and politically innovative set of opponents. Those movements, as Michael Denning has so persuasively argued in *Culture in the Age of Three Worlds*, were animated by a polyvalent desire for liberation: liberation from sexism, racism, heteronormativity, and the horrors of imperial/neocolonial war (eventually put on brutal display in Vietnam).[9] Collectively, these movements confronted the nation-state as their antithesis, arguing for reproduction and divorce rights, for an end to nuclear proliferation and violent colonial war, for expanded civil rights regimes, for an end to patriarchy in its multiple manifestations, and for more inclusive access to the arenas of public discourse and culture.[10] According to Van Gosse, what made this New Left strikingly "new" was its "pluralist character" and its grounding "in a deep if inchoate sympathy with the resistance of long-exploited peoples . . . who were themselves part of the New Left."[11] What Podhoretz views as "America hating," Gosse identifies as a moment in which the concerns of U.S. progressivism became complexly constellated among a vast number of activists and intellectuals working both within and beyond the U.S. political scene—or that it represented the historical emergence of which we might identify as a "stranger" Left. Furthermore, as Denning so deftly demonstrates, this "stranger" Left proved highly adept at linking its analyses of social and political marginalization to processes of massification, which Stuart Hall explored through his concept of the "national-popular," taking "up the question of how people are produced" via mass media and the cultural apparatus.[12] Cultural analysis, that is to say, came to drive the canon of New Left theory, as the work of figures such as Mills, Hall, Raymond Williams, Louis Althusser, Frantz Fanon, Pierre Bourdieu, Jacques Derrida, Michel Foucault, Edward Said, Gayatri

Spivak, Étienne Balibar and a host of others analyzed the "tropes and allegories of social discourse" that had allowed the modern nation-state to coalesce (and continually reproduce itself) as an exclusionary formation hostile to sexual, racial, colonial, and ideological otherness, thereby establishing poststructural, postcolonial, feminist, and critical race theory as the dominant analyses of social and political power for decades to come.[13] The Cubalogues, as I hope should be clear from the preceding chapters, anticipated many of the political and cultural concerns of these new liberation movements, and thus represent a valuable indicator of the polyvalent New Left's emergence while participating in a similar set of critiques regarding the national-popular and its enabling tropes of political and social discourse.

Despite the political and theoretical upheavals forwarded by the New Lefts, and the subsequent collapse of the Soviet Union, we are still living with the legacies of the Cold War era—especially in relation to Cuba. The truth of the matter is that Cuba itself has existed as a figment of the U.S. imagination for quite some time, as countless historical actors have attempted to circumscribe what the island might be or become, from the outside, according to one or another political or cultural outlook. In his recent *Cuba in the American Imagination: Metaphor and the Imperial Ethos* (2008), Louis A. Pérez, Jr. convincingly explores this notion of an imaginary Cuba in relation to U.S. foreign policy, spelling out the myriad ways in which the island has served as the laboratory for U.S. world-ordering ambition across a fairly sustained historical arc. Pérez asserts that starting in the nineteenth century—when American politicians, journalists, and capitalists began publicly lamenting the close proximity of a Spanish colonial possession to the mainland United States—Cuba has served as a fabrication of the U.S. political imagination, which has helped anchor U.S. national identity and multiple historical narratives concerning the U.S. role in/relationship to the world at large, especially since the Spanish-American War.[14] Oft-repeated metaphors, Pérez argues, have constituted the most prominent features of official/ mainstream accounts of the island from the nineteenth century to the present, securing the U.S. political imagination within a dissimulating "vernacular of empire" that justifies various appeals to paternalistic intervention.[15] As figures of thought, metaphors provide shape to our comprehension of the world, but as Pérez suggests throughout, figurative language often conceals as much as it reveals. In the words of Pérez himself: "Metaphorical representations are instrumental in shaping the cognitive context in which people apprehend the world about them, the way they arrive at an understanding of their time and place, often the very reason they choose one course of action among others."[16] But these metaphoric representations—which U.S. politicians and journalists have consistently employed as a "cognitive context" through which the U.S. citizenry could understand not only Cuba but the overall global imperatives of U.S. political life—work to "narrow the choice of perception to the one desired. Point of view [becomes] inscribed within the metaphor."[17]

Pérez goes on to reveal the three most dominant metaphors structuring the United States' tempestuous relationship to Cuba as such: 1. Cuba as brothel. 2. Cuba as disease and malignancy. 3. Cuba as child, or as a nation of politically rash and dangerously irresponsible children. These metaphoric figures of thought have in turn anchored appeals to altruism and U.S. national virtue—or to demands that the United States intercede in the island's affairs in order to liberate the helpless, underdeveloped, and persecuted Cuban people—thus overshadowing the true tactical and commercial desires of the U.S. political and interest structure, which has viewed the lack of sustained U.S. administration over Cuban affairs as a threat to national security and an embarrassing failure of economic/market expansion within the American hemisphere. In terms of the late 1950s and early 1960s, Pérez explores the extent to which the metaphoric rendering of Cuba as a rash child became projected specifically onto Castro himself, as *New York Times* columnists (so mistrusted by Ferlinghetti and Baraka) tended to describe the young leader as "an over-grown boy" and "an immature boy," thereby invalidating his revolution as impossibly whimsical, overly idealistic, and irrational in its political demands and expectations.[18] Castro was dismissed, in other words, in quite the same way in which the Beats were dismissed as childish, immature, and naive during the same general era by Cold War liberals such as Podhoretz, Daniel Bell, Mary McCarthy, and Diana Trilling.

This dual dismissal undoubtedly explains some of the initial appeal of Castro for the Beats and their fellow travelers, as Castro was in a sense cast within the Cold War political drama as a young, bearded, and politically rash Cuban beatnik. Moreover, Pérez's insightful unpacking of U.S. imperial metaphors echoes the insights of many of those who traveled to Cuba during the initial revolutionary period, especially Mills, Baraka, and Schleifer, whose Cuba writings respectively explored "Cold War analogy," the historical rootedness of the "cold light of reason," and the tropes of Kennedy-era New Frontierism as cognitive blocks within the U.S. imperial imagination. These writers also attempted to expose the ways in which figurative language and thought might occlude other viewpoints on the revolution, thereby authorizing particular courses of action in U.S. relations with Cuba; virtually all of the figures treated in this book were concerned with the extent to which mass cultural projections of Cuba came to circumscribe the meanings of Castro's revolution within a false or limited terrain of cognitive engagement passing as received wisdom or political common sense underwritten by the Cold War consensus. Collectively, they critically analyzed the "vernacular of empire" at the very moment it was being applied to Castro's young revolutionary government, suggesting that not only had Cold War anti-Communist rhetoric been wrongly superimposed over an anticolonial movement, but that such superimpositions had failed to completely displace alternative renderings of what was taking (and might take) place in the island's cultural and political life. The Cubalogues, that is to say, represent acts of counterimagination aimed at superseding long entrenched imperial tropes and the bifurcating rhetoric of Cold War politics that gave such tropes new life and relevance. Ultimately the Cubalogues configured Cuba as a transnational and collaborative laboratory—a site for experimenting with new and stranger notions of inter-American politics. Undoubtedly they were idealistic and utopian—and as is usually the case with idealism and utopianism, reality eventually refused to play along for a whole host of reasons—but the documents themselves nevertheless forwarded a vision of intellectual and cultural collaboration that refused to participate in the official discourses of neocolonialism and conquest, while suggesting that the budding revolution might have some wisdom to offer the U.S. political class and its overly obedient Cold War pundits.

Moreover, many of the issues raised by the Cubalogues (and Pérez) remain relevant today. Even in the wake of Fidel Castro's rule—which many who danced through the streets of Miami upon hearing the news believed would mark the end of Cuban Communism—Cuba remains a focal point of U.S. foreign policy and discursive maneuvering within the public sphere, a fact brought home ever so clearly during the latest U.S. presidential election. Not only would Castro, the recent retiree, not be vacationing in Miami at any time soon, but the legacy of his relationship with U.S. authorities came very much to the fore as the election season reached its head. In October of 2008, for instance, George W. Bush visited Miami in order to raise money for Republican electoral candidates, couching his plea for contributions within the region's still-pronounced anti-Castro animus. Despite Barack Obama's request that the Bush administration "at least temporarily lift the Cuba travel and remittances ban in the wake of Hurricanes Gustav and Ike," Bush maintained a hard line on the island, exclaiming that the travel ban and embargo shall stay in place until Cuba embraces democracy.[19] Republican presidential candidate John McCain took Obama even more directly to task over the course of the election season, repeatedly claiming that the Illinois senator was "too willing to talk to America's enemies," evinced by his professed readiness to lift the Cuban embargo and to engage in diplomatic relations with Raúl Castro.[20]

Adding fuel to the heated fires of disputation, Obama openly refused to refute McCain's charges, exclaiming that upon being elected he would meet with the younger Castro "at a time and place of my choosing," and that the time had come to "pursue direct diplomacy, with friend and foe alike, without preconditions."[21] The time had come, according to the senator, to reassess the grounding assumptions of U.S. diplomacy, starting in places such as Cuba—or we might say that the time had come to finally leave the Cold War imaginary decisively behind, as figures such as Mills and Ferlinghetti hoped to do decades earlier. But McCain was interested in doing just the opposite. Addressing a crowd in Harrisburg, Virginia, in October 2008, McCain waxed nostalgic about the Cuban Missile Crisis, exclaiming that "I sat in the cockpit on the flight deck of the USS *Enterprise* off of Cuba. I had a target. . . . My friends, you know how close we came to a nuclear war. America will not have a president who needs to be tested. I've been tested, my friends."[22] In this particular instance, McCain's reminiscence sutured Obama's "soft attitudes" on Cuba directly to the War on Terror, implying that Obama will eventually have to deal with a similar nuclear crisis generated in terroristic Middle Eastern states. Growing desperate as the race reached into the final stretch, the McCain campaign participated in some rather blunt fear-mongering in relation to U.S. national security, openly conflating the political panic of the U.S.'s current Terror War with the specters of Cold War Cuba and the political upheavals of the 1960s. At roughly the same time that the Arizona senator was reminiscing on the Cuban Missile Crisis and continually accusing Obama of "being soft" on the Castro government, his campaign unleashed a strategy that ultimately tested its credibility, as running mate Sarah Palin consistently excoriated Obama for "palling around with terrorists" as a result of having attended some fund-raising functions with former Weather Underground member William Ayers. Palin's accusations not only linked Obama simultaneously to New Left excesses and contemporary anxieties regarding terrorism, but went so far as to suggest that the Illinois senator "is not like us" and that "we see America as a force of good in this world," statements rife with racial connotations and xenophobia further extended by McCain's questions regarding Obama's longtime friendship with Rashid Khalidi, a Palestinian scholar and professor of Middle Eastern Studies at Columbia University. Mired in election season despair, the McCain-Palin campaign began race-baiting, New Left–baiting, red-baiting, and terrorist-baiting all at once, a fact that was not lost on the *New York Times*'s Frank Rich, who not only understood the racial connotations of Palin's accompanying appeals to the "real America" but failed to comprehend why McCain and Palin would feign confusion when gatherers at their rallies subsequently began calling Obama a "terrorist" and shouting "off with his head!," while engaging in the "uninhibited slinging of racial epithets."[23]

This explicit linking of the politics of the Cold War era to the War on Terror perhaps finds its most significant and pressing embodiment not in the campaign rhetoric of the McCain camp—which unjustly projected its hyperbole onto Obama as some sort of radical or terrorist sleeper agent—but in the Guantanamo Bay detention center. In our supposedly "globalized" present, the existence of the detention center has attested to the fact that certain cultural and political borders remain sacrosanct within the militarized logics of U.S. world-ordering ambition, whose reach into the Caribbean, and propensity for imagining it as an offshore holding pen rather than as a space of liberation, continues to allow for the outright denial of those forms of democratic practice that the nation claims to uphold—an especially ironic turn of events for those "suspicious" U.S. citizens held indefinitely by the military (without being charged of actual crimes) on an island that their own nation has continually accused of tyranny. While under U.S. jurisdiction, Guantanamo has remained suspended in a state of murky legality, a third space for anti-democracy justified by shadowy rationales unavailable to debate and redress.[24] The detention center represents, in other words, the very antithesis of what the Cubalogue writers initially hoped would unfold in Cuba, while speaking to the ongoing U.S. willingness to flex its military muscle in the Caribbean whenever it so chooses. To return to the assertions of Pérez, the detention center not only helps facilitate Cuba's standing as home to political pathology and inexplicable rashness that must be contained at the very cost of national security, but helps buttress the rhetorical conflation of Communism and terrorism literally embodied in figures such as Raúl Castro and the suspected enemies of the United States incarcerated in the detention center.

The ideological concerns of the Cold War yet endure, imbricated within the public rationales of the War on Terror through rhetorical cross-pollination and the quite tangible existence of Guantanamo as a holding pen. The discursive rationalities of the Cold War era yet endure, even after the turbulent 1960s and early 1970s when liberation movements (in which the Cubalogue writers played identifiable roles) presented U.S. world-ordering ambition and hawkish liberals with their most significant public challenge to date. Across the Cold War historical divide, appeals to national security through fear-mongering, along with exceptionalist platitudes regarding the unconditional superiority of U.S. political, economic, and cultural institutions (embodied most clearly in Palin's rhetoric), still tenaciously persist within the nation's public political speech. Ultimately, U.S. foreign policy in the wake of the Cold War era—spurred on in its earliest moments by George H. W. Bush's call for a "new world order" during Operation Desert Storm—has fully revealed the core of world-ordering ambition which remained somewhat cloaked within Cold War claims of Communist containment. While Obama's election signals a possible détente in U.S.-Cuban relations and an end to the pronounced unilateralism of the Bush years, we remain in momentous need of an engaged and significant public discussion on how our nation might abandon its long-standing inclinations toward presumptuousness (and even downright insolence) in the international arena and in turn learn to collaborate more fully with other nations on securing a more just and peaceful future for the inhabitants of the planet—a conversation that does not feel imperiled by discourses of freedom and democracy issuing forth from places other than the official hallways of the Washington power elite, the commercial imperatives of the corporate interest structure, or policy think tanks such as the RAND Corporation. In a sense, this was the collective dream of the Cubalogue writers, who were not nearly as successful at writing their concerns into Cuba's revolutionary history as they were at transforming those concerns into compelling forms of cultural and political activism that challenged the rationales of U.S. world-ordering ambition and what they saw as the nation's partially achieved democratic legacy.

The questions they posed, however, remain very much on the table, not only in terms of Guantanamo and the War on Terror, but in efforts to effectively deal with U.S. legacies of heteronormativity and white supremacy. In terms of the first category, social activists (of especially the past ten years) have been confronting sexualized limits on citizenship by arguing for the true integration of the "don't-ask-don't-tell" military and the expansion of marriage rights to same-sex couples. Moreover, these very issues came to the fore in the days after Obama's election as the LGBT (Lesbian, Gay, Bisexual, Transsexual) community, sent momentarily spinning in disbelief from the passage of the same-sex marriage ban in California, took to the streets in cities such as New York, Albuquerque, Minneapolis, Raleigh, and Obama's hometown of Chicago; these coordinated protests highlighted the continued status of heteronormativity as an orienting condition of democratic life in the United States, even as the nation was congratulating itself, and rightly so, for the historic election of its first black president. Obama, it appears, only deepened this chasm when he invited evangelical minister Rick Warren to take part in the invocation at his inauguration, as Warren had vociferously campaigned in favor of California's same-sex marriage ban from the pulpit of his Saddleback Church in southern California. Furthermore, as many commentators gushed over Obama's nomination and election as ushering in a post-racial United States and equally gushed over his adept use of the new electronic commons (or the digital public sphere) to mobilize the constituencies that got him elected, the legacies of racism still mark the very real landscapes of American life in the persistence of racialized poverty and healthcare gaps, substandard urban education, and the grim realities of police profiling and inordinate rates of incarceration among people of color (even as a racially diverse cast of media stars proliferates throughout globalized U.S. mediascapes as the Walter Whites and Edith Sampsons of their day).

In the aftermath of an historic presidential election rich in expectations—and in the subsequent wake of Obama's executive orders calling for the closing of the Guantanamo Bay detention center and for the curbing of the Cuban travel ban—the need persists for "stranger" and more expansive notions of democratic belonging.

# Notes

## Introduction

1. Cabrera Infante, *Mea Cuba,* 53.

2. Castro, "True Social Revolution," *Militant Online* 62.46 (December 21, 1998), http://themilitant.com/1998/6246/6246_15.html.

3. Ibid., 3.

4. Cabrera Infante, *Mea Cuba,* 67.

5. Fisher, "Narration," 265.

6. Ibid.

7. Ibid., 266.

8. Gosse, *Where the Boys Are,* 5–10. Gosse's work on "Fidelismo" and the FPCC has been an invaluable resource for this project, which, so to speak, stands on the shoulders of Gosse's work. *Where the Boys Are* provides a sweeping overview of the vast coalition of writers and intellectuals involved in the FPCC and related organizations, a coalition that he views as representative of an important historical passage from the Old Left to the New Left in the United States. The Beats, and some of the works I will be discussing in this project, are included in his purview. This book, however, thickens out Gosse's cultural history through more substantial readings of Ferlinghetti, Allen Ginsberg, Baraka, and others, while focusing far more attention on the inter-American relationship between Cuban cultural history and the evolution of Beat narrative forms, along with the extent to which that relationship reveals the limitations of U.S. political thought during the Cold War era (and seemingly beyond).

9. Ibid., 82–85.

10. Podhoretz, "Know-Nothing Bohemians," 484–88.

11. As quoted in Theado, *Beats: A Literary Reference,* 82–83.

12. Bell, *End of Ideology,* 301.

13. Ibid.

14. Even scholars to the left of liberalism have branded the Beats as apolitical, attesting

to the extent to which their political pedigree has become too firmly attached to the figure of Kerouac. In *Where the Boys Are,* Gosse asserts that "the Beat Generation of 1950s America had been thoroughly apolitical in its initial premises," which for Gosse consists of various expressions of orgiastic excess (183). This characterization is important to Gosse's narrative, which then argues for Cuba as a complete political awakening for the Beats. The Cuban experience was no doubt a political awakening for Baraka, though figures such as Ferlinghetti and Ginsberg had been engaged in a cultural struggle against Cold War political assumptions for quite some time. The legal struggle regarding *Howl and Other Poems* is an obvious example, though, as shall become evident in the pages that follow, there are others worthy of a deeper consideration. In any case, the logic of Gosse's argument regarding the Beats revolves around Baraka's "Cuba Libre," which is the only Cuban travelogue by the Beats that Gosse treats extensively (see pp. 184–87).

15. Charters, *Beat Down,* 480.

16. Ross, *No Respect,* 51. For other treatments of Cold War liberalism, consult Lasch's *New Radicalism in America 1889–1963,* 286–347, and Singh's paradigm-shifting essay, "Culture/Wars," 471–522. I will be mapping out my own thoughts on Cold War liberal philosophy, including its relationship to U.S. hemispheric and global ambitions, in each of the chapters that follow.

17. Ibid.

18. Rorty, *Achieving Our Country,* 15.

19. Ibid., 43.

20. Lott, *Disappearing Liberal Intellectual,* 28.

21. Baraka, *Home: Social Essays,* 16.

22. See Martinez, "With Imperious Eye," 33–53.

23. Skerl, "Introduction," 1–2.

24. See Belgrad, "Transnational Counterculture," 27–40.

25. Here is a brief but representative list of the scholarship I have in mind: John Carlos Rowe's *The New American Studies* (Minneapolis: University of Minnesota Press, 2002) and *Post-Nationalist American Studies* (Berkeley: University of California Press, 2000); Amy Kaplan and Donald Pease, eds., *Cultures of United States Imperialism* (Durham, N.C.: Duke University Press, 1993); George Lipsitz's *American Studies in a Moment of Danger* (Minneapolis: University of Minnesota Press, 2001); Paul Gilroy's *The Black Atlantic: Modernity and Double Consciousness* (Cambridge, Mass.: Harvard University Press, 1993) and *Against Race* (Cambridge, Mass.: Belknap Press, 2000); Lisa Lowe's *Immigrant Acts* (Durham, N.C.: Duke University Press, 1996); Lisa Lowe and David Lloyd, eds., *The Politics of Culture in the Shadow of Capital* (Durham, N.C.: Duke University Press, 1997); Walter D. Mignolo's *Local Histories/ Global Designs* (Princeton, N.J.: Princeton University Press, 2000); John Tomlinson's *Globalization and Culture* (Chicago: University of Chicago Press, 1999); Fredric Jameson and Masao Miyoshi, eds., *The Cultures of Globalization* (Durham, N.C.: Duke University Press, 1998); Peter Linebaugh and Marcus Redicker's *The Many-Headed Hydra: Sailors, Slaves, Commoners, and the Hidden History of the Revolutionary Atlantic* (Boston: Beacon, 2000); Thomas Bender, ed., *Rethinking American History in a Global Age* (Berkeley: University of California Press, 2002); Jeffrey Belnap and Raul Fernandez, eds., *José Martí's "Our America": From National to Hemispheric Cultural Studies* (Durham, N.C.: Duke University Press, 1998); John Muthyala's "Reworlding America: The Globalization of American Studies," *Cultural Critique* 47 (2001): 91–119; and Gary Reichard and Ted Dickson, eds., *America on the World Stage: A Global Approach to U.S. History* (Chicago: University of Illinois Press, 2008).

26. Duncan, "Writing at Home," 53.

27. See Balibar, "Racism and Nationalism," 37–67.

28. Macdonald's *The Root Is Man*—serialized in *politics* in 1946—serves as the philosophical apotheosis of the anarcho-pacifist movement, especially in regards to cultural theory. One of Macdonald's principal concerns was that the avenues of mass communication—film, radio, and the print media—had been effectively drafted into the militarized will of competitive Western societies. He argued, in turn, that a principled alternative to the emergent geopolitics of military aggression and growing atomic fear would need to be articulated in the small press and other alternative media venues. The mass cultures of modern nation-states, according to Macdonald's thinking, eradicated more extensive visions of human potential and community—or those forms of subjectivity and attachment excessive to the imaginary of national belonging. Indeed, at the outset of World War II Macdonald rejected the Trotskyite Marxism he had embraced as an editor of *Partisan Review* for a new political ethos of universal human emancipation; that is to say, Macdonald grew increasingly wary of proletarian struggle as the catalyst of emancipatory politics, as the militarized interest structure seemed increasingly able to enlist the agency of all of its citizens (not just "the proletariat") into its acquisitive will. A new oppositional politics, in Macdonald's estimation, would need to be based upon the development of human personality with as little external meddling as possible; in other words, freeing human potential from the will of culturally entrenched nation-states would be essential to the ongoing development of interpersonal relations across the national and ideological divides of an increasingly militarized world. Gregory Sumner's penetrating study, *Dwight Macdonald and the Politics Circle* (Ithaca, N.Y.: Cornell University Press, 1996), provides an extensive look at Macdonald's political evolution, while restoring Macdonald's work as an important precursor of the New Left and New Social Movements. For a more wide-ranging treatment of wartime anarcho-pacifism and conscientious objection, consult Heather T. Frazer and John O'Sullivan's *"We Have Just Begun to Not Fight": An Oral History of Conscientious Objection in Civilian Public Service during World War II* (New York: Twayne, 1996).

29. Taylor, *Modern Social Imaginaries*, 83–100.

30. Duncan, "Homosexual in Society," 209.

31. Ibid.

32. Ibid.

33. Hamalian, *Life of Kenneth Rexroth*, 105.

34. Lasar, *Pacifica Radio*, 33–36.

35. Cruse, "Negro Looks at Cuba," 20.

36. For Cruse's thoughts on absorption, consult *Crisis of Negro Intellectual*, 348–52.

## Chapter 1. Hemispheric Beats (in the Bay Area and Beyond)

1. Ferlinghetti, "One Thousand Fearful Words," 48.

2. Ibid.

3. Muste, et al., "Tract for the Times," 6.

4. Ibid.

5. Ferlinghetti, "Poet's Notes on Cuba," 10.

6. Ibid., 11.

7. Ibid., 12.

8. Ibid.

9. Ibid.

10. Ferlinghetti, "Muralist Refregier," 12.

11. Ibid.

12. Gosse, *Where the Boys Are*, 176.

13. Ibid., 183.

14. McClure, "From *Scratching the Beat*," 274.

15. Rexroth, *World Outside the Window*, 60.

16. Vale, *Real Conversations*, 210.

17. Silesky, *Ferlinghetti*, 56.

18. Ibid., 21–22.

19. Madoff, "Birth of a Poet," 148–49.

20. Hamalian, *Life of Kenneth Rexroth*, 214.

21. Stonor Saunders, *Cultural Cold War*, 157–58.

22. As quoted in Ginsberg, *Howl, Original Draft Facsimile*, 156.

23. McClure, "From *Scratching the Beat*," 274.

24. As quoted in Charters, *Portable Beat Reader*, 229.

25. McClure, "From *Scratching the Beat*," 275.

26. Ferlinghetti, "Between the Lines," 35.

27. Ibid.

28. Ferlinghetti, "Horn on Howl," 254–60.

29. Ibid., 261.

30. Silesky, *Ferlinghetti*, 98.

31. As quoted in Silesky, *Ferlinghetti*, 99.

32. Keylor, *World of Nations*, 94.

33. Ibid., 95.

34. Ibid., 99.

35. Guillen, "Satchelmouth," 16.

36. Ibid.

37. Davidson, *San Francisco Renaissance*, 32.

38. Little work has been done thus far on the transnational dimensions of Beat aesthetics. The one representative volume is James Campbell's *This Is the Beat Generation: New York–San Francisco–Paris* (Berkeley: University of California Press, 1999), which partially illuminates the transnational nature of Beat aesthetics. While Campbell's compassionate study of the Beat writers focuses some attention on Mexico City and Tangiers as critical sites in the Beat universe, most of his attention is focused on the three cities highlighted in his title. The Paris material is focused on the Beat Hotel, where William Burroughs worked out his theory of the "cut-up" with Brion Gysin. The Hotel also served as the Paris residence for many of the movement's other principal figures, whose ideas collectively resonated with French literary and intellectual trends of the pre- and postwar period. The Beat aesthetic echoed, in various ways, the existential concerns of Jean-Paul Sartre, the collage or "cut-up" experiments of Dadaists such as Tristan Tzara, the automatic or "spontaneous" writing of the Surrealists, and the explicit antiheroics and homoerotics of Jean Genet. The Cuban Revolution, however, does not fall within the boundaries of Campbell's transnational cultural geography, and his treatment of Mexico City and Tangiers focuses most of its attention on sexual exploits and the consumption of various drugs at the cost of a sustained study of local literary and artistic influences on Beat aesthetics.

39. Alegria, *Literature and Revolution,* http://www.webshells.com/jdoug/LitRev1.htm.

40. Ibid.

41. Parra, "Vices," 5.

42. Ibid.

43. Ginsberg, *Howl and Other Poems,* 39.

44. Parra, "Vices," 6.

45. Dickstein, *Leopards in the Temple,* 96–97.

46. Dickstein's penetrating study of postwar literary culture identifies a similar trend in the novels of Ralph Ellison and James Baldwin, both of whom rejected the politics of Richard Wright and the "protest novel" during the period in question. In the process, characters such as Bigger Thomas, who were working toward a manifestation of racialized class consciousness, were recast as the young, politically disenchanted (and usually pleasure-seeking) characters of Ellison and Baldwin.

47. Ferlinghetti, "Poet's Notes on Cuba," 12.

48. Guevara's experiences, which led to a political epiphany regarding Latin American poverty, were captured in his *Motorcycle Diaries: A Journey around South America,* translated by Ann Wright (London: Verso, 1995), which served as the basis for Brazilian director Walter Salles's 2004 film of the same name. Salles is now at work on bringing Kerouac's *On the Road* to the screen. This development might very well speak to the ongoing appeal of the Beat aesthetic in Latin America.

49. Mills, *Listen, Yankee,* 2.

50. Ibid.

51. In his "Letter to the New Left," Mills implored the emerging lefts of the 1960s to divest themselves of the "labor metaphysic" of the Old Left in favor of a more personal political optics opposed to extensive forms of human alienation and authoritarian governance (18–23). The Old Left had failed, Mills contended, precisely because it had wound its vision of estrangement and emancipation too tightly to the category of labor, epitomized in Karl Marx's notion of "estranged labor." Guided by Marx's theoretical vision, leftists had equated human emancipation with the emancipation of laboring potential for far too long. New activists, Mills contended, must instead be intellectually daring enough to think the world beyond militarism, race, gender discrimination, and nationalism, all of which had helped construct a prison house for human potential.

52. Belgrad, *Culture of Spontaneity,* 2.

53. Fisher, "Narration," 268.

54. Ibid.

55. John Dewey theorized the inherent limits on democratic publicness as early as 1927. In *The Public and Its Problems,* Dewey declared that the democratic publics of liberal nation-states are "organized and made effective by means of representatives who as guardians of customs, as legislators, as executives, judges, etc., care for its especial interests by methods intended to regulate the conjoint actions of individuals and groups. Then and in so far, association adds to itself political organization, and something which may be government comes into being: the public is a political state" (35). Dewey was concerned, in other words, with the extent to which democratic publics were called into being by modern nation-states whose ideological considerations regulated the contents of mass public conversation (even as they enabled it). An avowed liberal for much of his life, Dewey was nevertheless concerned with the discursive preconditions of liberal conceptions of publicness, as he questioned whether

the preservation of the national collective might in some instances jeopardize a candid conversation regarding social and economic ills.

56. Luis, "Exhuming *Lunes de Revolución*," 254.

57. As quoted in Luis, 255–56.

58. Ibid., 255–58.

59. Ibid.

60. Ferlinghetti, "Poet's Notes on Cuba," 13.

61. Ibid.

62. As quoted in Silesky, *Ferlinghetti*, 267–68.

63. Luis, "Exhuming *Lunes de Revolución*," 257.

64. Cabrera Infante, *Mea Cuba*, 66.

65. As quoted in Luis, "Exhuming *Lunes de Revolución*," 261.

66. Mills, *Listen, Yankee*, 142.

67. Ibid., 143–44.

68. Ibid., 144–45.

69. Ibid.

70. Ferlinghetti, "Poet's Notes on Cuba," 14.

71. Ferlinghetti, "Preface," xv.

72. Farber, *Cuban Revolution Reconsidered*, 1.

73. Ibid., 36.

74. Ibid., 37.

75. Ibid., 36.

76. Ibid., 37–38.

77. Ibid., 125.

78. Cabrera Infante, *Mea Cuba*, 52. My treatment of *P.M.* in the pages that follow is highly dependent upon Cabrera Infante's description of the film in *Mea Cuba* and Luis's brief description in "Exhuming *Lunes de Revolución*," as copies are nearly impossible to come by. Thus, virtually no one has written about it at length.

79. Ibid.

80. Ibid.

81. Ibid., 67.

## Chapter 2. On the Crisis of the Underground and a Politics of Intractable Plurality

1. Sukenick, *Down and In*, 22.

2. Cruse's revelation resonates with one of the principal characteristics of black Marxism, as explored in Cedric Robinson's compendious *Black Marxism: The Making of the Black Radical Tradition* (Chapel Hill: University of North Carolina Press, 2000). Robinson places Cruse within the black Marxist tradition which, among other things, attempted to complicate theoretically rigid notions of the proletariat and class struggle through the optics of race.

3. Cobb, "What Is Left?," xviii–xix.

4. Cruse, *Crisis of the Negro*, 5.

5. Ibid.

6. Harold Cruse, "Race and Bohemianism," 21.

7. Ibid., 23.

8. Ibid., 21.

9. Ibid., 22.

10. Ibid.

11. Ibid.

12. Sukenick, *Down and In,* 36.

13. Ibid., 37.

14. Cruse, "Race and Bohemianism," 25.

15. Di Prima, *Recollections of My Life,* 143.

16. Sukenick, *Down and In,* 20.

17. Cruse, "Race and Bohemianism," 25.

18. Cruse, *Crisis of the Negro,* 273.

19. Ibid., 274.

20. Ibid.

21. Ibid., 275.

22. This portrayal is particularly pronounced in articles dealing with the Beat aspects of a more general youth culture pervading the Village, as seen in the August 13, 1958, edition's "Hipnicks: Where Do They Bed-Down When the Sun Comes Up?" and J. R. Goddard's June 30, 1960, article "'Run, Beatniks, Run!' To Mecca, 1960," each of which is reprinted respectively in *The Village Voice: Our 50th Anniversary Issue,* L.53 (October 26–November 1, 2005), 8; 16. That same issue contains further support for Cruse's characterization of the early *Voice* in Jarrett Murphy's "Buying and Selling and Buying the *Voice,*" in which he explains that the weekly's earliest years were marked by intense inner squabbling between founders Ed Fancher, Dan Wolf, and Norman Mailer, and that "Mailer, who had declared himself 'General Marijuana,' started writing a column whose first installment dubbed the *Voice* 'remarkably conservative for so young a paper.' A couple of turbulent months later, Mailer ended the column, saying the *Voice* was too 'square'" (31). Mailer's overall impression was that the young paper was not politically radical enough and had "sold out" shortly after being founded (31). The *Voice* also featured a number of articles dealing with Kerouac's success following the publication of *On the Road,* though many of these articles portray him (and his devotees) with only a mild degree of seriousness, often stressing his drunkenness and his reliance on a Beat argot (full of references to "chicks" and "cats"), which belies his artistic achievements in a fashion similar to Podhoretz and Bell. Jerry Talmer's "Jack Kerouac: Back to the Village—but Still on the Road" and Howard Smith's "Off the Road, into the Vanguard, and Out," both collected in Fred McDarrah and Timothy McDarrah, eds., *Kerouac and Friends* (New York: Thunder's Mouth Press, 2002), 33–40; 55–60, epitomize this characterization. Two notable exceptions are Marc Schleifer's "Allen Ginsberg: Here to Save Us, but Not Sure from What," which appeared in the October 15, 1958, edition of the *Voice* (and has since been collected in Carter, ed., 2001) and "The Beat Debated—Is It or Is It Not?" published in the November 19, 1958, edition (and collected in McDarrah and McDarrah, eds., on 71–77). Schleifer, whose work as a Beat editor and journalist shall serve as one of the primary foci of chapter four, chose in the second of these articles to treat a November 6, 1958, reading and panel presentation ("Is There a Beat Generation?") at Hunter College by letting participants speak for themselves. Overall his article presents comments by Kerouac, Kingsley Amis, James Wechsler, and Ashley Montagu with virtually no editorial commentary.

23. Those familiar with *Raisin in the Sun* undoubtedly realize that Cruse's own reading of the play seems to have been limited for rhetorical effect, or for the needs of his arguments

regarding the racial outlooks of the Village's "older bohemia." The conflicts driving Hansberry's play are more complicated than Cruse admits (or cared to admit), as Beneatha Younger actually serves within *Raisin* as the voice of emergent black nationalism. Moreover, at the conclusion of the play Beneatha is still considering relocating to Africa with the Nigerian, Joseph Asagai, suggesting that the goals of domestic life, within Hansberry's theater, are not as monolithically "middle class" or bourgeois as Cruse suggests.

24. Cruse, "Negro Looks at Cuba," 20.

25. Ibid.

26. Ibid., 11.

27. Writing in 1960, Cruse believed that the revolution was proving true to its professed antiracism. It should be pointed out, however, that the extent to which the revolution actually realized its initial claims of racial justice has been decried by a number of scholars. In *Local Histories/Global Designs*, Walter Mignolo argues that Soviet imperialism in Cuba ultimately eradicated the promise of racial reform gestured at during the early days of Castro's revolution. With the advent of Soviet influence—which was solidified in the wake of the Bay of Pigs—dogmatic class analysis displaced the revolution's promise of a race-based revision of hemispheric colonialism, enacted domestically in the immediate outlawing of all forms of institutionalized racism in 1959 (335). In *The Origins of the Cuban Revolution Reconsidered*, Samuel Farber makes the similar assertion that the revolution was adept at recruiting Cuban blacks into its ranks, but in the wake of its explicitly Communist turn the black population felt increasingly alienated from the revolutionary program and Communism became merely a tolerated political outlook in the greater Afro-Cuban community (51–52). In *Castro, the Blacks, and Africa* (Los Angeles: UCLA Center for Afro-American Studies, 1988), Carlos Moore provides the most stinging (and perhaps most well-known) reassessment of revolutionary racial policy, arguing that the revolution's approach to race never progressed beyond populist platitudes and that Cuba's black population continues to suffer from wide-ranging inequalities, which the revolutionary elite continually refuses to address. In fairness to Cruse, his experience of the revolution occurred at its outset, and the ultimate importance of his Cubalogue rests not in whether Cuba actually lived up to his initial enthusiasm, but in the ways in which his early contact with the revolution's claims and excitement compelled him into an influential reevaluation of U.S. cultural and political life.

28. Cruse, "Negro Looks at Cuba," 18.

29. Ibid.

30. Ibid., 14.

31. Ibid.

32. Ibid., 15.

33. Ibid., 17.

34. Baraka, *Home: Social Essays*, 18.

35. Cruse, "Revolutionary Nationalism," 39.

36. Ibid., 40.

37. Ibid.

38. Ibid., 45.

39. Ibid., 60.

40. Ibid., 62.

41. Singh, *Black Is a Country*, 183.

42. Cruse, *Crisis of the Negro*, 483.

43. Ibid., 357.

44. Ibid.

45. Ibid., 474.

46. Ibid.

47. Klages, *Literary Theory*, 149–50.

48. I am thinking primarily of Césaire's *Discours sur le colonialisme* (Paris: Présence Africaine, 1953) and Fanon's *The Wretched of the Earth* (New York: Grove, 1963).

49. Cruse, *Crisis of the Negro*, 457.

50. Ibid., 458.

51. Ibid., 363–64.

52. Ibid., 347.

53. Kelley, *Freedom Dreams*, 61.

54. Cruse, *Crisis of the Negro*, 357.

55. Ibid., 380.

56. X, "Ballot or the Bullet," 359–61.

## Chapter 3. Unsettling the Democratic Score

1. As quoted in Saloy, "Black Beats,"162.

2. Jones/Baraka, "Cuba Libre," 346.

3. Ibid.

4. Ibid.

5. Ibid.

6. Ibid.

7. Kerouac, *On the Road*, 280–87.

8. Jones/Baraka, "Cuba Libre," 353.

9. Ibid.

10. Ibid., 352–53.

11. Ibid., 347.

12. Ibid., 353.

13. Ibid.

14. Ibid.

15. Ibid.

16. Ibid.

17. Anderson, *This Is Our Music*, 102–108.

18. Doyle, *Freedom's Empire*, 2–4.

19. Gilroy, *Black Atlantic*, 57.

20. Ibid.

21. I am referring here to Anderson's argument regarding literacy and national belonging in *Imagined Communities*, 1–47.

22. Jones/Baraka, *Blues People*, 1–10.

23. Jones/Baraka, *Black Music*, 12.

24. Ibid.

25. Ibid., 13.

26. Ibid., 19.

27. Ibid., 20.

28. Jones/Baraka, *Blues People*, 4.

29. Ibid., 80.

30. Ibid., 79–80.

31. Ibid., 96.

32. Ibid., 102.

33. Ibid., 125.

34. Ibid., 123.

35. Ibid., 235–36.

36. Jones/Baraka, "Screamers," 293.

37. Ibid.

38. Ibid., 292.

39. Ibid.

40. Ibid.

41. Ibid., 294–96; emphasis mine.

42. Ibid.

43. Panish, *Color of Jazz*, 130.

44. Ibid.

45. Ibid., 131–40.

46. Jones/Baraka, "Screamers," 295.

47. Singh, *Black Is a Country*, 206.

48. Denning, *Age of Three Worlds*, 39.

49. Hassan, *Contemporary American Literature*, 134.

50. Ibid., 166.

51. Ibid., 166–68.

52. See Singh's *Black Is a Country*, 202–11, and Kelley's *Freedom Dreams*, 85–99, on the complex relationship between 1960s black nationalism, global decolonization, and the modern Civil Rights Movement. I will have more to say regarding this relationship in the chapter's closing pages.

53. Negri, *Insurgencies*, 304.

54. Meiksins Wood, *Democracy Against Capital*, 193.

55. Ibid., 204.

56. Ibid., 205.

57. Calhoun, "Imagining Solidarity," 149.

58. Fontana, et. al., "Introduction: Deliberative Democracy," 1.

59. Ibid., 5.

60. Ibid., 8.

61. Jones/Baraka, "Cuba Libre," 353.

62. Tyson, *Radio Free Dixie*, 225.

63. Ibid., 227.

64. Barksdale, "Robert F. Williams," 76.

65. Ibid., 84–85.

66. Ibid.

67. Ibid., 86–87.

68. In a sense, Radio Free Dixie rode on the strategic coattails of Guevara's "Radio Rebelde," which broadcast from the secured territories of the Sierra Maestra at the outset of the Cuban Revolution. Guevara and his revolutionary compatriots also set up a small print-

ing press, which they used for printing newsletters and an irregular newspaper, distributed to a peasantry who had been taught to read by Guevara and his core of teachers. Guevara's establishment of an alternative public arena, which challenged Fulgencio Batista's iron grip over Cuban media outlets, was an essential component of the Cuban Revolution. Castro's subsequent decision to provide Williams with a radio frequency (and his subsequent support of figures such as Carl Marzani, Waldo Frank, and Cedric Belfrage) should be seen as an extension of these political aims, which were open to the insurgent possibilities of alternative media. See Peter McLaren's *Che Guevara, Paolo Freire and the Pedagogy of Revolution* (Lanham, Md.: Rowman and Littlefield, 2000).

69. Williams, *Negroes with Guns*, 65.

70. Ibid., 77.

71. Ibid., 76.

72. Ibid.

73. Ibid., 69.

74. Ibid.

75. Ibid.

76. Brown, "American Welfare State," 93–122.

77. Singh, *Black Is a Country*, 58–100.

78. Williams, *Negroes with Guns*, 114.

79. Schlesinger, Jr., *Vital Center*, 230.

80. Ibid., 232.

81. Ibid., 230.

82. Ibid., 235.

83. For a more detailed examination of this phenomenon, consult Mary Dudziak, *Cold War Civil Rights* (Princeton, N.J.: Princeton University Press, 2000).

84. Schlesinger, Jr., *Vital Center*, 190.

85. McAlister, *Epic Encounters*, 73.

86. Ibid., 71.

87. Williams, *Negroes with Guns*, 114, emphasis mine. Williams's text is not without a certain degree of discursive murkiness or dissonance, especially in those sections where he takes on the pacifist strategies of the NAACP and MLK. At times, Williams advocates a violent confrontation with, and subsequent occupation of, state power as the antithesis to pacifist gradualism. At other times, he seems to offer violence as a complement to the assimilationist and civic nationalist strategies of the mainstream Civil Rights Movement. In such moments, violence is offered as an expedient to civil rights reform. Rather than seeing these inconsistencies as a theoretical shortcoming, I tend to read Williams's text as a transitional text in a longer discursive history that bridges mainstream civil rights and the eventual advocation of violence (by groups such as the Black Panther Party) attributable to the failure of Civil Rights legislation to walk its integrationist talk. This difficult, and at times frustrating, political balancing act is also registered in the fact that Williams is but isn't a member of the NAACP, along with his assertion that he is both an armed revolutionary American and a Cuban anti-imperialist.

88. Negri's claim has been given incredible shape and depth by Peter Linebaugh and Marcus Rediker's study of the revolutionary Atlantic, *The Many-Headed Hydra: Sailors, Slaves, Commoners, and the Hidden History of the Revolutionary Atlantic* (Boston: Beacon Press, 2000). Linebaugh and Rediker's history of the long Atlantic revolution privileges the spectacle of

the "motley crew," the multiethnic and interracial coalition of workers and the dispossessed organized "from below"—or we might say an early plebeian counter-public that set the revolutionary storm in motion. This motley crew, the authors convincingly argue, was the driving force of eighteenth-century revolution. Revolutionary documents, and the U.S. Constitution to come, were Platonic documents that attempted to organize these revolutionary forces at the expense of their most radical demands—such as the immediate and unequivocal end to slavery. The Sons of Liberty, organized by the propertied classes to resist British rule, called for "orderly resistance" at odds with the "anarchy" threatened by various motley formations—but the founding culture of U.S. politics had already been shaped by a transatlantic and plebeian collection of wills and forces.

89. Jones/Baraka, *Jones/Amiri Baraka Reader*, 140–41.

90. Ibid., 130.

91. Tyson, *Radio Free Dixie*, 207.

92. Jones/Baraka, *Jones/Amiri Baraka Reader*, 130.

93. Ibid.

94. Tyson, *Radio Free Dixie*, 225.

95. Jones/Baraka, *Jones/Amiri Baraka Reader*, 145.

96. Ibid., 144.

97. Ibid.

98. Ibid., 131.

99. Ibid.

100. Ibid.

101. Sukenick, *Down and In*, 38.

## Chapter 4. Beat Publics and the "Middle-Aged" Left

1. Gosse, *Where the Boys Are*, 3.

2. Ibid.

3. Hornick, "*Kulchur:* A Memoir," 281.

4. Ibid, 281–82.

5. Jones, *Hettie Jones*, 199.

6. Ibid.

7. Schleifer, epilogue to *Negroes with Guns*, 127.

8. Ibid., 128.

9. Marzani, *From Pentagon to Penitentiary*, 208–209.

10. In *From Pentagon to Penitentiary*, Marzani claims that the "major recruiter of Reds into the OSS was Donovan himself" (102). Included among Donovan's "Red" recruits were Roberta Blatt, a known CP member who, along with Marzani's wife, Edith, initiated a labor movement among service workers at Macy's in New York, setting off a series of events that was highly publicized at the time. Donovan also recruited Milt Felson, a Lincoln Brigade veteran and unabashed socialist who later composed the memoir *The Anti-Warrior* (Iowa City: University of Iowa Press, 1989), and Don Wheeler, Marzani's fellow Rhodes Scholar. Wheeler, a "well known man of the left" (103) retreated from public life in order to run his family's dairy farm in Washington state. His papers are in the process of being collected at the University of Oregon.

11. See Smith, *Shadow Warriors*, especially chapters 7 and 8. According to Smith, Donovan

was not averse to hiring Marxists or Communists into the OSS. In fact, Donovan even attempted to initiate combined intelligence operations with the Soviet Union, which would have included stationing a NKVD officer in Washington and an OSS representative in Moscow, but his plan was dismissed after a rigorous public campaign by J. Edgar Hoover.

12. Marzani, *From Pentagon to Penitentiary,* 50–54.

13. According to W.E.B. Du Bois, it was Marzani's labor documentary, *Deadline for Action* (1947), that ultimately led to his imprisonment in 1949. As Du Bois adroitly explained in his preface to Marzani's Cold War revisionist history, *We Can Be Friends* (New York: Topical Books, 1952), the 1947 documentary—shot with Congress of Industrial Organizations (CIO) sponsorship as general striking erupted across the postwar American landscape—made the mistake of "naming names" (6). Playing upon the red-baiting rhetoric of the time, Du Bois contended that the film, which valorized organized labor as the safeguard against U.S. corporatism and global ambition, was "the best educational film ever gotten out by a labor union . . . [and] was immediately criticized as 'communistic' and attacked by the press and certain corporations mentioned in it. Within a few months Marzani was indicted for making a false statement [as a member of the State Department] in 1946 as to his alleged membership in the Communist Party in 1940" (6).

14. Marzani, *Reluctant Radical: Spain, Munich,* 131. *European Political Report,* assembled in conjunction with the SOE, was never declassified. Fortunately, Marzani's and Schlesinger, Jr.'s separate recollections of institutional feuding match up on the details most relevant to the arguments here.

15. Schlesinger, Jr., *Life in the Twentieth,* 300.

16. Ibid., 301.

17. Schlesinger, Jr., "London Operation," 62.

18. Schlesinger, Jr., Life in the Twentieth, 334.

19. Ibid., 402.

20. Ibid., 403.

21. Ibid., 232.

22. Schlesinger, Jr., "London Operation," 65.

23. Ibid.

24. Marzani's *Prison Notebooks* were named in homage to Antonio Gramsci. In fact, Marzani's translation of Gramsci, *The Open Marxism of Antonio Gramsci* (New York: Cameron Associates, 1957), represents the first English-language translation of the Italian political philosopher.

25. Marzani, *Prison Notebooks,* 178.

26. Marzani, *From Pentagon to Penitentiary,* 168.

27. Marzani, *Prison Notebooks,* 178.

28. Schlesinger, Jr., *Vital Center,* 166; emphasis mine.

29. Marzani, *Reconstruction,* 55; 59.

30. Ibid., 59–60.

31. Lasch, *New Radicalism in America,* 308–309.

32. Ibid., 309–10.

33. Schlesinger, Jr., "Memorandum," 186.

34. Ibid., 187.

35. Light, "Cubans in Exile," 5.

36. See, for instance, "China's basic policy: Get U.S. forces out of all East Asia" in *National Guardian* 11.13 (November 12, 1958): 5; Ursula Wasserman's "Ghana sets its goals in massive

development plan" in *National Guardian* 11.16 (February 9, 1959): 7; Cedric Belfrage's "Moment of decision for the continent of Africa" in *National Guardian* 11.23 (March 23, 1959): 7; "It was quite a year of Negro history—and there's more to come" in *National Guardian* 11.17 (February 9, 1959): 5; Louis Burnham's "Mississippi lynching and the untold horrors" in *National Guardian* 11.30 (May 11, 1959): 5; "Negro leader runs for mayor in Monroe, NC" in *National Guardian* 11.26 (April 13, 1959): 4.

37. Light, "World Reaction," 5.
38. Belfrage, "Eyewitness in Cuba," 1.
39. Gosse, *Where the Boys Are*, 221.
40. Schleifer, "Cuban Notebook," 72.
41. Ibid.
42. Ibid.
43. Ibid., 73.
44. Williams, *Empire as a Way*, 189–90.
45. Gosse, *Where the Boys Are*, 211–14.
46. Baran, "Cuba Invaded," 86.
47. Ibid.
48. Ibid., 88.
49. Huberman and Sweezy, "Notes from the Editors," contents page.
50. Ibid.
51. Schleifer, "Cuban Notebook," 79.
52. Ibid.
53. Ibid.
54. Duberman, "Havana Inquiry," 131–42
55. Fernández Robaina, "Brothel of the Caribbean," 257–59.
56. Pérez, Jr., *American Imagination*, 235.
57. Cirules, *Mafia in Havana*, 16–31.
58. Ibid., 127.
59. Schleifer, "Cuban Notebook," 81.
60. Lewis, et. al., "'Rehabilitation' of Prostitutes," 395–98.

## Chapter 5. (Back) Toward a Stranger Democracy

1. Ginsberg, "Interview with Clint Frakes," 543.
2. Schumacher, *Dharma Lion*, 420.
3. Ginsberg, "Interview with Clint Frakes," 535.
4. Ginsberg, "Interview with Barry Farrell," 57.
5. Cabrera Infante, *Mea Cuba*, 120.
6. Ibid.
7. Ginsberg, "Interview with Allen Young," 320.
8. Serra, *"New Man" in Cuba*, 9.
9. Guevara, "Socialism and Man," 148.
10. Ibid., 154.
11. Ibid., 156.
12. Ibid.
13. Arenas, *Before Night Falls*, 105.

14. Serra, *"New Man" in Cuba,* 144.

15. Ibid., 12.

16. Ibid., 19, 58.

17. Luis, "Exhuming *Lunes de Revolución,*" 255–58. For more on the aesthetic cosmopolitanism of Borges, consult Evelyn Fishburn's *Borges and Europe Revisited* (London: University of London, 2002) and Ion Tudro Agheana's *The Prose of Jorge Luis Borges: Existentialism and the Dynamics of Surprise* (New York: Peter Lang, 1984). In terms of these aspects in Cortázar's work, consult the Harold Bloom–edited *Julio Cortázar* (New York: Chelsea House, 2005) or the writer's own *Around the Day in Eighty Worlds,* trans. Thomas Christensen (San Francisco: North Point Press, 1989), in which Cortázar documents his artistic debt to figures such as Jules Verne, Edgar Allan Poe, Man Ray, Marcel Duchamp, Antonin Artaud, along with Charlie Parker and Lester Young, both of whom had a tremendous amount of influence over the jazz poetics of the Beat writers.

18. Serra, *"New Man" in Cuba,* 20.

19. Ibid., 5. It should be pointed out that one of the strengths of Serra's own inquiry is her demonstration of the subtextual stakes involved in many works, such as Edmundo Desnoes's *Memories of Underdevelopment* (1965) and Miguel Cossio Woodward's *Sacchario* (1970), both of which won the Casa prize, though, upon close reading, they each reveal nuanced critiques of the New Man ideology whose values they simultaneously purport to speak. They are, in the words of postmodern/post-structuralist theory, double-coded texts.

20. Saldivar, "Dialectics of Our America," 74.

21. Serra, *"New Man" in Cuba,* 20.

22. Coover, "Julio Cortázar," 270.

23. League of Militant Poets, "Statement," 5.

24. Ibid.

25. Ibid.

26. Ibid.

27. Portuondo, "New Art For Cuba," 48–52.

28. Poggioli, *Avant-Garde,* 26.

29. Ibid.

30. Editorial preface to Eisenstein, "Last Scenes," 104.

31. Bergan, *Sergei Eisenstein,* 338.

32. Ibid., 341.

33. Eisenstein, "Last Scenes," 114.

34. Cabrera Infante's *Carteles* writings are collected in *Twentieth Century Job* (New York: Faber and Faber, 1992).

35. McClure, "Fidelio," 53.

36. Ibid.

37. Gosse, *Where the Boys Are,* 190.

38. McLucas, "Letters from Cuba," 96.

39. Ibid.

40. Ibid., 98.

41. Ibid., 100.

42. Serra, *"New Man" in Cuba,* 135.

43. Ibid.

44. Fernández, "Dead Mother," 21–23.

45. Cabrera Infante, "She Only Sang Boleros," 28–29.

46. Serra, *"New Man" in Cuba*, 58.

47. Ginsberg, "Prose Contribution," 63–64.

48. Ibid.

49. Ibid., 62.

50. Ibid., 71.

51. Ibid.

52. Ibid., 71–72.

53. Ibid., 72.

54. Roderick Ferguson, "The Parvenu Baldwin," 235. Also see D'Emilio's, "Homosexual Menace," 226–40.

55. Ibid., 235.

56. Ibid., 254.

57. Hodges, *Alan Turing*, 497.

58. *Interim Report submitted to the Committee on Expenditures in the Executive Departments by its Subcommittee on investigations pursuant to S. Res. 280*, as quoted in Hodges, *Alan Turing*, 498.

59. Hodges, *Alan Turing*, 501.

60. Sherry, *Shadow of War*, 104–105.

61. Doherty, *Cold War, Cool Medium*, 222.

62. Ibid., 224.

63. Ibid., 223.

64. Schlesinger, Jr., *Vital Center*, 166.

65. Alamilla Boyd, *Wide Open Town*, 1–20.

66. Ibid., 5.

67. Ibid., 110–13.

68. Ibid., 111.

69. Ibid., 121–22.

70. Ibid., 3.

71. Ibid., 107.

72. Ginsberg, *Howl and Other Poems*, 9.

73. Ginsberg, *Howl, Original Draft Facsimile*, 21.

74. Ginsberg, *Howl and Other Poems*, 9.

75. Ibid., 21–22.

76. Ibid., 43.

77. Cabrera Infante, *Mea Cuba*, 70.

78. Luis, "Exhuming *Lunes de Revolución*," 256.

79. Bergan, *Sergei Eisenstein*, 346.

80. Kerouac, *Selected Letters*, 320.

81. Ibid, 427.

82. Duggan, *Twilight of Equality?*, ix.

83. Schumacher, *Dharma Lion*, 427.

84. Berman, *All that is Solid*, 189–92.

85. Cotkin, *Existential America*, 109.

86. Bahktin, *Dialogic Imagination*, 270–71.

87. Ibid., 424.

## Coda

1. Schleifer, "Here to Save Us," 5.

2. Podhoretz, *Ex-Friends,* 23.

3. Ibid., 27–35.

4. Ibid., 46–47.

5. Ibid., 47.

6. Wald, *New York Intellectuals,* 353.

7. Ibid.

8. Berman, *All That Is Solid Melts,* 311.

9. Denning, *Age of Three Worlds,* 225–29.

10. Ibid., 43.

11. Gosse, *Where the Boys Are,* 257; 255.

12. Denning, *Age of Three Worlds,* 89.

13. Ibid., 81–90.

14. Pérez, Jr., *American Imagination,* 1–2.

15. Ibid, 2–3.

16. Ibid., 14.

17. Ibid., 15.

18. Ibid., 241.

19. Mazzei, "Bush Firm on Cuba during Miami Visit," *Miami Herald,* October 10, 2008, http://www.miamiherald.com/news/americas/cuba/v-print/story/721709.html.

20. Michael Luo, "Cuba Is Topic as McCain Continues Attack on Obama," *New York Times,* May 21, 2008, http://www.nytimes.com/2008/05/21/us/politics/21mccain.html.

21. Jeff Zeleny, "Obama, in Miami, Calls for Engaging with Cuba," *New York Times,* May 24, 2008, http://www.nytimes.com/2008/05/24/us/politics/24campaign.html.

22. William Douglas, "McCain Recalls {ap}62 Missile Crisis," *Miami Herald,* October 21, 2008, http://www.miamiherald.com/news/front-page/story/735904.html.

23. Frank Rich, "The Terrorist Barack Hussein Obama," *New York Times,* October 12, 2008, http://www.nytimes.com/2008/10/12/opinion/12rich.html.

24. In *Black Empire,* Stephens engages in a similar set of arguments concerning the legacy of Guantanamo, though she is primarily interested in exploring its anomalous (though representative) standing as a site that restricts the movements of global people of color within a supposedly deterritorialized age. See especially 270, 279.

# Bibliography

Alamilla Boyd, Nan. *Wide Open Town: A History of Queer San Francisco to 1965.* Berkeley: University of California Press, 2003.

Alegria, Fernando. *Literature and Revolution.* Trans. D. Ohmans. http://www.webshells.com/jdoug/LitRev1.htm.

Anderson, Benedict R. *Imagined Communities: Reflections on the Origin and Spread of Nationalism.* 2nd ed. New York: Verso, 1991.

Anderson, Iain. *This Is Our Music: Free Jazz, the Sixties, and American Culture.* Philadelphia: University of Pennsylvania Press, 2007.

Arenas, Reinaldo. *Before Night Falls: A Memoir.* Trans. Dolores M. Koch. New York: Viking Penguin, 1993.

Aronowitz, Stanley. *The Death and Rebirth of American Radicalism.* New York: Routledge, 1996.

Bahktin, M. M. *The Dialogic Imagination: Four Essays.* Ed. Michael Holquist. Trans. Caryl Emerson and Michael Holquist. Austin: University of Texas Press, 1981.

Balibar, Étienne. "Racism and Nationalism." In Étienne Balibar and Immanuel Wallerstein, *Race, Nation, Class: Ambiguous Identities.* Trans. Chris Turner. London: Verso, 1991. 37–67.

Baraka, Amiri. *Black Music.* New York: De Capo, 1998.

———. *Blues People.* New York: Quill, 1963.

———. "Cuba Libre." *Evergreen Review* 4.15 (November–December 1960): 346–53.

———. "Cuba Libre," *The LeRoi Jones/Amiri Baraka Reader.* Ed. William Harris. New York: Basic Books, 1999. 125–61.

———. *Home: Social Essays.* Akashi Classics: Renegade Reprint Series. New York: Akashic, 2009.

———. "The Screamers." *The Moderns: An Anthology of New Writing in America.* Ed. LeRoi Jones. London: MacGibbon and Kee, 1965. 292–97.

Baran, Paul. "Cuba Invaded." *Monthly Review* 13.3 (July–August 1961): 84–91.

Barksdale, Marcellus C. "Robert F. Williams and the Indigenous Civil Rights Movement in Monroe, North Carolina, 1961." *The Journal of Negro History* 69.2 (Spring, 1984):73–89.

Bartlett, Lee. *William Everson: The Life of Brother Antoninus.* New York: New Directions, 1988.

Belfrage, Cedric. "Eyewitness in Cuba: It took 66 hours to smash invasion." *National Guardian* 13.29 (May 1, 1961): 1.

Belgrad, Daniel. *The Culture of Spontaneity: Improvisation and the Arts in Postwar America.* Chicago: University of Chicago Press, 1998.

———."The Transnational Counterculture: Beat-Mexican Intersections." *Reconstructing the Beats.* Ed. Jennie Skerl. New York: Palgrave Macmillan, 2004. 27–40.

Bell, Daniel. *The End of Ideology: On the Exhaustion of Political Ideas in the Fifties.* New York: Free Press, 1960.

Bergan, Ronald. *Sergei Eisenstein: A Life in Conflict.* Woodstock, N.Y.: Overlook Press, 1999.

Berman, Marshall. *All That Is Solid Melts into Air: The Experience of Modernity.* New York: Penguin, 1988.

Brown, Michael K. "Race in the American Welfare State: The Ambiguities of 'Universalistic' Social Policy since the New Deal." *Without Justice For All: The New Liberalism and Our Retreat from Racial Equality.* Ed. Adolph Reed, Jr. Boulder, Colo.: Westview Press, 2001. 93–122.

Cabrera Infante, Guillermo. *Mea Cuba.* Trans. Kenneth Hall. New York: Farrar, Straus, and Giroux, 1994.

———. "She Only Sang Boleros." *Pa'Lante* 1.1 (May 1962): 27–35.

Calhoun, Craig. "Imagining Solidarity: Cosmopolitanism, Constitutional Patriotism, and the Public Sphere." *Public Culture* 14.1 (2002): 147–72.

Campbell, James. *This Is the Beat Generation: New York–San Francisco–Paris.* Berkeley: University of California Press, 1999.

Castro, Fidel. "A True Social Revolution Produces A Cultural Revolution." *The Militant Online* 62.46 (December 21, 1998). http://themilitant.com/1998/6246/6246_15.html.

Charters, Ann. *Beat Down to Your Soul.* New York: Penguin, 2001.

———. *The Portable Beat Reader.* New York: Penguin, 1992.

Cirules, Enrique. *The Mafia in Havana.* Melbourne, N.Y.: Ocean Press, 2004.

Cobb, William Jelani. "What Is Left?: An Introduction." *The Essential Harold Cruse: Reader.* Ed. Cobb. New York: Palgrave, 2002. xv–xxiv.

Coover, Robert. "Robert Coover on Julio Cortázar." *Mutual Impressions: Writers from the Americas Reading One Another.* Ed. Ilan Stevens. Durham, N.C.: Duke University Press, 1999. 269–74.

Cotkin, George. *Existential America.* Baltimore: Johns Hopkins University Press, 2005.

Cruse, Harold. *The Crisis of Negro Intellectual.* New York: William Morrow, 1967.

———. "A Negro Looks at Cuba." *The Essential Harold Cruse: A Reader.* Ed. William Jelani Cobb. New York: Palgrave, 2002. 7–20.

———. "Race and Bohemianism in Greenwich Village." *The Essential Harold Cruse: A Reader.* Ed. William Jelani Cobb. New York: Palgrave, 2002. 21–26.

———. "Revolutionary Nationalism and the Afro-American." *Black Fire: An Anthology of Afro-American Writing.* Ed. LeRoi Jones and Larry Neal. New York: William Morrow, 1968. 39–63.

Davidson, Michael. *The San Francisco Renaissance: Poetics and Community at Mid-Century.* New York: Cambridge University Press, 1989.

D'Emilio, John. "The Homosexual Menace: The Politics of Sexuality in Cold War America." *Passion and Power: Sexuality and* History. Ed. Kathy Peiss, Christin Simmons, and Robert Padgug. Philadelphia: Temple University Press, 1993. 226–40.

Denning, Michael. *Culture in the Age of Three Worlds.* London: Verso, 2004.

Dewey, John. *The Public and Its Problems.* New York: Holt, 1927.

Dickstein, Morris. *Leopards in the Temple.* Cambridge, Mass.: Harvard University Press, 2002.

Di Prima, Diane. *Recollections of My Life as a Woman: The New York Years.* New York: Penguin, 2002.

Doherty, Thomas. *Cold War, Cool Medium: Television, McCarthyism and American Culture.* New York: Columbia University Press, 2003.

Douglas, William. "McCain Recalls {ap}62 Missile Crisis," *Miami Herald,* October 21, 2008. http://www.miamiherald.com/news/front-page/story/735904.html.

Doyle, Laura. *Freedom's Empire: Race and the Rise of the Novel in Atlantic Modernity, 1640–1940.* Durham, N.C.: Duke University Press, 2008.

Duberman, Martin. "The Havana Inquiry." *Left Out, The Politics of Exclusion: Essays 1964–2002.* Cambridge, Mass.: South End Press, 2002: 131–42.

Duggan, Lisa. *The Twilight of Equality? Neoliberalism, Cultural Politics, and the Attack on Democracy.* Boston: Beacon, 2003.

Duncan, Robert. "The Homosexual in Society." *politics* 1.7 (August 1944): 208–12.

———. "Writing at Home in History." *Derivations.* London: Fulcrum, 1968. 53–54.

Eisenstein, Sergei. "Last Scenes from the Screenplay of Ivan the Terrible Part III." Trans. Ivor Montagu. *Pa'Lante* 1.1 (May 1962): 104–24.

Everson, William. *Naked Heart: Talking on Poetry, Mysticism, and the Erotic.* Ed. Lee Bartlett. Albuquerque: University of New Mexico Press, 1992.

Farber, Samuel. *The Origins of the Cuban Revolution Reconsidered.* Chapel Hill: University of North Carolina Press, 2006.

Ferguson, Roderick. "The Parvenu Baldwin and the Other Side of Redemption." *James Baldwin Now.* Ed. Dwight A. McBride. New York: New York University Press, 1999. 233–64.

Ferlinghetti, Lawrence. "Between the Lines." *San Francisco Chronicle,* May 19, 1957: 35.

———. "Horn on Howl." *The Portable Beat Reader.* Ed. Ann Charters. New York: Penguin, 1992. 254–60.

———. "Muralist Refregier and the Haunted Post Office." *Art Digest,* April 15, 1953: 12–13.

———. "One Thousand Fearful Words for Fidel Castro." *Starting from San Francisco.* New York: New Directions, 1967. 48–50.

———. "Poet's Notes on Cuba." *Liberation* 6.1 (March 1961): 10–14.

———. "Preface." *The Essential Neruda: Selected Poems.* Ed. Mark Eisner. San Francisco: City Lights, 2004. xv.

Fernández, Pablo Armando. "The Poet to His Dead Mother." Trans. Jose Yglesias. *Pa'Lante* (May 1962): 16–25.

Fernández Robaina, Tomás. "The Brothel of the Caribbean." *The Cuba Reader.* Ed. Aviva Chomsky, Barry Carr, and Pamela Maria Smorkaloff. Durham, N.C.: Duke University Press, 2003. 257–59.

Fisher, Walter R. "Narration as a Human Communication Paradigm: The Case of Public Moral Argument." *Contemporary Rhetorical Theory*. Ed. John Louis Lucaites, Celeste Michelle Condit, and Sally Caudill. New York: Guilford Press, 1999. 265–87.

Fontana, Benedetto, Cary J. Nederman, Gary Remer, eds. *Talking Democracy: Historical Perspectives on Rhetoric and Democracy*. University Park: Penn State University Press, 2004.

Gilroy, Paul. *The Black Atlantic: Modernity and Double Consciousness*. Cambridge, Mass.: Harvard University Press, 2003.

———. *There Ain't No Black in the Union Jack*. Chicago: University of Chicago Press, 1991.

Ginsberg, Allen. *Howl and Other Poems*. San Francisco: City Lights, 1956.

———. *Howl, Original Draft Facsimile, Transcript & Variant Versions, Fully Annotated by Author, with Contemporaneous Correspondence, Account of First Public Reading, Legal Skirmishes, Precursor Texts & Bibliography*. New York: Harper and Row, 1986.

———. "Interview with Allen Young." *Spontaneous Mind: Selected Interviews 1958–1996*. Ed. David Carter. New York: HarperCollins, 2001. 303–42.

———. "Interview with Barry Farrell." *Spontaneous Mind: Selected Interviews 1958–1996*. Ed. David Carter. New York: HarperCollins, 2001. 54–66.

———. "Interview with Clint Frakes." *Spontaneous Mind: Selected Interviews 1958–1996*. Ed. David Carter. New York: HarperCollins, 2001. 532–45.

———. "Prose Contribution to Cuban Revolution." *Pa'Lante* 1.1 (May 1962): 61–73.

Gosse, Van. *Where the Boys Are: Cuba, Cold War America, and the Making of a New Left*. London: Verso, 1993.

Gray, Timothy. *Gary Snyder and the Pacific Rim: Creating Countercultural Community*. Iowa City: University of Iowa Press, 2006.

Guevara, Ernesto. "Socialism and Man in Cuba." *Che Guevara Speaks*. Ed. and trans. Joseph Hansen. New York: Pathfinder, 2000. 142–60.

Guillen, Nicolas. "Satchelmouth." *Thirty Spanish Poems of Love and Exile*. Ed. and trans. Kenneth Rexroth. San Francisco: City Lights, 1956. 16.

Hamalian, Linda. *A Life of Kenneth Rexroth*. New York: Norton, 1991.

Harris, William, ed. *The LeRoi Jones/Amiri Baraka Reader*. New York: Basic Books, 1999.

Hassan, Ihab. *Contemporary American Literature, 1945–1972*. New York: Frederick Ungar, 1973.

Hodges. Andrew. *Alan Turing: The Enigma*. New York: Simon and Schuster, 1983.

Hornick, Lita. "*Kulchur*: A Memoir." *The Little Magazine in America: A Documentary History*. Ed. Elliott Anderson and Mary Kinzie. New York: Pushcart, 1978. 280–86.

Huberman, Leo and Paul Sweezy. "Notes from the Editors." *Monthly Review* 13.3 (July–August 1961). Contents page.

Jones, Hettie. *How I Became Hettie Jones*. New York: Grove, 1997.

Kelley, Robin D. G. *Freedom Dreams: The Black Radical Imagination*. Boston: Beacon, 2002.

Kerouac, Jack. *Lonesome Traveler*. New York: Grove, 1988.

———. *On the Road*. New York: Penguin, 1991.

———. *Selected Letters, 1957–1969*. Ed. Ann Charters. New York: Penguin, 1999.

Keylor, William R. *A World of Nations: The International Order Since 1945*. New York: Oxford University Press, 2003.

Klages, Mary. *Literary Theory*. London: Continuum, 2007.

Lasar, Matthew. *Pacifica Radio: The Rise of an Alternative Network*. Philadelphia: Temple University Press, 2000.

Lasch, Christopher. *The New Radicalism in America 1889–1963*. New York: W. W. Norton, 1965.

League of Militant Poets. "A Statement by The League of Militant Poets." *Pa'Lante* 1.1 (May 1962): 5.

Lewis, Oscar, Ruth M. Lewis, and Susan Rigdon. "The 'Rehabilitation' of Prostitutes." *The Cuba Reader*. Durham, N.C.: Duke University Press, 2003. 395–98.

Light, Robert. "The Cubans in Exile." *National Guardian* 13.5 (November 14, 1960): 5.

———. "World Reaction to Cuba Invasion Hits Yankee Imperialism." *National Guardian* 13.29 (May 5, 1961): 5.

Lott, Eric. *The Disappearing Liberal Intellectual*. New York: Basic Books, 2006.

Luis, William. "Exhuming *Lunes de Revolución*." *New Centennial Review* 2.2 (2002): 253–83.

Luo, Michael. "Cuba Is Topic as McCain Continues Attack on Obama." *New York Times*, May 21, 2008. http://www.nytimes.com/2008/05/21/us/politics/21mccain.html.

Macdonald, Dwight. *The Root Is Man*. New York: Autonomedia, 1994.

Madoff, Stephen Henry. "Birth of a Poet." *Naked Heart*. Ed. Lee Bartlett. Albuquerque: University of New Mexico Press, 1992. 145–51.

Malcolm X. "From 'The Ballot or the Bullet.'" *American Protest Literature*. Ed. Zoe Trodd. Cambridge, Mass.: Belknap, 2006. 356–63.

Martinez, Manuel Luis. "With Imperious Eye: Kerouac, Burroughs, and Ginsberg on the Road in South America." *Aztlán* 23.1 (1998): 33–53.

Marzani, Carl. *The Education of a Reluctant Radical: From Pentagon to Penitentiary*. New York: Topical Books, 1995.

———. *The Education of a Reluctant Radical: Reconstruction*. New York: Monthly Review Press, 2002.

———. *The Education of a Reluctant Radical: Spain, Munich, and Dying Empires*. New York: Topical Books, 1994.

———. *Prison Notebooks*. New York: Monthly Review Press, 2001.

Mazzei, Patricia. "Bush Firm on Cuba during Miami Visit." *Miami Herald*, October 10, 2008. http://www.miamiherald.com/news/americas/cuba/v-print/story/721709.html.

McAlister, Melani. *Epic Encounters: Culture, Media, and U.S. Interests in the Middle East Since 1945*. Berkeley: University of California Press, 2001.

McClure, Michael. "Fidelio." *Pa'Lante* 1.1 (May 1962): 53.

———. "From *Scratching the Beat Surface*." *The Portable Beat Reader*. Ed. Ann Charters. New York: Penguin, 1992. 273–87.

McLucas, Leroy. "Letters from Cuba." *Pa'Lante* 1.1 (May 1962): 94–100.

Meiksins Wood, Ellen. *Democracy Against Capitalism: Renewing Historical Materialism*. New York: Cambridge University Press, 1995.

Mignolo, Walter D. *Local Histories/Global Designs: Coloniality, Subaltern Knowledges, and Border Thinking*. Princeton, N.J.: Princeton University Press, 2000.

Mills, C. Wright. "Letter to the New Left." *New Left Review* 1.5 (September–October 1960): 18–23.

———. *Listen, Yankee: The Revolution in Cuba*. New York: McGraw-Hill. 1960.

Muste, A. J., et al. "Tract for the Times." *Liberation* 1.1 (March 1956): 3–6.

Negri, Antonio. *Insurgencies: Constituent Power and the Modern State*. Minneapolis: University of Minnesota Press, 1999.

Panish, Jon. *The Color of Jazz: Race and Representation in Postwar American Culture*. Jackson: University Press of Mississippi, 1997.

Parra, Nicanor. "Vices of the Modern World." *Anti-Poems*. Trans. Jorge Elliot. San Francisco: City Lights, 1960: 5–8.

Pérez, Louis A., Jr. *Cuba in the American Imagination: Metaphor and the Imperial Ethos*. Chapel Hill: University of North Carolina Press, 2008.

Peters, Nancy. "The Beat Generation and San Francisco's Culture of Dissent." *Reclaiming San Francisco: History, Politics, Culture*. Ed. James Brooks, Chris Carlsson, and Nancy J. Peters. San Francisco: City Lights, 1998. 199–216.

Podhoretz, Norman. *Ex-Friends: Falling Out with Allen Ginsberg, Lionel and Diana Trilling, Lillian Helman, Hannah Arendt, and Norman Mailer*. New York: Encounter Books, 2000.

———. "The Know-Nothing Bohemians." *Beat Down to Your Soul*. Ed. Ann Charters. New York: Penguin, 2001. 479–92.

Poggioli, Renato. *The Theory of the Avant-Garde*. Trans. Gerald Fitzgerald. Cambridge, Mass.: Belknap, 1968.

Portuondo, José Antonio. "A New Art For Cuba." *Pa'Lante* 1.1 (May 1962): 48–52.

Rexroth, Kenneth, ed. and trans. *Thirty Spanish Poems of Love and Exile*. San Francisco: City Lights, 1956.

———. *World Outside the Window: The Selected Essays of Kenneth Rexroth*. Ed. Bradford Morrow. New York: New Directions, 1987.

Rich, Frank. "The Terrorist Barack Hussein Obama," *New York Times*, October 12, 2008. http://www.nytimes.com/2008/10/12/opinion/12rich.html.

Robinson, Cedric. *Black Marxism: The Making of the Black Radical Tradition*. Chapel Hill: University of North Carolina Press, 2000.

Rorty, Richard. *Achieving Our Country: Leftist Thought in 20th Century America*. Cambridge, Mass.: Harvard University Press, 1998.

Ross, Andrew. *No Respect: Intellectuals and Popular Culture*. London: Routledge, 1989.

Saldivar, José David. "The Dialectics of Our America." *Do the Americas Have a Common Literature?* Ed. Gustavo Pérez Firmat. Durham, N.C.: Duke University Press, 1990. 62–84.

Saloy, Mona Lisa. "Black Beats and Black Issues." *Beat Culture and the New America, 1950–1965*. Ed. Lisa Phillips. New York: Whitney Museum of American Art, 1996. 153–68.

Schleifer, Marc D. "Allen Ginsberg: Here to Save Us, but Not Sure from What." *Spontaneous Mind: Selected Interviews, 1958–1996*. Ed. David Carter. New York: HarperCollins, 2001. 3–6.

———. "Cuban Notebook." *Monthly Review* (July–August 1961): 71–83.

Schlesinger, Jr., Arthur. *A Life in the Twentieth Century: Innocent Beginnings, 1917–1950*. Boston: Houghton Mifflin, 2000.

———. "The London Operation: Recollections of a Historian." *The Secrets War: The Office of Strategic Services in World War II*. Ed. George C. Chalou. Washington, D.C: National Archives and Record Administration, 1992. 60–66.

———. "Memorandum from the President's Special Assistant [Schlesinger] to President Kennedy, April 5, 1961." *United States State Department, Foreign Relations of the United States, 1961–1963, Cuba*. Volume 10. Washington, D.C: Government Printing Office, 1997. 185–86.

———. *The Vital Center*. Piscataway, N.J.: Transaction, 1997.

Schumacher, Michael. *Dharma Lion*. New York: St. Martin's, 1992.

Serra, Ana. *The "New Man" in Cuba*. Gainesville: University Press of Florida, 2007.

Sherry, Michael. *In the Shadow of War: The United States since the 1930s*. New Haven: Yale University Press, 1994.

Silesky, Barry. *Ferlinghetti: The Artist in His Time*. New York: Warner, 1991.

Singh, Nikhil Pal. *Black is a Country: Race and the Unfinished Struggle for Democracy*. Cambridge, Mass.: Harvard University Press, 2004.

———. "Culture/Wars: Recoding Empire in the Age of Democracy." *American Quarterly* 50 (September 1998): 471–522.

Skerl, Jennie. "Introduction." *Reconstructing the Beats*. New York: Palgrave Macmillan, 2004. 1–12.

Smith, Bradley F. *The Shadow Warriors: OSS and the Origins of the CIA*. New York: Basic Books, 1983.

Stephens, Michelle Ann. *Black Empire: The Masculine Global Imaginary of Caribbean Intellectuals in the United States, 1914–1962*. Durham, N.C.: Duke University Press, 2005.

Stonor Saunders, Frances. *The Cultural Cold War: The CIA and the World of Art and Letters*. New York: New Press, 2001.

Sukenick, Ronald. *Down and In: Life in the Underground*. New York: Collier, 1987.

Taylor, Charles. *Modern Social Imaginaries*. Durham, N.C.: Duke University Press, 2004.

Theado, Matt, ed. *The Beats: A Literary Reference*. New York: Carroll and Graff, 2001.

Tyson, Timothy B. *Radio Free Dixie: Robert F. Williams & the Roots of Black Power*. Chapel Hill: University of North Carolina Press, 1999.

Vale, V. *Real Conversations 1: Henry Rollins, Jello Biafra, Lawrence Ferlinghetti, Billy Childish*. San Francisco: RE Search, 2001.

Wald, Allan. *The New York Intellectuals*. Chapel Hill: University of North Carolina Press, 1987.

Williams, Robert. *Negroes with Guns*. Ed. Marc Schleifer. New York: Marzani and Munsell, 1961.

Williams, William Appleman. *Empire as a Way of Life: An Essay on the Causes and Character of America's Present Predicament, Along with a Few Thoughts about an Alternative*. New York: Oxford University Press, 1980.

Zeleny, Jeff. "Obama, in Miami, Calls for Engaging With Cuba." *New York Times*, May 24, 2008. http://www.nytimes.com/2008/05/24/us/politics/24campaign.htm .

# Index